BO
THE BLITZ

Also by Colin Perry FCCA JDipMA FSS MIMC
Chartered Certified Accountant
Registered Auditor – retired

Non-fiction

Various factual financial volumes published

Fiction

The Telephone Rang

BOY IN
THE BLITZ

COLIN PERRY

AMBERLEY

To my son Lawrence,
my daughter Felicity,
my grand-children Helen, Gavin and Tamara,
and
Irrepressible Youth.

This edition first published 2012

Amberley Publishing
The Hill, Stroud
Gloucestershire, GL5 4EP

www.amberley-books.com

British Library Cataloguing in Publication Data.
A catalogue record for this book is available from the British Library.

ISBN 978-1-4456-0696-5

Typesetting and Origination by Amberley Publishing.
Printed in Great Britain.

Contents

Contents

Introduction

Colin Albert Perry was born in Camberwell, London, on 12 February 1922. He left school at fourteen in 1936. He had no qualifications.

His parents removed from Brixton to 14 Holmbury Court, Tooting, London SW17, in April 1939, being among the first tenants to occupy the flats. There was a purpose-built air-raid shelter under a central rockery for the residents. The rent for three-bedroom accommodation was about 28s 6d a week.

In April 1940 he was passed medically fit for RAF flying crew but was rejected as not being up to educational standard.

This remarkable diary of his experience as a teenager during the Blitz first came to the attention of the Imperial War Museum as long ago as 1969 when the author, with no thought of publication in mind, offered his narrative for the archives. *Boy in the Blitz* was first published in 1972 and was warmly received.

It was written in his home in Tooting and in the City of London where he worked. It is the only account of its kind and is published just as he wrote it in those never-to-be-forgotten times. As it is his own composition, intended for no other person, the words flow rapidly, for they are no more than the tangible expression of what was going on in his mind and of the sights he saw about him. It contains, therefore, no afterthoughts, only the youthful, untrained outpourings of a proud and totally insignificant Londoner. It spans what the Air Ministry was to call '... the Great Days from 8th August–31st October 1940' and the fifty-seven nights when the bombing of London was unceasing, the period enshrined in our history as the Battle of Britain – *the most momentous year for Britain in the twentieth century.*

This edition is testimony of what the Imperial War Museum wrote:

> ... it adds something fresh to a seemingly exhausted subject, the Battle of Britain
> ... it is as honest a self-portrait as can be wished for, without malice and without subterfuge ... It is a minor classic of the psychology of adolescence ... In one

On 21 March 1932, Colin poses with his younger brother Alan and their mother. (*Author*)

sense it is not your work, for the Colin Perry of 1940 was a different person: one great merit of the diary is that it has preserved him like an insect preserved in amber.

The wartime devastation inflicted is exquisitely portrayed in this edition of *Boy in the Blitz*, with over sixty images depicting London's suffering at the hands of the Luftwaffe during the summer of 1940. However, Perry's earnest and sincere writing style evokes genuine feelings of pride in readers both old and young. Thanks to being blessed with the naivety of youth, and writing with no intention of publication, he has created a work that accurately depicts not only the vast destruction caused by the Blitz, but also the attitude of the common Londoner.

The diary has dual appeal, as not only is it a day-by-day account, touchingly recording the bombings and their physical effect on the London populace, but it also gives an indication as to how British propaganda helped the English public to keep their faith and weather the storm that had subjected mainland Europe to Nazi occupation. Winston Churchill proclaimed in a speech heard by Perry, on 14 July 1940, 'We would rather see London laid in ruins and ashes than that it should be tamely and abjectly enslaved.' This led Perry to record at the end of his entry for that day, 'Churchill – well, he is England to me'.

Such a comment is typical of this work, which contains almost all of what survives of the journal Perry kept between March and November 1940 when he was eighteen years old. In February 1945 his ship docked in London and in the one night he spent at home before marrying his wife in Liverpool he destroyed a lot of the diary's manuscript for fear she should read and ridicule it. But Providence stayed his hand and saved the heart of it.

The diary concludes on 5 November 1940 and by 17 November the 23,700 gross tons P&O RMS *Strathallan*, with newly appointed ship's writer Colin Perry on board, left the pierhead with 4,500 soldiers for Port Said in Egypt; on the return voyage the ship went solo from Cape Town to Glasgow. On its next trip *Strathallan* returned from Egypt via Trinidad alone, seeking to avoid U-boats.

In 1941, when three days out of Cape Town bound for Bombay, into the ship's bureau walked chaplain Wintersgill, a bank clerk who used to work in the Royal Bank of Canada building in the City, as did the author. The *Strathallan* was 'dry', but crew could buy beer; crew quarters were out of bounds to troops. Perry invited Wintersgill to his peak forward, where he was one of six leading hands, and that evening was enjoying some beers when an army subaltern arrived with two military police, burst into the peak, cried 'Wintersgill!' with obvious relief, and escorted him away.

There had been a roll call of troops and Wintersgill was absent. Two destroyers were ordered astern to search for the supposedly missing Wintersgill. The Next day Wintersgill was court-marshalled.

However the ship's purser and the O.C. Troops on board were friends, and all was forgotten and Perry as ship's writer could not be involved in army procedures. The whole affair was hushed up.

On the day of the attack on Pearl Harbor (7 December 1941) the *Strathallan* had embarked in the Clyde with replacement crews for HMS *Prince of Wales* and HMS *Repulse* and sailed for Singapore. On 10 December 1941, when the convoy was two days out of UK, both of these capital battleships were sunk by Japanese aircraft in the South China Sea. The intended replacement crews were landed in Durban. *Strathallan* proceeded independently to Bombay and, after refitting, when Perry and shipmate Millman crossed the Western Ghats to Poona for the hell of it, carried Indian troops to Suez where Australian troops from the Western Desert were shipped in mid-February for Rangoon, as Singapore had fallen to Japan on 15 February 1942. There occurred exchanges between Roosevelt, Churchill and the Australian Prime Minister Curtin while the Aussie troops were anchored in Colombo, but the Australian Prime Minister insisted his troops be returned to Australia in defence of their country. *Strathallan* and other vessels were escorted by a British warship to Fremantle and disembarked the Aussies in Adelaide. *Strathallan* continued to Sydney, where the author met with his pen-friend Binnie Patterson in March 1942, but he and Binnie did not 'hit it off' and he rejoined his ship. After dry-docking in Cockatoo, *Strathallan* sailed to Auckland, where the author visited Rotorua. He left New Zealand on 8 April 1942 with some NZ troops and food supplies for UK and travelled via the Panama Canal independent of convoy. *Strathallan* completed a round-the-world trip in Glasgow on 10 May 1942.

Following another trip via South Africa, *Strathallan* was ordered from Suez via the Cape to New York, where the author travelled to Washington, saw the White House, and went in the elevator to the top of the Washington Monument. In New York he watched a baseball match between the Yankees and the Boston Red Sox, and by invitation of Music Box Canteen met with the stars of the then-popular film *Mrs Miniver*.

In October 1942, *Strathallan* departed New York and carried US Army troops for UK. She then embarked UK troops for initial Torch landings in Algiers. After a night's air raid alongside Algiers, the ship sailed for home for reinforcements. Next day, 25 November 1942, the author was on gun watch on the bridge at noon when, as he was about to enter the turret, the ship rolled and he fell from the turret onto a spike of the ammunition locker some 16 feet below. He was operated on without sedation on board, and on docking in Glasgow declined going ashore to hospital, and returned on *Strathallan* to the Mediterranean. *Strathallan* was Commodore of Convoy when she was torpedoed by a U-boat on 21 December 1942 in the early hours; HMS *Verity* picked up about a quarter of the military persons on board and these were landed in Oran. The surviving crew of the *Strathallan* arrived back in the UK on 1 January 1943.

On 13 February 1943, Colin Perry signed under Admiralty Service T124X agreement and enlisted in HMS *Mersey* in Liverpool. He was discharged on 10 March 1943:

> ...on account of being Below Naval Physical Standard. When medically examined he was found to have an ununited fracture of the left collar bone, which had been broken on three occasions. The X-ray report dated 15th February 1943 reads, 'There is an old un-united fracture of the left clavicle in the centre of the bone, with a false joint and cystic degeneration of the fractured ends.'
>
> [Signed] Lt Commander R Chapman for Commanding Officer (on leave) HMS *Mersey* 2 April 1943.

In May 1943 he was promoted to assistant purser in a troopship expected in Liverpool, together with another assistant purser, a Keith Wylie. Both were due to join SS *Orduna*, but the vessel did not arrive. Keith Wylie invited him Perry his home in Aigburth and he met his sister, Elaine, a nurse, about to be employed in the missing-persons' section of the Ministry of Defence. Perry

The Perry brothers outside the bicycle sheds of their home at Holmbury Court, London in 1944. (*Author*)

Colin and fiancée Elaine upon their engagement in Liverpool, 1944. (*Author*)

said he would help Elaine with her garden, but he was suddenly told to join SS *Empire Voice* in Hull in the full rank of purser on the 6,800-ton cargo ship, and sailed in June 1943. The *Empire Voice* had a mostly Indian crew and docked in Beira, Durban and Calcutta, including a three-week visit to the Seychelles with high-explosives for its defences (in 1943 the Seychelles was a British colony and remote). In 1944 the *Empire Voice* visited Palestine; in Haifa, he and the captain with three fellow officers taxied to Nablus, Bethelem, Jerusalem (including the Dome of the Rock) and Tel Aviv. Later he bussed to Nazareth. At the end of 1944 his ship docked in Venezuela, Aruba, Curacao, and left Georgetown, British Guiana, with a cargo of copper via Trinidad. She loaded sea-island cotton and general cargo in Grenada, St Vincent, Montserrat, Santo Domingo, and visited New York for bunkers (*Empire Voice* was coal-fuelled). It was when going on ship's business to the British Sea Transport Office in Manhattan that he astonishingly bumped into his young brother, whom he had thought was working as a reporter on *The Times* in London. His brother had arrived in SS *Queen Mary* that day and was off to Mobile to join an armed merchant ship.

Empire Voice left the next morning, 23 January 1945, and a US security captain commanding guards over the ship in Brooklyn said, 'Sure as hell we can see he is your brother and we aren't looking, and if he is on the gangplank at 10.00 tonight we ain't looking either.' His brother, without any pass, was enabled to join in dinner on board *Empire Voice*. 'Thank you, America!'

The author and Elaine were married in Mossley Hill Church, Liverpool on 13 February 1945 (the day of the Dresden raid by the RAF). They were married for sixty-four years with two children, three grandchildren, and eight great-grandchildren. They received a Diamond Wedding anniversary card from Her Majesty Queen Elizabeth on 13 February 2005. Elaine died in 2009.

The Journal

France has capitulated. Britain is alone.

The French Army has laid down its arms, M. Reynaud has resigned, and 84-year-old Marshal Petain is the new Premier. Comments come thick and fast: have the French turned Leopold? Is our second B.E.F., thought to be so well equipped with the latest weapons, cut off on the other side of the Channel without a chance? The French air force? Surely the Germans will not be allowed French aircraft. Tunis, Morocco, Syria? Will these countries down arms? Will Britain alone face the menace of Germany and Italy? If, as people ask, our Fleet is withdrawn from overseas for the protection of our own island shall we jeopardise the integrity of our colonial possessions? That would not be a British thing to do. Hitler is recognised for his quick, powerful action: will he therefore dally in offering us peace terms? More likely he will send his myriads of 'planes, strengthened by Italian forces, and try to bomb us into submission. Is it better to die, if we must, as an Empire and foremost world power, fighting to the last drop of our blood, or now, immediately, lay down arms and not hold our country and breed in lunacy of death for the sake of tradition? If our Government realise the situation is hopeless, is it right that they should risk the appalling loss of life which must result if we pursue our struggle to end this Nazi tyranny? Condemn him to hell who is responsible for bringing Britain to the verge of her existence – Britain whom we love, and whom our ancestors placed into the leadership of the world.

How surely will our Fleet win through? If France has failed to survive the impact of the German air offensive, can our ships survive the packs of German submarines which are surely to be launched against them? If the courage of the Italians may be called in dispute, none can accuse the Germans of anything but the highest order of bravery. Even should we withstand, as we shall, the bombing attacks, and maintain the supremacy of the seas, if our blockade of Germany is to be effective we are committed to a five years' war: in this time we shall be expanding our air armada, but even then we shall be without a battlefield, and a battleground there must be if a decisive war is to be fought.

There is impatience in the soul to even things up with the Germans. France said she lacked men and equipment. For ourselves, I do not know about equipment: but men! The call-up is the first consideration: there can be no excuse for the lack of manpower. Lately, everyone has been demanding to be taught in civvies how to use arms: to no avail. Here we are, with the war on our doormat, and still this indescribable muddle. We have been too long resting on our laurels: we have grown soft.

Red tape is our curse. Maybe I'm embittered at having passed the medical A1, just because I do not possess a school certificate I cannot get into the flying part of the R.A.F. In any case I do not for one moment think I am to blame: I haven't had the opportunity to sit for the exam. Yet I have more pep and fire, more ambition than the whole gang of them put together. But no, that is unfair: for our air force is magnificent. But still, my point is obvious: did Hitler, ex window-cleaner of Munich, have a certificate? Not on your life: yet he has risen from the ranks to be ruler of Germany.

We will eventually win this war, but if only Russia would aid us the situation would be less perilous. Perhaps Stalin will wait until we are conquered and then jump in and take all. Oh, it's an enigma, and none of this writing will enlighten any person other than myself. I have total faith in God, and perhaps this is His way of reforming a sinful world.

The evening grows late, the sun is casting its shadow over this paper, and the wind springs in the open window and sends the accumulating papers to the floor. I must partake of this beautiful evening in a crisp walk on the common. Yes, I'll go now. Who knows but it's a last chance, for the raiders are expected tonight. Ah well, time marches on.

18 June
My holiday! I bought an Orange Coach day return ticket to Brighton. Fare 5/6d return, cheap in wartime compared with the rail fare of 10/1d. Left Balham at 9.38 a.m. and arrived Marine Parade, Brighton at 11.30 a.m. Weather magnificent. Straightway I had a swim, which was superbly exhilarating, and, afterwards, while tanning myself on the beach, I got talking to another young chap of about twenty. We veered round to the R.A.F. He had been examined, physically and educationally, and passed. He was waiting to be called up. He said he had been given the opportunity of waiting a year and being accepted as a pilot or of being called up within the next five weeks to become an observer. He had chosen to be an observer as it meant his enlisting earlier: I should have preferred to wait, I think, in the hope that a demand for pilots would be coming before very much longer.

Two more swims before I returned, but the sun tanning was grand. Yes, the outdoor life suits me to perfection. I believe we ought to lead the life our fancy dictates, and my fancy is to live, perhaps only for a time, primitively, in the Australian Bush, with, I think, Binnie as my sole companion. Man and woman! Ta, tar, tah! I want power, of thought and action. Most of all action. I want to be able to dictate men's lives, to feel supreme in a moment of danger, oblivious, daring, alive, revelling: to steer a boat in a stormy sea, a sea of death, with my face set, slated by the salt wind: to feel at grips with the elements and to outride them. Power! Yes, more than money – a mere civilised liability.

In this country it is the people with the money who rule: the average commoner, such as me, is given no facility for rising. Everything in England is based on money, which is influence. The rich can never see the point of view of the poor, but it is the poor who suffer every time. In wars he is the other rank: whatever his ability he is prohibited from exercising it. Today I heard a story from one of the lads in the gallant B.E.F.: his officers – mainly, I take it, who had bought their commissions in peace-time – deserted their men when their ship was sunk by German dive-bombers. Terrible! Our army has something radically wrong with its organisation, whereas our navy and air force are superb. Why is this? Can Englishmen still squabble about personal and mercenary gains when their very soil is endangered as never before? No! Well then, let the commoner have his chance. Hitler. Did he matriculate? No. Of course, General Ironside did. It all goes to prove that it is not always the man with the academic standard who gets there: in all history it is the ordinary English person who has shown himself to be absolutely dependable in adversity.

Our Government is too slow. We should have military training for every man on his attaining the age of eighteen and until he reaches nineteen: thus many youths would be saved from the hardness of the world. Those who are undergoing studies could have their training deferred. At present we are split into three classes; the workers, the middle class, and the rich. Why should titles be hereditary? I know if ever I was fortunate enough to benefit the world I shouldn't want any subsidy or lavishes to be poured upon my son, if God should grant me one. No, he would have to work for his own way, not to be idle under a sphere originated by his father.

Away with the red tape, away with the idle rich, away with the foreigners. Make Britain for the British, concentrate upon the Empire and make that our life, independent of outside contacts if need be. The Empire should work together as one man. If trouble should arise in an outpost the whole weight of the Empire would fall upon the aggressor. By our might, our perfect understanding of each other, in our trust, we would rule the world, in peace. This war, I hope, will awaken our sleeping brain to the paradise we could achieve and for which we should strive. Last time we were promised a land fit for heroes to live in, said Dad, and for that he fought those long years through. Perhaps again we fight for the realisation of those same ideals: whatever may now befall, we shall see an England – a Britain – arise from her sleep of complacency, arise to victory.

29 June

I have started a cuttings file of 'Leaders'. These are the editorial columns which inspire me in the evening newspapers.

The *Evening Standard* articles are making a war diary for me: they are so excellent that I wrote to the newspaper and told them so. Someone, for the editor, wrote and thanked me for my observations.

I have now started on the task of getting T. E. Lawrence, the book on his life by Vyvyan Richards, *The Research Magnificent* and *The Fate of Homo Sapiens* (both by H. G. Wells), into one tangible and fulfilling story. It's some job, and will test my continuity and patience and, most of all, my intelligence. The prospect is so ambitious in its entirety,that it will take me goodness knows how long. Done, it will be more than satisfying. In fact, I imagine it will be after the style of Benham's *Research*. The trouble is that with every minute, at the awkwardest of minutes, new ideas flow through my head, demanding immediate recording.

9 July

Invasion daily becomes more threatening, air attacks upon our shores more devastating. All those people who flocked out of London at the beginning of the war are coming back and we seem to be the unofficial reception area now. But Dad says we've seen nothing yet. The *Evening Standard* tonight says all the lamp-posts should be torn down: it says in London alone 100,000 lamp-posts stand serving no useful purpose but to mock our discomfiture in the black-out: they would provide 20,000 tons of scrap from which to make guns. Dad said the lamp-posts would be useful to string the Jerries on.

Azario, the man who owned the pet stores at the bottom of our road, has lost his life on the *Arrandora Star*. It was only a few short weeks ago that my brother, Alan, took our canary to him to have its nails cut; and only a few short weeks ago that he bought weed for the goldfish bowl from him. Only yesterday, it seems, we were tormenting him over the alley fence as he returned our balls which always seemed to go into his yard. We used to be slightly amused at his long, straggling hair, his stooped shoulders and his characteristic Scrooge appearance. Then Italy entered the war. The pet man – as we called him – an Italian subject who had lived peacefully in Tooting for forty-two years, was immediately taken off in a police car for internment. His last words to his wife and daughter were: 'I shall never come back.' Funny, we thought, only the black-listed were interned immediately – and he went straightaway. But we merely shrugged our shoulders, off-handedly interested. Last week the sinking of the *Arrandora Star* of 16,000 tons was achieved by a U-boat (commanded by the man who torpedoed the *Royal Oak*) in the Atlantic, some hundreds of miles off the west coast of Ireland. Fortunately, there were no evacuee school-children on board her – only internees being removed to Canada, out of harm's way. Azario was on board. He lost his life.

Any scrap materials were extremely useful during the rationing period, and many children would collect all they could, to be utilised in some way or another.

That is all there is to this story: but I had to record it because somehow it just seems incredible that an old man who kept a pet stores in Upper Tooting Road has suddenly been snatched away, to forfeit his life in the Atlantic. I can see him now attending his pets...

A girl who regularly eats in the ABC café in Cheapside, almost opposite Bow Bells, where I eat my soup, roll, butter and cheese at lunch time, and in whom I have become increasingly interested, today – I imagined fondly – gave sly glances in my direction from her table near mine. I merely returned a cold, stony gaze, and I meant to be so friendly. She has black, shiny hair, no cosmetics (at least not that I noticed) and dark blue eyes, with good lashes. I wonder if I'll ever talk to her. I think of Binnie in Australia, and rebuke myself. I think of the impending invasion and think: 'Hell, why not ask her her name?' I think again of my desire to travel, and look stonily ahead. Then... well she does look pretty, and I wonder what it would be like to kiss her. Would she be full of life, of ideas, ideals? Or dull, girlish, demanding?

Would she care for walks, like London, see the world, as I? Slyly, I glance at her profile: definitely, she is outstanding, superior to those around her – but of course she would be, otherwise I wouldn't be looking at her so inwardly agog. Oh damn, as I get into my roll and butter, I suppose she is after all just a girl. And yet... well I can but throw a gamble, it would be a diversion, and like anything I desire to escape routine. But wait, she carries a gas-mask, and to lunch! Horrors. No girl of mine would display so frightening a taste. But wait! Does her employer require her to do so? Whatever the reason, she certainly does apppear to be one who has steady nerves, is cool, unflurried, unperturbed. Maybe I should appreciate the gas-mask as a truly feminine instinct and consequently I should loom the more manly (tut-tut) as I never carry one.

No, I don't admire that instinct. Ah well, it is but another fly on the flypaper, another ship in my sea – I suppose. If fate decrees it – well, what is to be will be. Anyhow she would probably be amazed if she knew I had spent several minutes in condemning her to my diary, if not flattered. The awful thing is that never having really aroused a second glance from a female in my life (bar in schoolgirl Kate – and Mrs Howarth) I cannot visualise myself doing so now – still, there you are.

This invasion again. Suppose Hitler does conquer us – will I ever know the true sense of travel romance? No, I fear not. Suppose I escaped from England before he grasped it – I mean by a British ship, for presumably our maritime fleet would evacuate our citizens to the New World: plausible perhaps, but would I go? If my people were here – no. Otherwise I should think twice, for I may be able to reach Australia. Again, if I were in the armed forces escape would be an impossibility: so should I seek to hurry my voluntary enlistment? Yes! For we are going to win, to conquer, to restore! But I do hope we shan't be too long about it, for I am impatient to get out East. Gosh, think of it – by twenty-six once travelled round the world, fought in a great, unprecedented war, and married – perhaps! Some hopes. Then again, to add one more item of insanity to an already insane diary, if England were (God forbid) conquered, maybe one day a liberator would arise...

Yet I want to know the joy of spending a week-end in gay Brighton, of ripping along in a car, of loving and taking a girl for a romp in the long grass on a hot summer's day, of dances, hikes, cinemas, shows, plays, tennis, cycling, visiting her people, meeting more friends and perhaps arousing jealousy in her as her best friend gives me the eye: of holidays together, of swims, of yachting, of continental travel. Oh so many things. Petty quarrels, making them up, etc – oh so typically ordinary, but so enjoyable. Yet that would anchor me and I MUST travel. All these things could be saved to Sydney – yet the Standard Oil Co. would be mighty fine, dictating to a secretary in San Francisco... a charming secretary, dictating personal letters, full of my war life to old friends or of inner thoughts to home, and her gazing admiringly, wistfully at me and I, the boss, pretending until the last moment not to notice the obvious. How I would love to write and pour dictation into her Yankee ears, about the glory of England, the sole fighter for world freedom – and how poor America would come in for criticism.

This will never do. I have brought to earth a terrible streak of vanity I never knew existed. But all creatures are vain, and few can control that vanity.

I finished *The Fate of Homo Sapiens* by H. G. Wells today. It has provided magnificent material which is manure for my intelligence. I have already succeeded, at a vast expense of rest, to type out my research and notes for a new world order. Many of my ideas which I would otherwise put in this diary are cemented in that research.

England today reminds me of David; Germany and her conquered lands of Goliath. The stream is the English Channel and the North Sea. It was David, so small, who slew the giant Goliath with a tiny pebble – England is David. It came to me, this reminder, as I visualised over a map that I was a watcher miles above the earth, viewing the German invasion of this country. Britain seemed so tiny, forlorn, that as I saw the waves of aircraft, the mass of shipping, converging upon her shores from so vast an enemy territory I could see nothing which could prevent the success of that invasion. The British were rushing hither and thither behind their barricades, bombed here, bombed there. The British air fleet seemed puny as it attempted to destroy and wreak retaliation on the enemy. I could see absolutely nothing which could stem the sadistic, degenerate, all-destroying Nazi war machine, as it descended upon those green, peace-loving shores. It was then that I remembered David slew Goliath, and God was in His Heaven, and I no longer feared. Indeed I lifted up my heart, and thanked God I was privileged to live in such momentous times, in such times when I was able to use my strength and mind to surmount the trials of mankind and to emerge, the better equipped, in experience.

Now for bed, and I hope tonight I don't dream the *Mauretania* has been sunk.

10 July

Reported engagement in the Mediterranean between British and Italian battle squadrons. The Italian Navy ran away, but one of our capital ships claims a direct hit on an enemy battleship. This news is welcome, for it shows the more plainly the terrific reputation our navy has; moreover it comes at an opportune moment, for events in the East are moving with rapidity, and not at all to the benefit of England.

Eire is considered our heel of Achilles; certainly de Valera deserves no sympathy from our Government – we should forcibly remove the menace at our back door. But once upset the Irish and by heavens we should be in for the devil of an amount of sabotage, etc. We should never (or do I mean 'ever'?) regret such an act. Maybe, though, even de Valera will call upon us if Eire is in danger of falling under the Nazi yoke.

The girl in the ABC was superseded this morning by 'the girl on the tube'. This girl I have seen on and off during the past year: she resembles Bette Davis, whom I like. She wore a large straw hat, bound with light blue ribbon, a royal-blueish dress, and a grey-blue coat: the colour combination looked quite attractive. Whether or not I shall ever speak to her I cannot guess, but I wonder if she thinks of me? Lately, it would appear, I am growing aware of the female sex, although I think it is a half-truth to say so for these observations are made in an off-handish way. I just think I would like to know a girl for – well, should I say by way of diversion, to broaden my scope of social life, which is exceedingly poor. Heaven alone knows I have no intention of kissing and that caboodle.

I must get in the R.A.F. and soon. I am endeavouring to ginger up the authorities, and shall visit them on Saturday. Service life would put me on my feet: office routine is too dull. If I do succeed in gingering them up it may again be abortive, for my lack of education has already prevented me from being passed for training as a pilot. If I wait, the demand for pilots may increase and they may not be so fussy. God, how I long to whirl around in a Spitfire.

I shall see!

Tonight is said to be the night for the German invasion.

11 July

Lunch time: just spoken on the telephone to the Croydon Royal Air Force Recruiting Depot re my enlistment:

First:

> As my name is already down for 'Air-Crew' I must wait; my call will come very soon.

Secondly:

> If accepted by the Selection Board (Air-Crew) I can state that whilst waiting to be called upon to train as a pilot I wish to become one of the ground staff, when they are sure to accept me. In any case there is nothing further to be done until I have appeared before the Selection Board.

So there I am. Despite my efforts I must wait. Well at any rate I hope I shall finally be accepted, for I admit the R.A.F. holds no attraction for me unless I can go up.

11 July (later)

Out of interest I list below all the girls I know, or have known, to date: my purpose is to record my 'social' life to provide me with some amusement in the future.

Kate Williams

Yes I really went 'mad' over her at Carshalton. Our meeting was quite romantic: she lived next door but one and threw me a note tied with blue wool to a stone over the intervening garden. Always quarrelling. Never kissed her – only once shook her hand.

Joan Taylor

Also of Carshalton. Good friends, lovely figure, nothing more. Just a phase.

Lise Schmidt

A German. Met at a Youth Hostel in Llangollen when I cycled there in 1938. Spent day and half 'showing her around' London. Charming and extraordinarily attractive, but I suspect her of fifth column work: she impressed me as clever and courageous (but I don't know why). She works for her country: I mine. Finis.

Binnie Patterson

Of Sydney, Australia. I have corresponded with Binnie for over three years and am resolved to meet her. Our common interests are immense and I am sure she will continue to play an important part in my life. Directly after the war is over I intend sailing to Sydney. I will not add more – I must see her to judge the strength and justification of my imagination and expectations.

Paula Starkie

Works in the same building as me. Has a 'bun' hair-do and sees a bank clerk at lunch times. She smiles at me, but I suspect in a condescending way. I may ask her to a show before I enlist. Absolutely no scheming ambition for her.

Girl in the ABC between 12–1 p.m. on week-days
How I look forward to lunching at the ABC in Cheapside. She appears serious and refined as she reads her book, alone amidst the tea-cups and the buns and butters, the waitresses and the crowd. I feel there is a mutual but unspoken understanding between us. We always sit near one another these days, half-way between the counter and the hot-press: she never used to sit anywhere specially. We seldom catch each other's eye, and, should we chance to do so, we both glance frigidly through our clandestine meeting. Each day I determine to sit *at* her table or, if I am first, *will* her to sit at mine. I doubt if she's my dream. I would I had the courage to speak to her.

Girl on the Tube
Gets on at Clapham Common, alights at Bank. Vivacious (I judge) and somehow appealing.

There is the list. I find them all a pleasant diversion from discussing *Homo Sapiens* and my world order. Putting them down has amused me, which in itself is a bit of fun. If I were 'ordinary' I would have kissed hundreds of girls and whistled thousands instead of wasting paper, ink and time in summing them up: as it is, I've only once shaken Kate's hand.

There you are, I like to pen things down – so much for stepping down and analysing myself.

12 July
Oh boy, oh boy, *Oh Boy!*

Just back from lunch and you can guess the reason for my jubilation. Or can you? Yep, you're right. It's the 'Girl in the ABC' – tra la lah la ... I am full of the joys of Spring, tra lah.

We caught one another's eye ... she looked, just dead straight ahead ... at me (of course) and I – well I did the same as her. A glimmer of a smile flickered round her face.

Her eyes, so blue, dark blue, flashed right across
my face;
I bashfully gave my lips to my hand
And executed the coup de grâce tra lah.
Whatever is said, and this I know,
She heated my heart and melted the snow.
And straightway I did glance away
Amused and pleased and quite amazed!

There you are. The ice cracked slightly, ever so slight, and I can hardly wait until Monday lunch-time. We each appreciated the other's amusement, of that

I am sure. Well now I do know, come hither go thither, I am resolved to speak to her sooner, or later.

It was a tremendous sensation – her smile. It somehow warmed 'the cockles of my English heart', and I hope I warmed hers, bless her heart. Tra lah lah…

14 July: 9.55 p.m.

I have just listened to perhaps the most historic and amazing news bulletin of my life on the wireless.

First, Churchill: '…We toil in the valley until we reach the dawn of a new day in the hills'.[1] And he said we are prepared that our offensives will begin in 1942! Great Scott. He commenced his rousing address by saying that today is Bastille Day, and he hoped that many of us would live to see that day dawn once again, representing an even greater event, the liberation of France![2] The liberation of the world! I query the *many*!

Then Charles Gardiner, stationed on the South Coast, broadcasting the progress of an air-raid at the moment it was taking place over his head: Twenty German dive-bombers accompanied by fighter escorts were attacking one of our convoys through the Channel – until our Spitfires came. I shall never forget it. The true spirit of British sport came right into its own through the magnificent boyishness of Gardiner. For all the world it was like a Cup Final or Derby, and how our boys cheered when the Nazis came down. Result: 6 Germans shot down, 1 British. Fine! All the while he was broadcasting anti-aircraft guns were pummelling away and machine-guns rattling. It was irresistible. I must be a fighter pilot – God, I must!

J. B. Priestley gave the postscript to tonight's radio news. He made us seem like little schoolboys saying things and then glancing up at Churchill to see if he, the headmaster, approved.

Churchill – well, he's England to me!

ABC tomorrow! Here's hoping.

17 July

Tonight we in our proud Island prepare ourselves for the word that the invader has commenced his attack. The air-raid wardens have passed information round that the Military at Tolworth will tonight throw up a smoke-screen, which will spread and envelop the whole Metropolis, blot out vital objectives, and generally throw invading hordes into confusion. At any moment – now, as I write this – the attack may commence. We are awaiting with calm fortitude for the inevitable. Airraids, massed murder, total devastation of beautiful buildings: the unknown: and gas, too, maybe, to poison our food and pollute our water. All these evil possibilities confront the people of England, now. We have witnessed countries torn to shreds by this Moloch of our age. We, alone, await his onslaught, calm, confident, determined.

Despite all this, which but a year ago would have sounded fantastic, my ordinary life continues. And today it is not the war which occupies the whole of my inner mind, but 'the Girl in the ABC'. I am callous about the war business. Certainly not in any degree scared or anxious. I am intensely interested. *Britain at Bay*, the film I have just seen, makes me want to join the army tomorrow. It showed our fair Kentish fields, the pleasant Surrey woodlands, the broad moors of Devon and Cornwall to the wild bracken of Scotland; from the smelly City to the remotest village hamlet – this is the 'frontline': this is where we stand to defend our right with all our might. Somehow it is magnificent and terrible in one. But the Girl...

I always lunch at the ABC on the corner of King Street and Cheapside, and whenever she is there always near the Girl. It is a mutual arrangement – I think. Neither of us appears the slightest interested in the other, yet somehow I have that all-elating fire: it is hard to describe my feelings. If, as I fervently hope, we like each other, then if I postpone talking to her much longer the invasion may be upon us and my chance have gone. Yes, I will sit at the same table tomorrow and I'm damned if I don't break the silence. She smiled at me over the waitress's shoulder today and I, drinking a cup of tea, grinned back. I hope she has a pleasant voice.

18 July

A bare fourteen hours ago I was emptying my heart of its burden of occupation with 'the Girl in the ABC': now, the lunch hour planned to break the stalemate has been and gone, to no avail. Indeed it is the irony of Fate. I had led myself to believe in all honesty that the girl and I had a 'mutual understanding,' that she did care for me, a little, and that at last Fate had offered me a flaming star: but CRasH! my dreams are smashed to atoms. It was all make-believe.

I took the ABC by storm, and sat myself in shapely order at the regular table. I waited ... the tables began to fill, and 'Ah,' I thought, 'she will have to sit next to me.' Alas, she entered and the incredible happened. She sat on the opposite side of the room. If she had been in the least interested in me she would have sat near me. I plodded with heavy heart through a roll, butter and cheese, and a cup of tea. I carefully avoided looking in her direction. Soon I began to write some notes – I looked up and she was gone. So I went too, and lo and behold there she was at the cash desk; she saw me coming and, wonders, (could it have been to waste time?) she bought a bar of chocolate. It was teeming with rain, providentially, and so I sheltered in the porch. She came out and too sheltered, right near me. In the movement of the people we brushed against one another. Oh! I cannot tell of my feelings: I could have swept her off her feet and hugged her tightly – she must be good for me to feel that way. I wanted the rain to pour continuously, but in what seemed seconds it gave over, and I ventured miserably to the doorway. I walked despondently away. Suddenly, irrespective of the fact that the rain had started again, I turned and charged back to the ABC. She was still there ... If she had thought of me she would have quit as soon as I had gone. I dashed past her, and bought a bar of chocolate, then came out carefully counting my money. I was pretending I had left some change behind. Well I stopped again, but immediately she sallied forth from the doorway and into the rain, with never a glance at me.

19 July
I heard from the R.A.F. this morning, a maddening circular, identical with all the correspondence I have received from the Services, postponing any application by me for 'Aircrafthand/Air Crew' until at least a month. I do want to get in the Services before the winter, as I shall then save myself the price of a new overcoat, hat, etc.

I have needed to look at my money lately, and because I cannot think of anything worth while writing about today I'll note my position:-

Cash in box	£2.10.0
Dad owes me	£11.0.0
Saving stamps	7.0
War Certificates	£1.10.0
Old coins	£1.0.0
Cash in pocket	2.6
Note in wallet	10.0
Total	£16.19.6

Weekly pay £1.10 less 1/7 insurance, therefore, £1.8.5 net income distributed as follows:-

Mother (for keep) 8.0 (should be at least 10/- but she won't take it)	
Lunches	4.0
Season ticket (Trinity Rd. to Bank)	5.3
Haircut (once a fort-night)	1.3

Therefore

Carried forward	18.6
Brought forward	18.6
Pictures	1.0
Alan	6
Incidentals	2.0
	1.2.0
Savings	6.5
	£1.8.5

This is good for a fellow my age. But as I am now doing very much more responsible work – for the past week I have virtually been cashier for the London office of California Standard Oil Co. – I think it is high time I had an increase. If the R.A.F. reject me, I shall ask. An extra five shillings a week is nothing to the company but it's an awful lot to me. Naturally if I had a girl I should spend more and damn everything: I wish it were that way sometimes. It's nice spending money on people you like. It is true that I often go rash but I do not feel I enjoy myself as I should for I have no one to share my enthusiasm for life with. That's why I wish the 'Girl in the ABC' would speak to me.

20 July

I have bought another bicycle!

Who, who knows me, would believe it. But there it is. After breaking my collar-bone three times, and it now has an ununited fracture following my smash two years ago almost to the day on my old B.S.A., the family said I wasn't to have another bike. But there is something about a bike that gets me, and this morning I awoke with the sudden desire to get into the saddle again and to be mobile to see events between now and when I join up.

First I 'borrowed' a very old and rusted machine from the cycle shed in Holmbury Court: I finally got it to go, but no sooner had I mounted it – with eyes skimmed in case the owner saw me, whoever he might be – than the back tyre blew out with a loud, short bang. And that was that.

Then I set out for Boots Library in Streatham. I saw two second-hand bicycles standing outside a dealer's next to Trinity Road Tube. I went in and asked the price. I inspected the machines. I thought. Next moment a pound note had changed hands and I was the sceptical possessor of an ancient but rideable bicycle.

Mounting, I rode home (and what Mother had to say) and then went as far as Westminster Bridge and back, calling, incidentally, at another cycle dealers to see what price they would give me for my new purchase. 'Should get a pound... Good adjustments...' the man said. But of course I was not selling, only making sure I could get my money back if I wanted to.

This evening I cycled to Hackbridge. In the playground of the Central School L.D.Vs. [Local Defence Volunteers] were drilling: it seemed incongruous. Then as I went round the roads – my old haunts – I saw her. Kate was cycling towards me with another girl, and I knew I had secretly been hoping I should see the pig-tails and pale face of the girl who had once made eyes at me over the garden fence. I think we may have deliberately avoided looking at each other in the hope that the other would have called out first: whatever it was we passed each other by without any sign of recognition, and I thought of the time four years ago when she asked me to marry her. 'Oh, I shan't marry until I'm twenty-eight,' I said. 'I don't mind waiting,' she had smiled, demurely. And now we pass as strangers. What an odd world it is.

23 July

Oh boy, I feel a new man. This ancient crock which is my bike puts new life into me. Tonight I cycled via Wallington to Woodmansterne, and the evening was so heavenly. The sun beaming on the trees, the glorious fields full and pregnant in their harvest. Oh, it was so grand. As I began to smell the tar, feel the sting of dust, and delight in the wind flaying my legs, I began to feel once again how really superb life is. And all this only half-an-hour from the oppression of Tooting, and all for a quid!

There is no denying a bike is my desire. I felt my blood surge through my veins as I pedalled full speed homewards downhill through Carshalton Beeches: surely these were the good old days, the days of calf love, of the overwhelming fire to 'burn up the road'. Ah, it all came back to me as though it were yesterday. Yes, two years ago this very day I hit the rubble head-first, flat-out, on the south side of Leith Hill, and thus bade adieu to the song of the wheel. And now I ride again once more...

Passing Hamworth's in the Wrythe, his mother happened to see me, and in I went. Hamsie has been in the army six months and likes it more than anything else. I'm glad, he was always a jolly fine sport at school. Wait until I'm in the R.A.F ... Imagine it, pilot killed, rest wounded, and I, air-gunner Perry, assume command, but we are shot down in Germany. I escape and capture an enemy plane, which somehow I manage to fly; then, freeing fellow captives, I take off for England. Am set upon over Kent by Hurricanes, my companions bale out, but I, flying brilliantly, bring the aircraft safely to earth, a rich treasure for the country. Consequently, I am awarded the V.C. and given a commission as a fighter pilot... Hacha!

The 'Girl in the ABC' came back into my heart ... tomorrow – p...e...r...h...a...p...s (sez I).

Thursday, 25 July

Contemplating upon my proposed step to enlist in the R.A.F. I find it all very well, but sometimes as I visualise myself hurling the hell into eighty Messerschmitt 109s (which although some may dispute, I could do, for I would revel in that higher ecstasy which only I can know. The speed, the danger, ah, I long for it) I have a slight regret. In war, one can no longer experience that tremendous elation to be achieved by leading a victorious army into a town or village: you know – bands playing, banners flying, a bandage round the head, the jogging horse, the cheering men. To feel sublime, all-conquering, all-powerful; every man must surely long to hold power. No, this is the age of machines and not of *those* armies. But – and here how true today – we should have those bands, and the tunes which ooze Collingwood, Raleigh, Drake and the ghosts of old.

In the tube (half-an-hour ago, on my way to work) I suddenly amazed myself by discovering I still held a shred of feeling for Kate. Probably it is because I am a sentimentalist. If, and rarely these times, I find her creeping into my head I discharge her memory with a thrust. Why? I put it down to one of two reasons: first, I am annoyed with myself for letting her slip through my fingers, for I honestly *did* like her. Secondly, because I recall her changeable disposition. Really I cannot say – but whatever it is I refuse to entertain and suckle her in my inner self, and she is suppressed vigorously. If she were not suppressed this journal would become awfully or delightfully tainted. One moment and Kate is everything and next, absolutely nothing. Moods I guess. Of course I speak of her as I knew her two years ago.

2pm

Wasted ten minutes outside ABC and no girl. Went in and lo and behold there she was sitting at the same table I usually sit at. Here, then, was my chance. Admittedly, there was a near vacant table next to her, but remembering my determination I sat next to her, facing her over the table. My hand literally shook whilst I ate my bread and butter. She was reading *The Spring Term* (which, read upside down, may have been a chapter heading) by Pearl (?). Her library ticket was issued by Beckenham Public Library (Good, at least she lives south of the river). Her name is Lyle (I think) and initials J.L. (to the best of my knowledge): that means she is a Joyce, most likely. I am not keen on that name. Well I caught her eye once, but she dropped her gaze immediately. Blast. She went at 12.30 (so she couldn't have been very interested in me, unless of course she had to go back to work earlier) and, after fumbling in her handbag, she drew out a letter and then put it back, just before she asked for her bill. I reckoned it was from a boy-friend from the style of the writing, although she gave me the idea that she wanted me to glimpse her address from the envelope. But I wasn't able to and – Good Lord! Stop! Don't breathe, maybe she was letting me know she does in fact have a fiance in the forces. If so she would surely have removed herself to some other part of the cafe because she must know that a silent sense of intimacy prevails between us. Unless ... Never mind, a girl's ways are complicated in the extreme.

The times I've meant to breeze in and sing out, 'Good morning, kiddo...' etc, only to dry up at sight. Maybe she feels like me. And she is quite exquisite at close quarters. I wondered what it would be like talking with her. Damn it, there must be a sequel to this story.

Sunday, 28 July

Last night I mouched around the West End. Piccadilly, Shaftesbury Avenue, Frith Street, Greek Street, Soho, Tottenham Court Road, Oxford Street, Air Street, Haymarket, Trafalgar Square, Strand, and so on and I was struck with the amazing cheerfulness, the ordinariness, of the people. Czech, French, Polish, Dutch, Norwegian uniforms, with pilots, sailors and soldiers everywhere. Yes, it was all gay.

This morning I cycled to Kingston, Morden, Carshalton, etc, in my shorts. I saw Mickie Hutton by chance, and heard about several old friends from schooldays. While talking with him I saw a lovely young girl (about fifteen or sixteen years) dressed in a sailor's suit. Usually such an outfit would annoy me, but this girl had oomph: she looked at us and smiled; I hoped it was at me. She had dark hair, a very brown face, and, I believed, brown eyes. A single-decker bus going along the road to Carshalton Beeches stopped and picked her up, and she was gone.

Just heard Dorothy Thompson's fine broadcast comparing Hitler and Churchill. It was magnificent.

George Ivers telephoned me last night at 10.30 and today I am going to his home in Chancery Lane for tea. He lives with his parents, who are caretakers at the top of an office block owned by an insurance company.

Monday, 29 July

I met Ivers at Chancery Lane Tube yesterday afternoon and proceeded to his flat for tea. His room is truly delightful, having a Noah's Ark roof; ideally furnished, with books, odds and ends, autobiographies, etc. This room would suit me admirably: it is within minutes of the West End and City, and a stone's throw from Fleet Street.

The sun gleamed through the windows, barred to prevent any possible accident for the flat is very high, and as I sat reclining at ease in a grand chair, head tucked in my hands and gazing into the sun's eye I saw myself as Raleigh in the Tower, exiled, alone. But I was content with my thoughts. An exile, as such, would be rather magnificent. The view looks upon an ancient building, high up, and in the distance the Law Courts climb skywards, lofty and dictatorial. Here I was in the centre of London, the centre of the world's eye, the hub of the Empire; here in a City threatened with unprecedented air-raids, invasion, and all other kinds of peril. But here, in this City, the greatest brains had worked for the benefit of mankind, the greatest adventurers had lived and gone forth. And I was an aspiring adventurer, alone in my ideals, my visions, with a plan for a new world order. Here on top of London, alone in a tiny room, barred, sat the unknown thinker: unknown in 1940, but perhaps someday the world will find another great man – me. I want power, I want to dictate men's lives, be responsible for the expansion of world education and reform. I am not out for personal gain – money is merely a symbol, an evil symbol but possessed of the highest ideals I see a world working together for the well-being instead of the destruction of man.

The balloon barrage rose over the roofs, soft, flabby, silvery floating elephants, and Ivers entered, and brought me back to earth.

'You are out for personal achievement. Your vanity is rising,' he commented, as I spoke some of my thoughts. Yes, perhaps my vanity has something to do with it, but certainly not in my World Order: nothing will impair that. But I admit I want my name shot across the sky and felt in every corner of the globe, and above all I want to fulfil my dream of youth.

Ivers has just returned from doing some farm work in Wales, where he is establishing himself as a conchie. I do not hold with him, and he knows it.

I am convinced a Heinkel came over last night.

Called in the Air Ministry on Sunday afternoon. That form certainly doesn't promise a pilot ... I'll wait.

I am beginning to like Betty Lampson in Holmbury Court. She was born in Sydney, and wants to return there. She is voluptuous, exciting, sensible, intellectual (I surmise) and an adventuress! Many men have said how they would like to spend a night with her; I may spend more than one! Seriously, it is not for sex alone that I am interested in her although naturally that is an added inducement. When the raids start I might see her to the shelter.

In discussing my affection for Kate with George Ivers, he was firm in his belief that· I am making a 'mythical Goddess' out of her because I haven't got a girl. 'You'll soon lose your feeling for her,' he said.

I believe he is right. I don't know her really and perhaps I am building a castle out of a hovel, so I'll try and forget her. There's no hurry.

29 July (later)
While typing a list of salary requirements in the office today, Miss Mann discussed my wages with me. She said I ought to be getting two pounds a week, and I should. The last person to do my job assisting Miss Mann as cashier got three pounds.

Mr Lebkicher[3] said to me just before he went back to the States: 'Those who have patience and work on will find all will come right in the end.' I hope so. But thirty bob a week is hard to live on: it's a good thing I can find my enjoyment in writing instead of in pleasure which must be paid for.
Miss Mann also said that if I get into the R.A.F. I am entitled to have my money made up by the company. I mentioned I should earn much more in the lowest rank of the services than I get from the office. I sure wish Mr Lebkicher was back here.

30 July
This morning the Press carried an announcement that an examination would be held to select 1,200 candidates for emergency commissions. I applied at the Recruiting Inspector's Office outside the Mansion House. The announcement was new to them! I telephoned the War Office at Whitehall 9561, to be told to telephone Whitehall 9400, extension 1000: but the person who spoke to me at that number was also extremely vague about it. After a lot of enquiry I was referred to Abbey 7361 and 16 (the extension I had been told to ask for) was absent: finally I was put through to extension 24. Here at last I was able to grasp the text and nature of what the announcement intended.

I should write to the Under Secretary of State for War, War Office (M.T.4A), Horse Guards, Whitehall S.W.1 and list my qualifications: a pamphlet setting out the requirements for these commissions is obtainable from H.M. Stationery Office.

My thoughts about the air force were put on one side as I went in the lunch hour to Kingsway. 'A commission, oh boy,' I said to myself. But no one in the Stationery Office knew about the pamphlet: it was not on sale.

I posted my letter to the Under Secretary of State for War asking for details as to how I may take the examination for a commission.

10.30 p.m.

I had just settled to read *Honourable Estate* by Vera Brittain when suddenly a saw-like chatter broke out over Holmbury Court (H.C.).

'Dad, I bet that's a Jerry,' I shouted, leaping down the stairs into the court two at a time. As I did so, bursts of machine gun fire echoed against the walls and, sure enough, I saw that the beams from all the searchlights were concentrated over the flats.

I stood, eagerly expectant, thrilled, supreme. And not a hair of my head turned in this my first touch of the reality of war.

I decided this solitary raider (for I am convinced it was a Jerry) approached London at a great height engaged on reconnaissance work and, gliding over central London, slithered down below the low cloud ceiling to find itself confronted with a real or anticipated barrage balloon, at which it fired in its haste to escape.

The searchlights were on for a few seconds only: perhaps their intention was to feign a rural district so as not to give away London.

Incidentally, I heard that some houses at Mitcham are already converted into 'pill boxes'. Maybe tonight will come the invasion! If so, many personal problems are solved!

31 July

I arrived home from work and found to my joy three letters from Binnie waiting for me. I went into my bedroom to read them quietly when the telephone rang and it was for me. It was Michael Stokes, who I knew in Southampton. He is in the army and he told me he was passing through London from Hitchin, on his way home for two days' leave. He had found me by looking-up our number in the telephone directory. While Mike had not the time to meet me – he was speaking from Waterloo station – he reminded me that he will be twenty next month. He seems to like me. I am glad. I like him too.

I hurried back to Binnie's letters. How I love her witticisms, her expressions, her thoughts and her ideals. She is admirably suited to me. There and then I sat down and wrote four pages of tiny writing to her. I long to meet her. I see her as the mother of my son, for whom I shall have the highest ambitions. And I seek such a woman wisely, with diligence, and with my heart. Lust I know, but it will not stand to produce a son of mine. He will be intelligent, intellectual: he will

23 Radstock Road, Itchen, after a raid on 24 September 1940. (*Jeffery Pain*)

enjoy the things I have missed: and he will be the leader of something or other. Most of all I shall want his happiness. As for myself, I am afraid my chance to act my dreams is unlikely to materialise. But I am rocking with my World Order...

It has been confirmed that it was a German bomber over London last night. So my belief was right. The machine-gunning put out a searchlight! Miss Spindler, the office secretary who lives in East Sheen, also heard the bomber and saw the searchlights: she said a man who was walking with his dog in Richmond Park found himself suddenly surrounded by tracer bullets. Some bombs were dropped on Esher last night and two houses were demolished; five people killed or injured. Well, the invasion looks like coming off very shortly; reports say German troops are massing along the Channel ports. Good. Let's get it done with one way or the other. In Japan, too, more Britons are being arrested – but what can we do to prevent it at the moment. Our hands are pretty tightly bound at home.

I feel as if I am heading straight into disaster! I am going into it with my eyes wide-open. I can still apply the brakes...[4]

Invasion Imminent

Friday, 2 August

I am beginning to look upon this war with the interest of a reader of a novel. I finished reading *Honourable Estate* by Vera Brittain today. I am very fond indeed of this type of book, it attracts me and I am at home within its covers. I want to read her *Testament of Youth*. Sometimes I feel as though I joined up with Dad (in 1911, good heavens) and fought with him in 1914–18. The feeling is real and like the novel.

Last night I changed into my sports coat and shorts, grey socks and walking shoes, with an open white shirt. I had no idea just where I was going, but as is so often the case I found the wheels turn towards Carshalton. I cut a good speed and arrived in under half-an-hour in River Gardens; here I chanced upon Jean Doville (the little girl who always said she loved me). She called 'Hallo, Colin' and I thus became engaged for quarter-of-an-hour's enjoyable conversation. She is now thirteen, with fair, curly hair, freckled face and pale blue-grey eyes. I should very much like to see Alan meet her, when my brother is a bit older, of course. Then I went hell-for-leather back to Wandle Green where I gathered sufficient courage to dash past Mrs Howarth's and Kate's. As fate would have it I saw Kate: she did not appear to see me. Reaching Hackbridge, I became resolved to see her again. Consequently I rode back fast through the High Street and down Nightingale Road, where she was approaching the railway arch. I then slowed down, put on an air of nonchalance, and produced a terrible, croaking whistle. She saw me after I had passed under the bridge, and we stared full at one another. Then she began to smile, and so did I. She laughed. I shouted 'Hallo' and skimmed round in front of a 77 bus and came up to her.

I experienced very mixed, nervous feelings. However, she at once put me at my ease. She said she had seen me on a previous night. I did not say I had seen her – I never dreamed she would want to speak with me again. Apparently Kate would have spoken when I saw her the other night, only she imagined I had no desire to speak with her. Mutual thoughts. Well, the ice was broken. I wished fervently that I hadn't my shorts on; I looked no blasted older than fourteen, I swear. Her eyes twinkled in her amazing, fascinating way; so Bette Davis-like I always thought. Her face was white, very pale, but her skin was delicious. Her attitude became infectious, as I have so often discovered. She wore a neat fawnish-brown costume, stockings and high heels. I asked her how her young men were progressing, with a mighty big lump stuck in my throat. I learned she has many, as I can fully believe. We stayed talking for half-an-hour when I said I would have to be going. She must have been going to meet someone, but she chose to stay awhile with me. I wonder? Naturally, I asked her to come over to our place – to my delight she said she would, and nearly had the other day. Speaking to her took me back beyond the dark horizon to the sunny days I once knew. We were surely back in 1935–37? But no, horrible reality had to be stared at. They always say a war makes up for petty squabbles: I believe in that. Yet I would not change that moment for any other. I am older now, more mature. I know my own mind, I can voice my thoughts, pen my deeds, begin to see my future – I now know that I still love Kate.

Before leaving her I meant to say so many things; I wanted to arrange further meetings; tell her of my moods; tell her everything. My first vision of Kate was of a straight-haired, scholastic little girl, dressed in gym-slip and blue blazer, opening the front gates of her house for her father's car to drive through. I knew instinctively then that somehow that girl was my fate. I cannot possibly explain why. I don't wish to – it is enough to feel that way. After this we threw notes over the garden wall, waved secretly out of the bedroom windows of a night. In 1938, after my accident, I really thought we were together again – then the devil of intense jealousy pervaded, conquered and possessed my soul. I quarrelled and swore. We moved then, but she wrote to me. I scorned to reply. I can write pages of her, and nothing will compensate for the fact that I have lost her.

In bed last night I simply could not sleep. I threw off the clothes; listened to the snarling roar of a German bomber and from a far, remote existence, saw the searchlights sweep the heavens. Kate was everywhere; jumbled as a jig-saw. I tried in vain to piece her together. Throughout the past year I have always thought of her. In my school-days at Carshalton I suffered agonies of mind over her. I vow never to again. Always she has been present; as I've wandered round London, seen beautiful things, become sunburnt, done daring deeds – as I've gone to shows, to the West End Corner House, rowed on the Serpentine – as I've walked in Surrey, made poems, wrote articles, felt all-powerful – as I've thought complex thoughts, read books, seen pictures – I have always felt her presence and wished she had been with me to share my joys. It is not as if Kate was intellectual: candidly, she is not. I honestly do not believe she would understand my high ambitions, my perplexing thoughts. Binnie would, I am confident – but I love Kate. I haven't any earthly idea why.

Finally I grasped my plan. I would telephone her and ask her to come for a hike this week-end. I would not write – I remember all too vividly the fate of my last letter. It thus became the consuming desire to arrange a meeting.

Friday, 2 August (later)

I telephoned Kate's home at 5.20 p.m. just before her father gets home and, I hoped, just as she did. I was doomed to failure. Mrs Lucas (who reminded me she is Mrs Williams, to me she never will be) informed me very haughtily and finally that Kate was not home. I have rarely spent such an embarrassing few minutes as this conversation required of me. I thanked God when it was done with. I know the woman doesn't approve of me – but I care nothing for her. If it were the late Mrs Williams it would be so different: I would then feel awful.

My idea was to take Kate out into Surrey, talk to her, explain everything. I intended telling her my whole life story, of my moods, depressions, desires, how I felt about her, what she meant to me. I wanted to hear Kate's story (and I believe the truth would be hard, for me, as well as for her to tell. I realise Kate has an undercurrent of deceit, but I am aware of its implications and I still love her). Then I fondly imagined us kissing. I could feel her within my arms, feel her face against mine. We gaily skipped away over the grass hand-in-hand. At least I should have kissed one girl in love – the only girl I have ever really known. This day of fulfilment has been aching within me for years – I thought the golden chance was here.

I have never bodily desired Kate. My kiss would be of love, exotic love. Perhaps it would have tasted of passion. But I feel for Kate the most sublime, beautiful love. I confess I have succumbed to a passionate embrace before now: but love and lust are two vastly different contrasts. I want a girl – Kate. I want to tell her of the good within me, want her sympathy. I feel I want to demand and am entitled to her understanding. But if Kate doesn't love me, I would still love her. I would not even now think of encroaching upon any loyal attachment she has towards any male – but I am convinced she has not. But I believe for me she has. If we both love the other is red tape going to stop Colin Perry? No! I literally trembled with feeling for her last night, a feeling never known before. Tonight is another perfect sky, the kind when I always see Kate most clearly. Tonight is Kate.

Sunday, I had prayed, was to have been the day of realisation. That day, 4 August, I feel may be the day for invasion. I can imagine nothing more indescribably beautiful than Kate and I alone in Surrey whilst the hordes of evil pour over the countryside, death pours from the skies. If I should die with her contentment would forever be mine. I can see myself now – sheltering her from the forces of evil alone in Surrey – her song would ring true, her song of childhood:

'If you were the only boy in the world, and I was the only girl...' I somehow feel that may one day be true. I always have. Suppose it was Sunday...

Saturday, 3 August

A grand summer's day. I cycled to Box Hill and Leatherhead where I had heard the Canadian Army are headquartered, and I wanted to see if it were so. South from Banstead I saw machine-gun posts, barbed wire barricades, and trenches which flung themselves into contrast with the soft green fields. Army lorries rumbled by every few minutes; despatch riders with crash helmets, rifles, revolvers, gas masks, packs and an assortment of paraphernalia screamed their motor-cycles along the road and some, perhaps more self-conscious of civilians, would bang out a deafening roar of exhaust and race all-importantly out of sight. Some bombers made themselves heard – there they were, almost invisible, flying at what seemed a tremendous height. No time to look at them, though. A very stern, efficient looking soldier paused in his duties of directing convoys to tell me, 'Move on, come on now, keep moving.' I did so, wonderingly, unbelievingly. Who, a year ago, would have foreseen the fall of France and who among the thousands of people taking their tea on Box Hill would not have thought it fantasy, madness that such a fate should now loom here? And if Box Hill was the more scenic without the holidaymakers it was somehow sad, as though its life had been taken away.

A Canadian soldier on a motor-bike roared up to me, 'Which way Dorking?' he asked. I told him, and with a gay wave he was off, full of life and beans. I envied him. I should like to be on guard defending Surrey if the invader comes.

I lay thinking on the grass in the hot sunshine on the top of the hill. With the exception of two pill-boxes being built on the railway embankment far below, the view was, as always, quite superb. I could not see any sign of obstacles on the fields below me, so that it seemed enemy aircraft would have little difficulty in landing on them. But I did not feel worried by the prospect and concerned myself with tracing the route I often walked from Ranmore church to Leith Hill where, in the distance, I could see the tower standing out of the trees. I mused that my route was now in the front-line.

I mounted my bicycle and was soon pedalling down the goat track, although with some care as my brakes would never have halted a mad onrush down that hill. The countryside was delightful.

Bearing left at the foot of the goat track I entered the village of Burford Bridge. As I did so a procession of armoured cars rumbled past, streams of army motor-cyclists, wireless cars: under cover of the bushes tanks of terrific sizes thrust their snouts; lorries, ambulances, camps, men – they were all there – almost invisible. I thought, somewhat wistfully, how much more exciting it would seem if only these were the days of cavalry and gay cavaliers: today, war holds little glamour. I turned for Leatherhead now, much to my surprise, practically a garrison town. Military police were in full control: the army ignored the traffic lights and made fun of them and it did not seem possible a bad smash could be avoided. The troops were nearly all Canadian, so that the reports I had heard were now confirmed. As much as anything, I think it was the absence of sign-posts which caused the Canadians confusion in the centre of the town.

An ear-splitting bang made me look round. Oh boy, a column of motor-cycle sidecars, with Bren guns mounted on the sidecars and manned by tough, boyish-looking Canacs burst upon the scene. This was war, certainly. I wished there had been a band. The young, female shop-assistants had all quit the sultry boredom of their shops and were revelling in their newly applied cosmetics, smiling seductively at the soldiers. Lucky Canadians! One lorry, filled with noisy, laughing, hatless soldiers dangled a small, live rabbit in the face of some of the shop girls – what merriment ensued.

I arrived home at 7 o'clock. I never thought the old bike would stand up to the ride. At any rate, I have had my money's worth out of it. The trip has opened my eyes to events and London does not appear nearly as war-like as the Surrey countryside.

Tonight I saw *The Masquerader* starring Ronald Colman at the Classic cinema. Very good.

Before going to bed I gazed at the stars on this beautiful, clear, moonless night and thought of Binnie even then awake in the daylight of another day. I wondered if this was our last day of freedom, tomorrow being 4 August. Twenty-six years ago we declared war against Germany – surely on such an anniversary Hitler would make his attack. If he does not, I doubt if he will invade us this year. I believe Hitler will launch his offensive against Britain just before midnight tomorrow. I looked at the stars and mused if on every one of those specks of light life (if life there was) was endangered by wars. What held those stars in their places? Why did we revolve on a ball through space? What is space? Is there a God? What use is life if we simply come and go? Who made God? Who made that power? Oh, life is an enigma, beyond reasoning.

Sunday, 4 August

This was to have been the day when Kate and I would fulfil the promise of our youth. However it is not to be, and I will not bemoan my fate.

I cannot understand why she has not rung or written me by way of explanation. Being concerned on her behalf I waited an hour outside the cemetery at Carshalton this morning until I saw her father's car drive up (I know Mr Williams always visits the late Mrs Williams' grave each Sunday a.m.) together with Mrs Lucas. This is what I had been waiting for. I sprang into action, and tore to the telephone kiosk in the High Street. 'Wallington 58762 please' I asked the operator. No reply. I tried again, impatiently, again to meet the rebuff, 'I am sorry there is no reply.' By all my powers of reasoning Kate should have been at home cooking, or engaged in some other housework, and I should be able to have my private chat undisturbed with her. I cycled to the station and 'phoned once more. Again no reply. I gave it up – if she was interested she would have gone out of her way to ring me. Too bad.

Went in car to Box Hill tonight. (Gosh poor old Dad going down the goat track!) Glorious evening.

If the invasion is to materialise this year I believe Hitler will launch it at 11.55 tonight. He loves to be ironic.

5 August

The invasion did not come – but I would not be too optimistic.

I managed, by dint of gentle persuasion and a little oil, to coax the old iron bicycle to Epsom, Ashtead, Headley, Walton Heath and Wallington. It ran splendidly until then, when the tyre felt flat and the chain kept slipping. A glorious free-wheel all the way to Beddington Park put it in better spirits, and it was not until Tooting that the chain slipped again. The ride was grand. How glad I was to get free of home today, the place stank of tobacco smoke – which I hate.

The air over the Downs was filled with aircraft.

The ride was wholly beneficial, and I feel glowing and radiant as a result. I carried my blue sports coat on the handlebars, and wore my blue shorts, white shirt, brown shoes. People think me very young; this time next year I will be in the King's uniform.

Thinking things over I am convinced that after all Kate is not my type. I was carried away by the glamour of the story the other evening – still I will keep it in this journal, and hear what Lawrence or Anne[5] has to say in 1967. Binnie is by far the more intelligent. Ivers is right. I have built a castle out of a molehill, as the molehill is the only thing I know, and can only see with impatience the castle from afar.

Poland has today signed a pact of Military Alliance with us. How fine these Poles are, so sensitive with their music, so fine in thought, so hard in battle. I am glad they are our friends, and hope the day will dawn when Europe will benefit from their sacrifice. They withstood the hell of the Germans better than any other. The flower of their manhood, outlawed, finds sanctuary in our island – God give them strength, courage, freedom and above all, their country. Always shall I respect, admire the Poles, and not a little do I envy them their quiet calm, peaceful in the knowledge that theirs is the right cause, and that they do their duty so splendidly by it.

Long live Poland.

Wednesday, 7 August

Mother was really upset last night. Money. Damn it! People think because we have a car we are well off. Vice versa. It's a firm's car, and Dad has all he can do now to make ends meet. He owes me £13.5.0 and goodness knows if I'll ever get it all back. I always save my money, and never spend it unnecessarily, but this little capital, about £16 in all, I hold most dear. I want to open a savings account but I must keep the money to hand in case Dad wants to borrow any. Mother hasn't had any really new clothes for years, and we seldom ever get out. Poor little Alan yesterday paid sixpence for a goldfish, and being anxious to repay mother who lent him it he sold some of his schoolboy books to a bookseller. I really like to see my capital and to think that I have earned it with my own hands. I want it to reach £25 so that after the war I shall be able to pursue my cherished world ambitions, and see Binnie. That money represents the life of my dreams. In any case I shall need the money to buy civilian clothes after the war. The California Standard are real swell in offering to make-up my money every week if I volunteer for the services. I only get 30/- a week, and am worth a lot more. Miss Mann and I are the busiest people in the office – I would ask for a rise, but they may misinterpret my meaning and think I am trying to make more money if I join up. But honestly I cannot afford to buy a suit or anything, and soon circumstances will force me to ask. It annoys me to think I work the hardest (relatively speaking) in the whole office for the least wage. I literally sweated myself out for them during my first year, and for only 15/- a week. Still they are a grand firm in their intentions and I should hate to leave them. In any case my next job will be in the armed forces. I wish I could pay Mother more. I was so upset last night that I today sold some highly prized stamps for 18/- and thus I hope to make her a present of some few shillings. I will sell more this week. If only Dad could win some money.

I bought a Penguin *Lawrence of Arabia: Zionism and Palestine* by Stom. I must recommend this to Pewsham. Yesterday I lent Miss Spindler my *Seven Pillars*.

Ivers and his people are quitting Chancery Lane for Newquay. Hell, that fellow is now growing a beard, wearing blue corduroys, a red shirt, sandals, and his hair even longer. I have suddenly seen him in his true colours. He is an actor, to himself as well as to others. He makes himself believe that he thought up other people's views. He is an impostor. A rotten conchie. Many times he has let me down, yet only last night he rang me up to invite me to lunch with him and to bring some foreign stamps for him to sell and said we will go fifty-fifty on profits. Does he think me mad? I can get 100% alone. His people have money – mine haven't.

Everyone expects the invasion tomorrow. Well, the Englishman is completely unperturbed, and goes about his business as usual. Incredible, amazing, magnificent.

8 August

Two letters from Binnie this morning. These are the letters I imagined had gone to Davy Jones' locker. It is increasingly obvious that Binnie is my Utopia. More is unnecessary.

R.A.F. wrote – must reply in seven days if I want still to be considered to join R.A.F.

War Office wrote – publication of instructions for that commission business is to be issued shortly by H.M. Stationery Office. It emphasises the age limit – 18 in January next. Hell, can I try a gigantic bluff?

Dad has lost or mis-laid his Old Contemptible badge. Gosh and I had treasured that for years – wanted it for Lawrence or Anne.

Dad's Aunt wrote to say Auntie Beatie is in Santiago, due to an earthquake in Peru. Apparently Auntie Beatie thinks if Hitler conquers here (which he won't) he will only have to telegraph to Chile to pull off successfully a conquest in that country. The Chilean air force, army and navy are all pro-Nazi, and the country swarms with Germans and Italians. Beatie is anxious to return to Peru or the Argentine as both these countries are extremely loyal and pro-British.

The Italian attack is progressing favourably for them so far in British Somaliland. If we cannot dig in at them out east we are going to lose an enormous amount of highly important prestige. I would give anything to be fighting out east – a second T.E.[6] perhaps. I love the desert, the heat, and the army. Sweat, sweat, sweat. AH!

The *Evening Standard* Military Correspondent writes that the attack by the Italians must be the signal for the German offensive against us. This is zero hour for Britain too.

Last night in the A.R.P. wardens' post G.65, an old rugby blue who played ten years for the London Irish asked me what college I attended. Hell. This tie (red stripes on black) I wear certainly looks like an old school tie, which is why I love it so.

I feel really good lately; my hair is fair and anyhow, my face is tanned, ah if only Binnie could see me ... I love her saying my letters reek of Colin – just me!

9 August

The invasion did not come yesterday. Now people think Hitler will try today or tomorrow, both dates of which are favourable to his star. I maintain he will strike on the 22nd of this month now. Thus his schedule to be in London on August 15 is delayed – forever.

Our R.A.F. shot down 64 planes yesterday. We lost 16 fighters.

The Italian advance in the Somaliland has been halted.

The dropping or spraying of germs from the air, besides using gas in large quantities, is a possibility to be expected from the Nazi strategy. If not, and we stem the invasion, our blockade will be responsible for the spreading of pestilence all over Europe, and we will have to keep and prevent anyone from landing here, or the pestilence will overtake us also. I have heard several people are taking the precaution of being inoculated against typhoid etc.

Wrote umpteen pages to Binnie.

Sold some more foreign stamps for a good price – £1.10.0. Gave Mother 10/- from the proceeds.

Reading *Medal Without Bar* by Richard Baker. I like reading books about the last war in this one.

I must ask Storrs about that bird tapping on T.E.'s windows – something is contradictory in his version.

I *will* enlist – anyhow I shall be in action this time next year.

Saturday, 10 August

Last night I cycled to Carshalton. I saw 'Professor' Black, and had most interesting one hour chat with him. Surprising – he was the most 'bullied' fellow at school, is skinny etc, but now I have proved my argument. He is quite intelligent, and derived from that is a knowledge of the world situation. He is prepared and anxious to get in the army; it is apparent, I told him, that all these 'tough' fellows at school, bursting with brawn and apparent guts, are nothing but impostors. When a test calls for real courage they are right in the back line: they simply have not the mind to grasp the stupendousness of the whole affair.

I told Black of my fears for Chamberlain; namely that in the event of a severe British defeat – God forbid – he would be produced like Laval and old Pétain. I cannot understand just why Churchill does not kick him out, or is that version that 450 M.P.'s support Neville Chamberlain true?

America's *Time* of 22 July is most interesting and historic. It sums up just what the significance of the downfall of Britain would mean to them. They are now able to realise how dependent they were upon us. America would not help us at all by entering into this war. They are in greater danger from the Nazis than ourselves if they only but realised it. Riddled with fifth column, a bastard race, with a conflict of opinion they must maintain a two ocean Navy which they can't. Their country is so vast that the movement of troops could be a most hazardous, almost impossible task. The big industrial cities are wide open to bombardment. They have a tiny army, and an obsolete air force. They ponder as to whether they should send us all their resources, or keep them for home defence. Let me say now, if we are beaten America is too. They shouldn't dally; they ought to give us everything, or go right ahead with their own preparations, though I very much doubt if the American would give up so much for his country as we do in England.

10 August (later)

I am in my beloved room, sitting on the brown, orangy-coloured bed, in navy shorts, white, untidy dust-stained shirt, grey socks and a most comfortable pair of black, box-calf shoes. My appearance is that of a person 'off the track' and, indeed, I am. My hands are black with grease, my legs the wont for dust, my eyes ache from the wind; my hair is splendidly ruffled. Oh I am so happy – I sing from the housetops. Why am I happy? I have felt once more the pleasure of my soul. I have bent my body low over my old bicycle, I have pushed those pedals round harder than they ever went before. I have smelt again the exhaust of engines, the dust rising from the road, the smell of new mown hay, of the slowly changing trees and heath; the glories of inhaling greedily, anxiously, the fresh air, as it sweeps over hill and over moor, untainted by the smoke of factory and mill. Again I have heard the crash of machines, the squeal of brakes, the bird on the wing, the wind softly whistling as it is bustled along like some cantankerous old lady, trying to hurry on the dawning young winter, so that she may again play her tantrums on us poor humans. The steady hum of well-tuned engines vibrated the ever-changing sky, and powerful, swift, lean, dark aircraft played amongst the scurrying clouds. England was at rest, if only for today.

I commenced with the objective of visiting Brooklands. Riding into the teeth of a strong, unabating wind, I sped through S. Wimbledon, along the Kingston by-pass, up the gradient of Esher, and out into the land of my dreams, Surrey! I pushed hard on the Portsmouth Road, enjoying eagerly the sensations I thought never again would be mine. The bicycle, surely only used to steady plodding on a regular route by a labourer, bore up cheerfully to its unforeseen burden of youth, with his energy and freedom that imposed such enormous strain on its antiquated iron frame that a few weeks before had reposed undignified outside a suburban second-hand shop. This seemingly dilapidated iron responded magnificently, uncomplainingly, as if it too was discovering another, better existence, and bounced proudly along, passing all corners, and disdaining to look right or left. Perhaps it appreciated the well-meant intentions of its youthful rider, realised the value of its burden, the untold enjoyment it again found itself capable of giving. Certainly the rider appreciated the sudden strain he was asking, but he was relentless and considered himself alone. On along the rolling road until I eased my speed and turned off for Brooklands.

Brooklands presented the war. Aircraft roared continuously overhead. The buildings, hangars, outhouses, were all camouflaged in green, brown, black. Over the roofs were gigantic nets covered entirely with artificial leaves. The actual racing track, and the sand-banks behind, were also draped in these rather picturesque nets. At least the war had brought a measure of beauty to those stark white sand cliffs. I had understood that the German bombers had destroyed 'hangars at Weybridge' but I never saw one scratch. On my way I had branched off at Esher to view the destruction of three houses by enemy bombs. The 'plane responsible was the one which had popped off its guns directly over us – I might never have written this! Heavy damage had resulted: three cars had been blown through a wall etc, but amazingly enough only five persons had sustained cuts. I would add this was my first impression of the reality of war.

I glanced again at the seething workshops of Brooklands. Surely fate had been kind in directing those loads of death upon such a mission of 'peaceful' destruction, for if they had fallen on those Brooklands buildings…! Cars were parked everywhere. I became sentimental. Some of those cars, the majority, belonged to the aircraft workers – others, I contemplated, on just the other side of the fence, to our pilots and gunners who fly into hell – yes, sometimes a car would be driven away by a different man. Yet there must be something all-fascinating in an airman's life – that bond of friendship – eat, drink and be merry, for tomorrow we die. If I cannot be a pilot, I will accept an air-gunner's responsibility, knowing full well death will ride at my elbow and at its leisure rid this world of that which makes Colin Perry. It will be 'honour in character' which will make me ride with that dark compatriot. Of course I may be a pilot, and live to see the fulfilment of my innermost dreams.

I turned my faithful iron around, crossed the main road, and struck off on new ground. The heather, ferns, hedgerows all impressed themselves upon me. The wind blew crossways, and the iron squeaked objection to this unfair demand. Ah, as I sped down hill, this was the very essence of my existence, this control of a machine propelled by personal exertion; those people who passed me by in their fast, elegant cars, were they so peaceful and content as I: they in luxurious saloons and me on a ramshackle old iron which cost but one note? I very much doubted if they were. Why at any second the front tyre, with its smoothness, its cuts and exposures, may burst asunder in defiance of this uncalled strain. But I gave it no respite.

I was in the tall, dark, lofty pine woods now. The sweet-smelling fragrance imbued my soul. Yes and there, through the clearing, was the final fulfilment – a clear, rippling lake. I laughed, alone in my solace and solitude. Old iron you may rest – I carried her, my precious life, to the edge of the lake. I pushed the reeds aside, and trod the mud; a stagnant affair; on, over cones and needles, through bushes and more reeds, until I came upon the relaxing sight of enviable children splashing and shouting at the water's edge. How I craved to plunge my body, naked, into the fresh coolness of its depths. Floating in the centre of this beautiful lake were green trees, which enhanced the paradise. Their purpose seemed sinister. I immediately arrived at the solution: it was to prevent the invader landing by seaplane. I preferred, then, to omit this unpleasantry, to forbid the reality and urgency of the day to creep in and deprive me of my ecstasy. This, I learnt, was Wisley Hutch, and Guildford was southward only 8 miles; Cobham and Riply were at hand. My route, to my glee, lay to the east some 6 miles to Effingham. Old iron you did not know then how far we had journeyed.

It was a winding, tree-protected, quiet country lane which bore the weight of my desire. I happened upon a companion in the form of an elderly gentleman bound for Bookham. I would have preferred my solitude, but did not wish to appear unkind. Effingham and the parting of ways was only but a short while. I struck straight on, through a lane, so peaceful and lonely in pre-war days, contending with an encampment of lean, jovial Canadians. Some, in the shade of the woods, were writing to their loved ones across the sea; others played a form of baseball; several were shaving, and one having his hair cut. All were conscious of the side glances and open admiration of a party of girl cyclists. As I wistfully imagined myself away on some foreign field in the service of my dear country, I wondered if I too would have been so cheerful. I prayed that these lads from the prairies, the mountains, creeks, towns and villages of Canada, standing here on my noble Surrey hills also loved my country. I was glad that Surrey and this particular lane had the joyful responsibility of caring for her brothers from across the sea. I rode the more gladly; I inhaled willingly the smell of their camp fires, listened to the soft rolling of their accents. The view to the south was lovelier than ever before.

The leaves scurried and entangled themselves in old iron. Ranmore next was still as lovely, the ferns even prouder. I saw two gaily dressed girls upon chestnut horses. One was attractive, finely featured, proud; I wanted to talk about my thoughts to her. She, however, strong, clean and splendid, glanced not in my direction, and Bette Davis-like rode sternly, superbly, haughtily ahead, her orange blouse billowing in the soft, playful wind, and the thud of her horse carried her out of my sight.

It leaves me with a very unsatisfied feeling to have met so many shallow girls with whom most men are so obviously pleased. How I wish I could meet a good, kind girl, full of strength and knowledge and enthusiasm, in earnest about life! There must *be* such! And I wondered truly, and trusted, and hoped of Binnie. I lay on the summit of Ranmore, on an open hill, feeling the caress of the wind and the hand of the sun. I watched the huge, forbidding clouds sweep onwards to another night, and I saw wherever there is darkness a light must follow, and I wondered exceedingly in the evolution of time, and of the ultimate destiny of mankind. Wescott below, Leith Hill grim, imposing on the horizon, the Sussex Weald unfolding before my gaze. This land of my birth what extent of debt I owed thee, and will I be called upon to pay, soon? Willingly I will, for you Surrey, pay any price. The earth was hard, but warm, and the country real, yet afar. Was I, lying there so profusely in thought, ever to realise at least one ambition of my youth?

On to Burford Bridge. Make haste, the old iron groans. I attempt the Alpine-like goat track, and in elation succeed in climbing her scaling heights without standing on the pedals. You groaned, but too, I say, revelled in your achievement – Ranmore steeple was now astern, Box Hill departed under your haste. Over Walton Heath, anew in vitality down through Burgh Heath you went, so splendidly. We noticed now glances from the mass, and were satisfied, but ran on helter-skelter, proud, renewed. Through Sutton, and on, passing the crawling, hopeful, egoistical humanity that filled those houses, walked those streets, rode in the buses and drove those cars. Steadier now, old iron, you are growing tired. Past Tooting Broadway you fail once more, but a dash and a pat and we're on once again, and home!

Thank you old iron for a most magnificent 40-mile run. Get some sleep and we'll do it again. I end right here – still sitting on my bed, but I too am tired, and go now, into bed.

Sunday, 11 August
I only ambled to Reigate Hill this afternoon, along with Alex, whom I had no desire to accompany and listen to his ignorant and animal senses, drivelling

sex. I hate sex, its mystery and superficiality, its intrigues and obsession. Yet too it provides so great a pleasure – but its awful undercurrent, ever subdued, ever cultivated, drives me mad! Why is the human race so decadent, stupid, in this life-giving force? If only I was Lawrence, whom I strive to emulate, and could derive my satisfaction from denial instead of indulgence. I fight in moments of extreme desire to 'save myself' and I think of Binnie, and I am full of my children to be. I pray God that I may, in love, generate two children, Lawrence and Anne.

As I write this tonight, in nineteen hundred and forty, my ambition seems remote; I see the desert I must first traverse, its trials – corruptness, lust, stagnation of dying and mangled bodies on the field of battle, my balance of mind and the subjection of my intellectual faculties, of frustrated ideals, and the burning of my world order – all this strikes hard, and my survival is to be submitted to the balance of right and evil, but I feel, despite the evil gnawing, that my soul will be moulded more firmly, and I shall pass through the desert, unscathed, and enter the oasis, which as yet is but a mirage.

Tonight the people in Holmbury Court discussed the war. They think that America and Japan must enter into the conflict; Russia will remain isolated, aloof, until the carnage has subsided, when she, strong in her virginity, will sweep in and seek to command all. The war will last many, many years. Personally I care not for Life or Death, and indeed I wonder what Life is.

13 August

Ah well I feel more stable today. My pensive mood reached its climax last night, and as I cycled round Wimbledon, Putney, etc, I blew the remnants away. Funnily enough I am becoming more and more pensive of late – I gave Vera Brittain a rest, for it is her kind of books, along with Wells and Lawrence, which arouse my powers of thought. I am thinking more about things, things in general, than ever before. I try to trace everything down to its deepest foundation. I started reading *Surgeon's Log* by Abrahams, and this only sufficed to make me utterly miserable as I realised how futile contemplation of foreign travel is today. Anyhow the book stank of Pewsham.

I delved into *Letters of T. E. Lawrence* last night.

Dad has his bottom teeth out by gas this afternoon. Horrors.

Of all the luck – Stonehams sent in their bill today for the *Empty Quarter* I purchased a year ago last February. The book was too full of technicalities for my digestion.

I guess there are two things in this world I am really scared of – sex is the first, and I would like to blow it all sky high. The second is that I shall never get the chance I have been waiting for to prove my powers of intellect.

Portsmouth has had some bad air-raids in the last two days. Our R.A.F. has accounted for 128 enemy planes in two days – the Jerry now sends over 500 or so at a time. Evidently this is the prelude to the invasion, directed to smash our channel ports and endeavour to blockade us from the air. A New York report says we have a new-fangled invention, comprised of shooting steel nets high into the air, which prevents the raiders from penetrating our shores. I am very sceptical about this; mainly because at the moment Hitler has no wish to penetrate inland, but seeks to batter our ports to smithereens. I am sorry to write there appears to be no raids over Germany these last few days. Why? A German airman shot down yesterday said 'the war will soon be over if you keep up the raids over Germany' – this may be propaganda – none the less I see no reason why we should abate our raids. After all this time of war why do we not send out hundreds of 'planes over enemy territory? Naturally, after the invasion has been attempted, our losses will be enormous, pilots will be fewer, and as the war progresses into 1942 the demand for pilots (when our air force will be nearing, I hope, its peak of expansion) will be urgent. I hope then to come into my heritage, and conquer the air. Offensive action too, then, not defensive. Yes I am glad I haven't replied to the RA.F. at Croydon, for when I re-apply I shall bluff that I went to a secondary school, did not leave before 16 years, and have passes in trigonometry etc. They'll not bother on checking up. Of course if in 1943 I am serving out in the China seas; fighting against the Japanese, I may get wounded, drafted back to base (Sydney maybe) and find Binnie as my nurse. Such fond dreams. Which reminds me – the girl in the ABC was back today: my deductions were right I feel sure, she has been on holiday; but I am uninterested now – slim, petite (?) Binnie is my star afar. Pewsham is writing to Binnie – about me and the chances of finding himself a correspondent like her. Suppose the four of us settle in Sydney in the years to be!

13 August (later)
Oouch! What an awful lot I have to say for myself today. But isn't it after all an eventful day? You bet.

I am now convinced that the war against Britain is on. The Germans have sent wave upon wave of bombers and fighters over today; our ports undoubtedly have suffered damage, along with our North Sea convoys. According to the 9 o'clock news we have kept up our average, by again bringing down 67, and our losses are only 11. Of course the side launching the offensive is prepared for the greater number of casualties – but such a loss is extremely bad to the Nazi morale, even supposing a guess at their correct figures is obtainable by the Luftwaffe.

The German airmen shot down have made some very interesting remarks. One said if we continue our raids on Germany the war will be over within three weeks. Another looked at his wrecked 'plane, gesticulated 'a million marks gone!' and still the stories pour in. Obviously their morale is badly shaken. It is amazing to think that Germany has conquered such a vast territory, and yet, with only this island to contend with, finds herself in imminent danger of losing the war. Perhaps after all this war is not so terrible – yet. In 1914-18 in

A group shelter in an underground station during an air raid. The 'wave upon wave of bombers and fighters' sent over seems to be having little effect on the morale of these Londoners.

launching offensives millions of men were wantonly sacrificed – now, at the most only 3-4,000 men are 'sent over' in 'planes, and the effect may be even greater than the loss of division after division on the field. Those men in the 'planes surely cannot feel worse than the infantry who 'went over the top' last time. Therefore these raids should be treated in the same perspective as 1914 trench raids. The tragedy is the danger to the civilian population.

Our continued success in holding the air attacks is of tremendous significance. It is being proved, now as I write this, that the vaunted German air force has failed to gain local superiority, and until this has been obtained any invasion will fail. Remember it is our 'frontline' aircraft which is wreaking so much havoc – true as yet the Germans seek only to smash and paralyse our ports and apply their air blockade, but we have countless hundreds of machines waiting to take the air as soon as large scale inland bombing is commenced. Oh yes, I am very happy about things in general today. As regards our relations with Japan – candidly all this sudden outburst of anti-

British talk would cease immediately if we showed marked success in coping with Germany. Even now, beleagured as we are, Japan is nervous. We have only to smash the German air force and Japan, America – everyone would forget their jitters, their jeers, and acclaim once again England and the Empire forever. Yes, we have really started to win the war – but still I would like to see us a trifle more Socialistic inclined. Russia may then be appeased, conciliated. No – I hate that Chamberlain word – appeased.

Cycling tonight, in shorts. Over Wimbledon Common, across Putney Bridge (how admirably they have camouflaged a pill box there – to match the grey stone church) to Fulham, Chelsea, Battersea and home via Clapham Common. I prefer the Woodmansterne run however.

Dad's teeth out OK and he sure is pleased.

Reading *Testament of Youth* by Vera Brittain. The *Evening Standard* carried excellent article by C. E. M. Joad on Pacifism. The time is 11.25 p.m. and I am the only one up – so I'll turn in.

* * *

This story is circulating as an office joke:

INVASION

Hitler, so the story goes, has looted Michelangelo's 'Moses' from the Louvre and carried it off to Berchtesgaden.

When asked why he had stolen this panicular treasure he replied: 'Oh, it is a great piece of art, you know.'

But one of the Gestapo, spying on the boss, has reported another explanation. He saw the Füehrer on his knees before the great Jew and he was saying 'Dear Moses, tell me how you got across that Strip of Water.'

* * *

[Extract from letter sent to Binnie in Australia; dated 14 August, 1940.]

...As I write to you this evening the war is gradually coming closer and closer. We are within 30 minutes' flight of the vaunted German air force. Really, Binnie, you've no idea how proud we are. I have watched, at first distantly, and with ever increasing interest the development of the Nazi regime. Naturally in the early years I was not in the least concerned with politics; school and play were my preoccupations; now however, since 1935 I have felt a desire to study the world and its peoples. In 1937, the full significance of the constantly arming Germany, read about in papers, told me by people returning, presented itself to me. I grew apprehensive. There was a prelibation of the inevitable crisis, and I became alarmed by the nonchalance of our leaders. I never felt much faith in Britain since we failed so ignominiously over the Abyssinian outrage.

I recall Abyssinia well; I was only 13 at the time, yet I remember vividly my disappointment, alarm, despondency, when my country failed to champion the cause of those poor, unprotected, ignorant savages. Maybe I did look upon it in 'story-book' fashion, but my mind, from that moment onwards, became centred on politics. Please don't think for one moment I feign to be a politician. Oh no! I am not clever enough. Personally I do not think I would be content if I were – you see I like to feel I have achieved something by dint of physical prowess; that is why I am such an ardent admirer of T. E. Lawrence, that great personality who combined to perfection physical endurance and intelligence. Something irresistibly appeals to me as I read of his rides in the great desert wastes, his juggling in politics, and his love of speed, together with the enveloping cloak of mystery he so dearly loved to don.

Perhaps, Binnie, I have served to illustrate my point. I do hope so. Thus it followed that all my reading resulted in my yearning to visit this new Germany last year. I wanted to meet these Nazis, see exactly what this culture has done to their country. Lise, whom I met in North Wales, only stimulated my desire. Well, in August, just a year ago, I was to have fulfilled my ambition. However destiny decided that it was not to be, and circumstances over which I had no control prevented my going. I merely spent my holiday in Cornwall, and but for health I benefited not in my attempt to 'get a line' on Nazism. On 24 August, 1939, came the world-shattering Russo-German non-aggression pact, accompanied by its trail of havoc and chaos, and the plunge into darkness on 3 September, 1939. My last glimmer of hope that I would see and understand a Germany under Hitler in peace vanished instantaneously. Now if I ever visit Germany it will be a land of misery, horror and devastation. I will not see any Nazi 'culture'. I will not be treading in the land of a foremost world power. It will be a Germany without an army, a navy and an air force, without its own Government; a country which never again through the signing of an armistice, will be allowed to rise and hold the very essence of the world and freedom in jeopardy.

Thus you see, I have lived a very interesting life. I have witnessed the growth from a seed to a flourishing tree – namely Nazi Germany. And I shall help in its destruction, and can already see the sun shining down where shadow is now cast. (That last sentence is of course supposition.)

All this is inclined to ramble, but the purpose of an introduction is achieved, and I trust you will see the following the more clearly.

During the past few days our island has been subjected to constant and heavy bombing attacks. It may be the commencement of the German attempt to blockade us by air, to destroy all our coastal ports, destroy our air force, smash the Navy's blockade, and affect the morale of our people. As some newspapers point out ... it is most probably a prelude to a large scale invasion. Tonight it is announced that 17 parachutes have been discovered in the Midlands, and efforts by police and Home Guards have failed to trace their ownership; also there was a report in the *Evening Standard* yesterday that 12 airmen had baled out of a bomber we had shot down. It appears as if a sprinkling of Nazi parachutists are already entering our island. Despite all this I am confident the war is being won for us – now! Why? you ask. First, the magnificent R.A.F. is bringing down an average of 60 Germans a day, 78 yesterday to be exact. Secondly, the captured German airmen have all testified that the morale of the Luftwaffe is badly shaken, and our bombing raids over Germany are producing terrifying effects. Thirdly, our stupendous successes prove that the Germans have so far failed to establish 'local air superiority,' and until that is secured an invasion is doomed to defeat. Fourthly, both America and Japan will have violent repercussions in their respective countries as to the potency of our effort to fight. America will gain confidence, and see that Old England may yet keep the Nazi hordes from infringing American shores, and hasten to release to us those 50 destroyers, at present wasting in their shipyards. Japan will not be so anxious to ferment anti-British demonstrations, and certainly if an invasion is launched against us, and fails, as it will, Japan will fall over herself in getting into our good books. As for Russia – God only knows what is instilled in their minds but they can but inwardly admire Britain for her lone fight against tyranny. Seriously, can Germany, a country who would rob the world of truth, ever be allowed to dominate the world? For the future of mankind the answer is: No!

I confess, Binnie, the air-raids on Southampton have upset me a little. The beautiful, proud, fascinating town, in whose precincts I spent some of the happiest days of my youth, surely cannot possibly be in danger of destruction by aeroplanes? The stately Civic Centre, the lofty flour mills on the re-claimed land, the New Docks, and the ancient Bargate, surely they are immune. Highfield, the lovely residential district, can that too be bombed? I may seem a little fantastic, but the bombing of a town in which one has lived for so long, brings the war home in startling reality. Yet London I love most, and if it fell in ashes tomorrow, all those traditional emblems of our progress, those fine buildings and lovely parks, beneath the German bombers, I would not be dismayed, for I know some day it would grow again, finer, as the centre of a free loving world.

A touch of humour ... two more typical examples of the Englishmen's calmness. Newspaper contents bills chalked up by vendors say: EAST COAST INVADED – BY JELLYFISH: and another: MON. TUES. WEDS. (with total enemy bombers shot down against each) then 'NO PLAY'... All these air battles are ... likened by us to a football final at Wembley. We have reached the final, and are leading 3-0 at half-time. That saying, if England was reduced to rubble tomorrow the Englishman would still find a place in which to dine, is assuredly true. Thank God I'm English.

Thursday, 15 August
It's a simply glorious day. Hitler would have had a grand time stalking through here today; dictating his peace terms in Buckingham Palace, etc.

The Bargate is just visible in the distance, as two children sit amongst the desolation in Southampton. *(Jeffery Pain)*

God what a hope! That man really thought he would be in London today. Haw-Haw[7] has apparently promised us that this week-end will surely see the commencement of the invasion. We've heard that one before.

59 parachutes have been found abandoned in the Midlands, N.E. and S.W. yesterday and today. Home Guards, Police and Military have scoured everywhere. If enemy agents have landed and found the hide-out of a fifth columnist, their system certainly must be unique, infallible.

Placards this lunch-hour ran 'America faces gravest Crisis.'

Yesterday the subject of a rise for me was broached; Braithwaite, only 15, gets 20/- a week: I, 18 plus, only 30/- a week and I am assistant cashier! Sheila, who did my job (then not so busy) before the outbreak of war, drew £3.5.0 p.w. Miss Mann came in this morning very indignant about it, and thinks it grossly unfair my wage should be so low, and I have been here for 3 years. Next week, whilst I am on holiday, Miss Mann is going to ask for me. Good old Miss Mann.

The ABC girl made to speak today, but I was reading Vera Brittain.

It's a perfect evening, and looking out of the office window the balloons are the only reminder of war. Post letters to Binnie.

15 August (evening)

I arrived home at 6.5 this evening, and met T.C. on the steps. We agreed to go for a 'loosening up' on our bikes, prior to an all-day cycle on Saturday. I changed into my flannels and sports shirt, and whiled away an odd moment playing Alan darts in the Court, whilst awaiting Tom. Suddenly the air-raid warden beckoned me, and asked me to pop round and tell Dick in the wireless shop that a 'yellow'[8] had just been received. I did this, and dismissed it. A 'yellow' is a regular occurrence. I continued my game of darts.

Overhead a hum of aircraft became audible, and I looked upwards into the slowly setting sun thinking to see a 'Security Patrol'; then I saw three whirling 'planes, and Alan yelled 'Look! see them, it's a German!' and by God it was. I tore hell for leather to the top of our block of flats, and standing on the window-sill of the hall-landing I looked out over Surrey. Yes, thunder alive, there over Croydon were a pack of 'planes, so tiny and practically invisible in the haze, and – by God! the Hun was bombing Croydon Airport. I yelled down to Mother, roused the Court, 'Look Croydon's being dive-bombed' and I rushed to commandeer my excellent vantage point. Machine-guns rattled over the still air, and there, only a few miles away bombs commenced to drop. At last, the war was here! At last I was seeing some excitement. Anti-aircraft

Colin's youthful innocence, portrayed in the diary, is captured in this photograph with his young brother Alan in Southampton 1933. (*Author*)

guns threw a dark ring around the darting 'planes, Spitfires and Hurricanes roared to battle. A terriffic cloud of smoke ascended from the town; two more fires, obviously slight, rose on the wind. Boy, this was IT! 'Alan, mind those darts' I shouted, for he had forgotten all about them in the heat of the moment. His friend said 'I'm going down the shelter' and ran down the stairs. 'Yes Alan,' I said, 'You'd better get down too,' but he had no desire to miss this long anticipated moment.

The excitement was passing, and cooling my enthusiasm, I deigned to look about me. Workmen on a nearby house calmly continued repairing a guttering; trams still bore the city workers homeward; the women and children walked nonchalantly on their way. It dawned on me that although the bombs had dropped only a few miles away; the noise to the crowds below had not been discernible. It seemed so utterly fantastic. I glanced at Croydon again, where but an hour later I would have been winding up hill on my old iron; smoke was rising from three spots, but evidently damage had not been great. I feared the number of casualties in Croydon would be great, for of all times to have an air-raid this was the worst; workers would be thronging the roads, traffic congested, and the factories changing their shifts. The awful part was that no sirens had been sounded. No sirens! gosh I hated the very thought. I jumped down from my lofty perch and I told everyone my tale. Heads were all craning out of the windows of H.C. but I laughed; they were too late, the fun was over.

My hat, I simply ached to write Binnie about *this*! Only an hour before I had posted her two letters, but even so I would have to load her with the burden of another. A raid was not an every-day event. I munched an apple and went out armed with my enviable story. I didn't get far though, for a whine, fluctuating, grew from afar to a sudden deafening crescendo. Only the air-raid sirens. Hell, they were a bit behind time, the damn raid was over. Least I was convinced it was, and it happened I was proved right. Still people were not to know that, and all the milling throngs calmly drifted to their nearest shelter. The wail died away, and the roads, practically deserted, made way for a police car speeding along the Upper Tooting Road at something like 80 m.p.h. complete with a whirring, piercing siren. Just like G-men on the films, I thought. The wardens efficiently took up their action stations, and I, well I still sat munching my apple on the steps, thinking well at last a bit of excitement had hit the everyday routine, and somehow it certainly stimulates one, and surprisingly enough even Australia and Binnie attracted me not at that precise moment. My one regret was I had to be an onlooker; boy, if only I had been in one of those Spitfires – oh Hell! those 'planes got me; I must be a pilot! Hallo, the roads were not so deserted after all; a few idlers and soldiers on leave passed by oblivious of the impending danger; cyclists still hurried home – to their evening meal. I really felt content; I popped upstairs and donned my jacket, stuffed my pockets with a book, knife, wallet stocked with my 'worldly wealth,' and glanced at my brief case packed with my 'treasures'; no I needn't bother with that this time and I left it in my room. I wanted to write to Binnie whilst that raid was 'on,' but the activity below I could not miss.

The study of the people who filled my everyday existence was fascinating. Old Barrows was the first to scurry below, white-faced. Davis too was a trifle unstable. Mrs Hawkins even shed a tear because her young daughter was out cycling. Peters, who had witnessed the latter part of the raid along with me, soon departed upon the sound of the siren. The naval lieutenant wounded at Dunkirk never even bothered to leave his flat. Tom C. wandered miserably about, bemoaning the fact that his cine-camera had not had a telescopic lens, and kept muttering 'I'm sure I could get that column of smoke,' but he never tried it. Dad saw Mother and Alan into the shelter and returned to finish his writing[9] and dress to meet the South African officer, as they are going to the second house of the Palladium tonight. I went across to the cycle shed and Peters arose from the shelter, so we had a game of darts. He was winning when the 'All Clear' sounded some few minutes later, and the uprising of the people from the bowels of the earth stopped our game.

I suppose it was now 7.45 and T.C. agreed it would be futile attempting Croydon tonight, for the roads would probably be cordoned off. We vowed we'll have a decco on Saturday.

We roped in a few inhabitants of H.C. and enjoyed an hour's cricket before going in for the news. Joy of joy! Magnificent, stupendous, terrific! 88 German raiders down up to 5 o'clock this evening. Great Scott, at this rate Hitler must be having a pain right in the...! The Luftwaffe will not be liking the white cliffs of Dover much longer. We only lost 19 fighters, and four of our pilots (13 I believe) are safe. Cheers! By crikey I wouldn't give a jot for the chances of the crew of that bomber (or bombers) which reached Croydon, although if the truth is known I bet they were so keyed up, so fascinated, that the bullets from our machines served not to distract their attention. Ah – thought so, one of our new 'traps' fetched them down. By George, I bet they would have given anything to have got back to their base and told their tale, of how they actually saw St Paul's and Westminster Abbey, the Battersea Power Station etc. To me, though, it still seems utterly fantastic, yet so commonplace. Whoever would have visualised the air above peaceful Croydon would be contaminated by bullets, anti-aircraft fire, and the town smitten by bombs. The news said the damage was slight, but the smoke is still very thick, although it is not thick and dark enough to signify an oil dump. Peculiar, only last Sunday I stood on Reigate Hill with Alex and remarked, as I picked Gatwick aerodrome out in the distance, some ten-odd miles to the south, how awe-inspiring a raid on that 'drome would appear from such a highly magnificent viewpoint. Yet today that musing became reality, only the relative view obtained from H.C. was infinitely superior than any Reigate Hill could have provided.

On leave in 1943, Colin and Alan pose for this photograph on Wandswoth Common. (*Author*)

Well, I hardly imagined that my journal would ever bear such an interesting story. I would mention that I was absolutely the first person in the whole of our district to spot the raiders and definitely the first by far to witness the actual bombardment. I think it was the most exciting moment I have known for a very long time, yet somehow it all seems normal. Perhaps it is because we have been so well prepared to face such episodes; well at any rate H.C.'s morale is no different than it was (or would have been if it had been built in the peaceful years of the 1930's, when war was as remote as ice in Hades). I am glad, too, that I was quite a central figure in tonight's affair. First in Wandsworth to see the war of 1940! Oh boy, won't Pewsham be jealous!

Mother just tried to 'phone Mrs Howarth, but all the lines to Wallington are engaged. Naturally, all the papers will be hot on the trail. By God why on earth didn't I 'phone to the Express an eye witness view of the bombing? Hells bells I might have got my name in the paper. Ah, well, it's too late now. And so comes the night... and a heavenly moon – and searchlights. So this is London in 1940!

16 August

Last night's raid on Croydon caused hangars, houses and a scent factory to be damaged. Twenty-odd German dive-bombers accompanied by fighters were

It was often the case that a raid could result in the destruction of the majority of one's possessions. *(Jonathan Reeve)*

engaged. How on earth they managed to get so far inland without causing the sirens to be sounded is beyond my comprehension. Casualties were numerous in Croydon.

Graham Spry[10] asked me to tell him my tale about the raid, and he even asked if he could read my diary account; so I showed him the copy I was sending to Binnie.

Lunching at 12.25 today the sirens sounded. In the ABC I scarcely heard them, and the people continued with their meal in the normal manner. The Girl went out just before they started, much to my disappointment. By George it would have been swell, for I could really have spoken to her, and stayed in a shelter with her. Just my luck! and I am on holiday next week... blast. I left the ABC and the streets were clear of all but a few people; I ambled down Cheapside, along Old Jewry, and so to the office; here I had to go down to the sub, and quietly cursing I had to bury myself in a book for half-an-hour. I read Time and Life all through. Paula Starkie was down there but I felt no stirring of interest. Damn, and I could have been with the Girl in the ABC!

Oh, a story. Whilst standing on the hall-landing last night watching the raid, Booker came along and inquired what we were looking at. 'The Germans bombing Croydon' I retorted, 'can you see?' 'It's alright, thanks,' he said, 'I can see better from my flat' and calmly, unconcernedly went into his flat, as if a raid was a daily occurrence. Afterwards I had to laugh.

Am typing this whilst an air-raid is in progress. We had the warning at 5.25 p.m. and all trotted down to the Royal Bank's shelter. I therefore scrawled out a short line to Binnie, until hearing the tube stations were open I decided to go home. However, the Bank Station is unfortunately closed, so as I have a season ticket I must await for it to re-open. I am all alone in the office typing this; according to a press report enemy bombers were approaching London in large numbers this morning, so there may yet be a spot of excitement. Looking out of the window I see two yellow gas-caped men on duty on the Bank of England; taxis still tear around, and buses, packed, carry people homewards, oblivious of the threatened danger. A number of people are still walking about in the streets, all unconcerned, although a repetition of that Croydon raid would send them all scattering. It's quite fascinating being all alone in a threatened capital, so unreal.

I gather the sirens were only sounded after the raid in Croydon last night to clear the streets for ambulances and firefighting units. Ah, the jolly old gas-caped man has a large rattle strapped around his waist. Mr Spry read my diary entry describing the raid and wants me to re-write it, cutting personal items, and send it to Mr Hamilton[11] in San Francisco. I must do that. He has also mentioned me in his diary, which in itself is an honour. My name will thus go out all over the New World as a witness of the 'Great Croydon Raid.'

Am now going on the roof of the Royal Bank of Canada to overlook London in an air-raid.

Saturday, 17 August

I scribbled a few lines to Binnie whilst down the Royal Bank's shelter last evening, and then heard the Tubes were running. Consequently I made to go home, but was stopped at the door and told the Northern Line and Bank Station were closed; I might have realised this, as the flood gates are closed upon receipt of a warning. I did not relish retiring to the shelter again, so instead went on the roof. I looked out all over London, but nowhere could I see smoke indicating the dropping of bombs. It was rather a superb moment up there on the roof; I thought that tomorrow the world would know London had had two air-raids in a day, and meanwhile here I stood on the top of the City during one of those raids. However, whilst meditating on this score the 'All Clear' echoed forth, and I had to run down 8 flights of stairs to the sub to grab my book, back up another five to the office, then down again (no lift working) and hasten along Princes St to the Tube; but my hopes of being first in the queue were instantly dispelled. As I thought, the moment the 'All Clear' went the crowds rushed to secure front line places. After 15 minutes I managed to struggle my way on to the Northern Line platform, and another 15 minutes' fighting found me a place in the train. After Kennington it stopped in the tunnel between stations for a hell of a time; people were perspiring, and leaning against the doors. I read the *Standard* all through from cover to cover, *Time* I finished off, but I simply couldn't face my book, so I just stood, sticky and longing for my dinner. I finally reached Trinity Road at 7.20 p.m., the journey having taken an hour; normally it takes 25 minutes.

I found Holmbury Court quite excited. The German bombers had been right over home, and Alan and Mother, both ignoring the warning had rushed up to the top block to see if Croydon was getting it again, and had seen 5 fires started by incendiary bombs just a little way away. Naturally they then took cover. The guns on Clapham Common were in action for the first time, and the shells burst all around H.C. 'planes roared continuously overhead. The crump of falling bombs vibrated all over our neighbourhood. I gobbled my meal, and then packed into Dad's car and 'went exploring.' We had to double up all the side roads as Tooting Broadway was being cordoned off; no tube trains or road transport being allowed past. We turned off just past Mitcham Green and into St Helier's. The atmosphere was a trifle tense. At Morden Station crowds were seemingly miles long waiting in vain for buses; these City workers, munition and aircraft men, didn't arrive home until very late tonight. We went in the direction of South Wimbledon, but the Home Guard would not let us pass. Streams of people were hiking along the Wimbledon–Morden road, so we parked the car and continued our exploration. On top of the Morden Halt railway bridge we saw a factory slightly damaged, and further along several houses were demolished. We could progress no further. I had expected more damage – but I hadn't heard the news.

I obtained full details this morning in the papers and heard Dad's own account, for alone, with his Press pass, he had been allowed through. The papers described the raid on S.W. London: descriptions and statements by eye witnesses filled the main story, the Official Version being confined to vague comments. I had better set this out in two sections, no three – first the newspapers, then Dad's account, and next unconfirmed stories.

1. *Press reports* – 'Nazis first Bombs on London Suburbs' 'South West London Bombed' and so on, ran the headlines. If it is possible I will send Binnie copies of the newspapers, but it is rather difficult to obtain more than one copy of each paper these days. Goering apparently has ordered his Luftwaffe to bomb all points of military importance in the closer neighbourhood of the big cities. That means us. The raid – the Nazis machine-gunned the streets of south London, dive-bombed Morden Station, machine-gunned a train, demolished a large pub on Shannon Corner, simultaneously damaging the Odeon Cinema. Houses were wrecked on a council estate, and bomb craters 30 yards wide were blasted on the roads. A number of people were killed and injured.

2. *Dad's Account* – Dad was 'phoned at 12.15 a.m. and in view of the raid he had to be in the office at 4.30 this morning. He woke me up; as he was getting the car out Jerry was busy roaring around in the slowly greying dawn; I listened to him for some while until the throb-throb of his engines lulled me to sleep. Dad had a good look around and telephoned Mother. He concludes that, contrary to Press statements, about 70 people were killed. New Malden suffered pretty badly. South Wimbledon Underground lost the majority of its frontage. One man, woman and small son were sheltering in an Anderson shelter when it sustained a hit by a high explosive bomb. The husband was killed, the woman's brain turned, and the child had the whole of his right arm lacerated. (This is not glamourous or exciting; it's war, forged by a cold-blooded butcher.) Another young fellow upon hearing the warning at Shannon Corner chanced to run the 14 yards from a building to his home. He went five and fell with a splinter in his head – dead. I haven't seen Dad today yet, so I will have to write more later about this.

3. *Unconfirmed stories* – Richmond Park was bombed. (Canadians stationed there.) A raider was thought to have been shot down over Wimbledon, but an investigation did not bring it to light. Morden Halt line was hit.

Personal observations are that the morale of the people is merely strengthened. Theobald, an aircraft worker in the flats, refused to go down on receipt of the second warning yesterday. He had been working all night before, and is on night shift indefinitely. His wife implored him, started crying, and he had to go to the shelter. It's awful, for these men are absolutely dead tired. It is increasingly obvious that the men who work in the City, provided with magnificent shelters, are worried in a raid as to the safety of their families. No longer do the womenfolk have to worry about their men, but *vice versa*. Quite a number of men went home to burning ashes last night. I think it high time a new system of warning was devised, for from Epsom to Barnet the sirens are under the control of the Metropolitan Police; this is unsatisfactory, for if a raid is over Croydon only Tooting, Mitcham, Streatham, Sutton, Carshalton, Purley, etc. should be troubled; instead Barnet, 25 miles away, has to take cover, and unnecessarily be alarmed. Two men walking to Morden from Wimbledon last night, I heard say 'Yes the A.F.S[12] will start earning their money now,' the other nodded 'Wish I could do something, only I am disabled, I did try to join' – just what everybody is doing these days, joining a service unit.

I have since learned details of the Croydon raid, from Dad, and Graham Spry, who secures his information direct from the Home Office. As the raiders started to peel off to divebomb, our fighters took the air, climbing at colossal speed, and slithered down on the tails of the Nazis. In the first wave a stick of bombs straddled the hotel and control tower, blowing ten cars and a bus sky high, and bashing a gigantic crater in the tarmac of the 'drome. The hotel itself suffered only the loss of all its windows. The troops on top must have had a highly exciting time, equipped with their Bofors for just such an attack. The second bomber pan-caked all the bathing huts of Purley Way swimming pool (closed for the duration) and dented the bath. Yet a third pounded its way on to the Redwing aircraft hangar, destroying a valuable repair plant. Houses opposite (unfortunately working class, the rich never seem to 'get it') were demolished, and the road strewn with debris. A scent factory suffered a direct hit, and went up. Shepphmore saw one bomber crash a quarter-of-a-mile from his place, on the Downs. None of these raiders returned to their base, all were shot down. In which case I cannot understand why we gave such information to Germany. For news of this raid I suppose Jerry had to rely on our M.o.I.[13] Dad is of the opinion that 40 persons were killed, but I am sceptical. I'll have a look this afternoon.

* * *

A paragraph in the press today requests people to write their return address on the backs of envelopes to facilitate their return in case of non-delivery. Reading between the lines the real meaning is obvious – in case the addressee is no longer there to receive it, i.e. if the house or residence is removed by bombs.

Damn! Through showing my account of the raid to Spry yesterday he has just asked me if he could have it. My diary is therefore to be 'boosted up.' He is sending it to Mr Lebkicher in San Francisco. I wanted to cut out the personal items etc. but didn't have time. That means I will have boringly to type out another copy to Binnie. Hell! and I wanted to do so much this weekend. However the Croydon raid stirred me so much that I simply must let Binnie in on it. She may be interested. I am glad though Roy Lebkicher is getting a c.c. for he's a great guy.

Well it's thrown my schedule out, but I don't mind, in fact I am rather honoured.

Sent cuttings of Croydon raid to Binnie today.

It's an amazing sensation to feel when I quit the City today. I am entering the danger zone. The bombers will probably bash around somewhere today. Tom C. and myself are to tour around viewing damage on our bikes.

17 August (continued)

Dad saw Malden station this morning which had been dive-bombed yesterday. According to his opinion there were at least 50–90 casualties, mainly fatal. It was such a mess that bits and pieces of humans were unceremoniously pitched into sacks.

Well it was a splendid, magnificent day, not a breath of wind, and a tropical sun. Tom and I started our cycle at 1.30 p.m. approximately. Unfortunately I was unable to have the morning off. We packed a few tools and a puncture outfit, and got underway. First we agreed we just had to visit Croydon. So very expectantly we made our way out through Mitcham and Beddington to Purley Way. We were now in the bombed area. I suppose I was surprised, but the people and traffic were absolutely normal; no evidence of alarm or tension, but just a perfect day and everyone was happy. Ah, there was a white patch ahead. Funny, no cordon of Police, Home Guards or anything. Remarkable, I had expected quite a little excitement. We alighted just outside the Redwing hangar, and commenced our scrutiny, all very peaceful and we were not disturbed by anyone, or asked for our identity cards. The only stipulation was that no cars were allowed to park outside the 'drome. We studied the whole show minutely, and our findings were:

The row of Redwing hangars, camouflaged to appear like rows of dwelling houses, has sustained a direct hit in the far corner. Twisted girders, charred bricks, wrecked aircraft, and every form of debris was scattered far and wide. Two medium-sized craters indented the enclosure ground, and workmen were busy tidying up. Nurses and First Aid units grouped in the centre of the tarmac appeared busy, although the last casualty must long since have been attended to. Over the whole scene lay a white covering of powder. I glanced across the road, and instead of houses razed to the ground I found merely the roofs off and shattered windows. All the concrete bathing huts in the Bath had been flattened out, but even they withstood the turmoil firmly. The large council estate stretching from the opposite side of the control tower appeared to have had the worst, but naturally I could not trespass upon the property of private individuals so I made no attempt to discover more. We walked a little further on, and saw where part of the aerodrome proper had sustained direct hits, but the substantial material had stoutly resisted. Not one single window in the hotel was broken, which is miraculous considering high explosive bombs had fallen on each side of it. We wandered on, past a small boy swinging his legs on a seat, past rows of soldiers and airmen basking in the brilliantly hot sunshine, past soldiers opposite the airfield lazily digging new Lewis Gun posts, and finally we took a last look around this bombed area, staggered that everyone for all the world took it as a normal event. I did not see the scent factory, which may have been worse. However I am delighted and relieved Sir John Anderson is investigating the reason for the non-sounding of the sirens, which was responsible for so many deaths.

We continued out through Purley, Coulsdon, along the Reigate Road for two miles, and turned off across country to the Reigate Hill Road. It was most perfect, and the sun streamed down. Yet all the time we were bang on the front line of a war unprecedented in the history of the world. Perhaps for that reason alone we enjoyed our ride the more fully. Between Chipstead and Margery Lane all fields looked pitiful bearing their burden of ungainly naked poles to prevent enemy aircraft landing. Reaching M. Lane we turned in the direction of Burgh Heath and rode fast, until our interest was directed to an army convoy, and we watched ammunition vans roll by for a few minutes. Across Walton Heath, exceedingly hot and covered with haze, and on to Box Hill. We sunbathed on the steep slopes of the goat track, overlooking the winding road, twisting and turning between the white and green hills, shrouded in deep green oak trees every few yards, until the urge to be on dragged us away. Down the hill, into Burford Bridge on to the coast arterial, past more barricades, tanks, lorries, and marquees, left turn and through West Humble, and into the hay, pig, manure fragrance of the real farming country. We admired the view from the summit of Bagden Hill, and then sped down to Great Bookham, now swarming with Canadians, much to the elation of the village belles, who, no doubt, found all their needs satisfied. Striking across to Effingham Junction we were halted by a diving, gliding bomber sailing to earth. A German? No, just in time it banked and went soaring aloft, to expose itself as a Wellington. We watched it land at Brooklands ten miles distant. Continuing at a leisurely pace along shady lanes, past village ponds, we approached the tall, sweet-smelling pinewoods which marked Wisley Hutch. Time was drawing late so we increased speed along the Portsmouth Road, beyond Esher, past a patrol of police cars armed with rifles, and so to the newly-bombed suburbs of Wimbledon. We could not by any trick succeed in passing the police on the road to Shannon Corner, and were diverted a mile round. We glimpsed torn houses through the trees. Coming out south of Carters' seed factory we saw the anti-aircraft guns, ready, pointing their grim, deadly muzzles skywards. Here damage was apparent. We passed over a huge patch in the by-pass, and guessed that twenty-four hours ago one bomb had fallen there. A garage, heavily sand-bagged, with its roof caved in, was still serving out petrol. Further along, near Dorien Road, a house had been visited by an incendiary, but bore bravely up, aware of its new significance. I rode very cautiously here, for my front tyre was practically threadbare, and

Areas cordoned off due to unexploded bombs were a regular sight in Southampton *c.* 1941. (*Jeffery Pain*)

glass littered the road. Riding through Raynes Park district, people were still gaily walking around, but the worst was yet to come.

Traffic was diverted at Morden Halt station, but unostentatiously we slipped past the alert police, and mingled with the pedestrians. Looking east from the level-crossing we saw where a bomb had smashed the line, and where the train had been machine-gunned. Wardens prohibited persons in one part, as an unexploded bomb had been discovered. Wreckage was strewn everywhere. I ploughed through glass. Greengrocers smilingly served out their vegetables through smashed windows. Sweet shops through boarded windows. 'Dear Bruvver Syd, when you R.A.F. boys visit Germany next time please remember us – Merton and Wimbledon, and return the compliment, Your luvving bruvver. P .S. Give Adolf the biggest eggs you have, and remember our Spitfire fund' ran a chalked notice outside a newsagents. A clothier's front proclaimed 'What we haven't got outside, we've got inside. Come up and see me sometime.' A second-hand dealers, 'We buy anything – except Broken Glass – we have plenty' caused much amusement. Numerous placards such as these decorated nearly every bashed shop. The local car dealer did not have the chance to display his art; he had been buried amongst his cars, all grim and charred. People packed the road, all laughing, curious; the shops did a roaring trade to their new customers, who enjoyed the novelty of being served from a shop littered with glass. The cold meat store had established its bacon-slicer on a ledge nearly sticking out of the window. A house opposite the splintered fire-station had been blasted away to nothing. I simply could not get over the people – I wish Hitler could have seen them. Honestly, it's unbelievable. They are just having a look around like a child looks at a new toy. It's just a commonplace happening. There will never be any breaking the British morale; we do not get jittery, only harder, grimmer, and determined the more. Every story which is told about the complacent Englishman is true to its deepest foundation. Thank heavens I am such, for I haven't felt any stomach rolling, nervousness, or fear at all; candidly I am just the same as a year ago, in the best of health and spirits, and the raids – well they're just raids. That's all.

Along every side-turning gruesome sights confirmed the ferocity of the raid. Smashed homes were everywhere. Many roads were closed, as bombs or danger from collapsing houses made passage perilous. The whole area of some five square miles bore the signs of the bombardment. Between two houses a bomb had exploded, reducing everything to pulp, except the Anderson shelters, which defiantly stood out above the ashes. These shelters are worth their weight in gold. I could write for days about this havoc, but it would not do any good. Once past South Wimbledon Tube the ordinary business of Saturday night continued unimpeded. Five minutes later I was home, enjoying a boiled egg and a cup of tea for quickness's sake, and then playing a makeshift game of cricket.

Summing up this raid on S.W. London, just three or four minutes from home, and along the route I traversed daily whilst at Coombe, and of an evening when cycling, I mention a few extra details. New Malden Station was dive-bombed, not Morden, and it was from here I travelled with Spike Spurlock (now in Al Khobar) and R.L. whilst at Coombe Cottage[14]. Many people were killed, and the whole station totally destroyed. A lorry driver who left his lorry to get some goods from the station just after the warning, has never been seen since. The police have visited every hospital, every mortuary, but no sign. Guess he was blown to nothing. This morning three delayed action bombs exploded, fortunately no casualties. As H.C. must look like a military objective from above, with its wireless aerials on the roof, and

'Keep calm and carry on'. Southampton locals trudge through the destruction at Six Dials on their way to work during the blitz. (*Jeffery Pain*)

as Jerry comes over here regularly, I suppose eventually we will get one. But of course we may be more lucky; Jerry doesn't bomb military objectives.

Well, wholly an interesting day.

Sunday, 18 August

We had just settled down to a delightful dinner – chicken, marrow, peas, new potatoes and baked potatoes, stuffing and gravy, when the air-raid sirens started. Dad and Alan both took their dinners down the shelter. I, only dressed in pants and singlet, took some four minutes to dress, and hugging my brief case I too toddled off down. Aircraft were roaring overhead, and I didn't have time to survey the scene. However, having deposited my belongings safely below ground, I came up to the surface. I went across to No.1 block to the top floor, and sure enough Croydon once again was in smoke. A big fire also showed in the Wimbledon direction. Putney too appeared to have been hit, but it may have been a factory chimney. As I was looking out I heard a terrific roar approaching, and being from the north I could not see anything from where I stood, so I ran into the court, to the shelter, where everyone was busily scanning the sky. Then I shouted – first again – some 30 or 40 enemy bombers, accompanied by fighters, were sweeping in a direct line for

Croydon. They were indeed very near us. It presented an amazing spectacle, like a swarm of bees surrounding their queen; fascinating, most certainly. A puff of smoke and the sound of a gun signalled our retreat down the shelter. I fancied I heard the whine of dive-bombers, most assuredly we heard the guns and the crunch of falling bombs. I imagined this was the real commencement of hostilities against the British Isles. After a few moments I again came up; I wanted to stay in the flat all the time, but for the sake of my parents I went down. Davis tried to keep me down, but my answer to him, if he tries again, is that I am eighteen years of age, old enough for military service and to fight and die for my country. Fellows only a year my senior are up there shooting the raiders down, and within a year I too hope to be there. That is good enough for him. I popped indoors and finished off my dinner, and went once again to the top floor, but the smoke had cleared, and nothing was to be seen. Evidently not a great deal of really substantial damage had been done. The 'All Clear' sounded soon after, and we went back to cold chicken. Damn, the only time for months we have had a chicken and then the Nazis have to spoil it.

In the afternoon I started out on my bike to explore. Firstly to S. Wimbledon, for I wanted to take copies of all the witty phrases chalked up by the shop owners; I could only just manage to squeeze past the police by the tube station though, and by no trick could I succeed in passing the extra guard further on. I had to make the detour through Wimbledon proper. All the roads in this area were cordoned off due to the discovery of more unexploded bombs. The previous night I had visited all these roads! I am at least consoled by the knowledge that I viewed the damage in its entirety. The efficiency of the organisation effected to restore normal conditions in these bombed areas is remarkable. I continued on past Coombe Cottage, but Malden is definitely barricaded off, much to my annoyance. I cycled back across Wimbledon Common, and nothing else was worth note; except of course the nonchalance displayed by people all taking the air as large as ever over the common.

Dad won £1 odd down the air-raid G.65[15] post this after-noon; this compensated him for being fined for speeding this morning [*sic*]. His first time. One would hardly imagine in a bombed city the police would still rigidly observe their laws. Such is the backbone of England. A 'yellow' stopped the game, and at 5.35 p.m. the sirens blazed forth. As Mother remarked, this is now a regular feature; the raiders come at lunch time, and again about 6 p.m. Well I'm glad they stick to schedule. We had no fun this time, and were left unmolested.

I wonder what Binnie will think about all this?

19 August

Seeing as I have the remainder of my holiday this week I decided to accompany Dad to the newly-bombed areas this morning. I woke, thanks to a hovering German bomber, at 4.30 a.m., and after a deal of debating I finally managed to get up. A wash in cold water and a cup of tea soon put me right, and as the dawn was just beginning to break we got the car out, and made our way to Dad's office.

The guns on Clapham Common loomed very forbidding in the grey light; through the sleeping City, over the temporary Waterloo Bridge; the Thames looked gaunt; and so to his office in Floral Street. Whilst Dad attended to business I wandered round and looked at early morning Covent Garden; plenty of food here; but all this was boring for I've seen it so many times, so I obtained a morning paper, and sat in the car. 140 down yesterday; they made to converge on London but were thoroughly routed. Those squadrons which did penetrate dropped their eggs around us.

About 6 a.m. we were well on our way to South London and Kent. Purley Way was closed, and even Dad with his Press card could not get through. We were diverted round back doubles. I had assumed a high explosive bomb would blow an ordinary house to Kingdom Come, but here only the sides were blown in and the roofs off. The general air was calm: milkmen made their early morning round, the paper-boy delivered his news. Bombs? one would never think so. Proceeding along the main Purley-Coulsdon road we were again diverted; ahead lay more unexploded bombs, and passage was forbidden. On this same stretch I counted four houses partly demolished by bombs. Coulsdon proper was entirely cut off, a time bomb was buried amongst the wreckage of a newsagent's and was expected to go off at any moment. The police forbade entry, but we were permitted on the understanding that we did so at our own peril. Rather thrilling that sentence. We stopped by the particular shop for some five minutes, and I enjoyed the 'peril' business. Dad was quite pleased when we were out of the danger zone.

Purley station was open to southbound traffic only, as a bomb had destroyed a part of the line to London. Several shops hereabouts were shattered. Continuing out in the direction of Kenley, the aerodrome which had been bombed and where so many R.A.F. personnel had met their death, we saw how narrowly a bomb had missed a power house to land harmlessly on an old outhouse. Near Godstone one house, in a row of some thirty houses all joined together, had been demolished, yet every other home was standing intact. There was a touch of the uncanny about this. From the main road we commanded a view of the valley and Farthing Downs; in the valley and on the slopes of the hill, here and there a bungalow lay, a twisted heap of ruins – as if a hand had stretched out and struck it. I could have looked at this sight for hours and still not comprehend why it was that a bomb just dropped out of the sky and chose any one particular house. Silly as it may seem, I felt as if – as if God had smote down that spot.

Our progress was arrested for some ten minutes by a bomb which had destroyed the roadway. I explored the crater for a souvenir, but came away empty-handed. I learned afterwards that the bomb, in whose crater I had stood,

Portland Street, Southampton, where a number of buildings, including a solicitor's office, suffered irreparable bomb damage. (*Jeffery Pain*)

had been a delayed action, and had exploded only ninety minutes earlier. We again had to make a detour, and navigated a narrow path across fields to do so. I was surprised to find a mile further on that the long white cement road to the coast had been entirely covered with dull grey gravel. The prominent chalk pits were shrouded in camouflaged nets. All this of course was to prevent enemy raiders being assisted to their objective. Climbing Caterham Hill we were halted, but were allowed through on the password 'Press' and placed 'on our honour' not to go further than Dad's business of selling *Daily Heralds* made absolutely necessary. I found a deserted road, and saw a yawning crater bang in the centre. Notices were prominently displayed 'Danger. Gas.' Evidently the bomb had fallen on a gas main. Upon further enquiry I learned that in the crater, only 70 yards from me, lay an unexploded time bomb, and being in a rural district the authorities were waiting for it to explode. As I gazed I heard a bugle sing out from a nearby military camp, the roar of aircraft overhead (ours) and the radio from a cottage broadcasting the 8 o'clock news bulletin, announcing damage done etc. near which I was standing.

8 a.m. on the 19th of August – it would be 6 p.m. in Willoughby, New South Wales, and I wondered, as I so often do, what Binnie would be doing, and thinking, and had she heard that S.W. London had been bombed? Only patience will tell me, I guess.

We again passed all the same sights on the way back. I arrived home at 10.45 a.m. returning via Croydon and looking at the burnt-out scent factory (in which some 300 were killed and wounded) and the 'planes on the aerodrome ready and waiting. I am now very tired, not being used to getting up at 4.30 in the morning, so will want to get to bed early tonight. First though I must jot down a few observations.

Rumours. Last night I was 'told for sure' that 6 Nazis had been shot down on Mitcham Common (2 miles away) and that a bomb had fallen near Beddington. Another Nazi had hit the ground near Rosehill. All this proved false, and goes to prove how utterly unreliable information by 'people who saw' is, for they see perhaps one plane at 10,000 feet, not knowing whether it is British or German, and instantly collar' on to a yarn about a dog-fight. They do not say this because they are scared; on the contrary, they are simply bursting to say 'they've seen a scrap' and convince themselves that they have. Everyone is so keen to be in an air-raid that they exhort themselves to prodigious lengths to realise their ambition.

The German Official High Command state today that 'Croydon is again in flames; Sutton bombed: Planes destroyed at Biggin Hill and Croydon etc. etc.' Speaking from first hand I can say that Sutton has yet to be bombed. Croydon isn't and never has been 'in flames' and the German story of Biggin Hill is a gross exaggeration. I have only this morning been all through Croydon, Wallington, Sutton, Carshalton, and we need have no more worry on the German reports. As for morale ours will never be broken. We are English, and I need say no more.

The damage caused so far by their bombs, and as seen and witnessed by me (and I've seen a lot) is relatively slight. In the raid on S.W. London, the worst so far is just four minutes from Holmbury Court. I am afraid casualties are rather high. As for the raids yesterday – I am astonished at the slight destruction they caused. The German bombs cannot possibly be made of the best high-explosive chemicals. I heard two little boys in Kent on their way to school this morning, say: 'All the school windows are broken' to which the other replied 'Let's hope so' and they both ran off shrieking with laughter. I am afraid that Hitler, having lost 142 in yesterday's battles alone, is going to realise very soon that desperate measures will be necessary to 'destroy the English.' Consequently I suppose poison gas will be used. We are ready. I give the 'Invasion' date as 22 or 23 August, the date on which in 1914 the Germans launched their first successful offensive.

I am now very tired. I commenced this with the idea of completing my diary. I have concluded, I think, addressing the story to Binnie. The grammar I have made – as I am hopeless at nouns and pronouns, adjectives and conjunctives etc. – is a flood of ignorant rambling. I'm tired as hell. I like to think ·when I write to her I need have no control over convention, and just tap down anything I like. I cannot tell how much I enjoy this liberty, it's good to think that if I say anything a bit nonsensical or unconventional she'll not jump down my throat. That is how a real friend should be. Oh hell what am I raving about. Let me stop now.

20 August

Cycled through 'bombed' Sutton to Burgh Heath yesterday afternoon and scouted everywhere for a sign of the 'crashed German bomber' to no avail. I continued across Walton Heath, pausing a few moments to admire the wide stretch of purple heather, broken here and there by clumps of trees. I seemed the only person for 'miles' around. It began to rain, so I lay beneath a large, spreading oak. Horses jostled each other under the shelter of apple-trees, and poultry cackled amongst the leaves tearing around in whirlpools. The scene came almost from a picture-book. Frequently the weak sunshine would penetrate a break in the clouds, and as it briefly swept the expanse of short wiry grass, it was as a mother smiling upon. her child. The rain sheered off, and a sudden whim took me pell mell back into town. Passing through Carshalton I saw Mr Howarth, just back from a fortnight in Dorking on holiday; Mrs Howarth, too, was extremely well. What a lot can never be said. Reaching home it was not long before I got into bed.

Quotations from the *Daily Express*:

This is our finest hour. This is a story of a little island, hardly bigger than Borneo, fighting a whole continent. Two thousand years from now they will tell this story, but we are living it, too close to this tremendous event to see how big it is.

As homes are crumbled and householders take the brunt of the Nazi attack, the cry breaks out again BOMB BERLIN! The clamour is natural, but foolish. Why should we bomb Berlin? We are not fighting this war to kill the German people, but to crush the German war machine, to cripple the Hitler method of life. Our objectives are such things as the great synthetic oil plant at Leuna, and every Messerschmitt, Heinkel and Junkers factory. We are not out to stiffen the Nazi will to beat us by murdering deluded German innocents. But let Hitler know this. Every man or woman killed or hurt by his bombs, every child killed, hurt or frightened by his bombs does no more than harden our purpose. Which is to obliterate him and every foul thing he stands for from this earth. "Give us just three days" said an authorised Nazi spokesman in Berlin, "and the German air force will hammer home decisive blows on Britain." Referring to the results of the first day of "total blockade" of Britain he added, "She is cut off from the world, and in particular from the resources of her Empire. She stands alone in a hostile world." (A theatrical pause.) "The air Blitzkrieg will be resumed with increased fury today or tomorrow, or the next day." Hitler wants three fine days to beat Britain. When Napoleon threatened to invade England, he looked across from Boulogne and said to his commanders: "Let us be the masters of the Channel for six hours and we are masters of the world."

All this I find only makes us more proud, more tough; prepared to a point of fineness attainable on only the finest steel. I await today with unperturbed confidence.

Am lunching with Pewsham.

Wednesday, 21 August

Yesterday, as arranged, I met Pewsham at 11.30 a.m. at the Bank Tube. I admit I was very sceptical about how he would turn out after ten months, but he is still the same old Pewsham. We wandered up Moorgate, and I showed him Binnie's portrait, and heard all he had to say about Australia. We then lunched in the ABC. The girl was there. She seemed very stand-offish, and we progressed not at all. In fact we both felt very conspicuous and foolish. Afterwards Pewsham said he thought she must be about 20, having that 'mature' look about her. I shuddered and felt even worse. I believe my two months' illusion is shattered. Thinking of Binnie I am glad. When she left at 12.25 we settled down to my notes on *Homo Sapiens*, but we postponed real discussion until later, in a more secluded atmosphere. We walked up Cheapside, into St Paul's (I bought two more postcards of T.E.L.[16]) once round the interior, then down Ludgate Hill, through the delightful Temple, and on to the Strand. Here we became intrigued at an armed guard on a public building, and we ventured through the imposing gates. It was only Somerset House. We continued down the Strand, up the Haymarket and along Piccadilly, Me remonstrating persistently on my 'indefinable ideas' which I told Pewsham almost all about. He is sympathetic and understanding, and I would never tell anyone else. Yet I was disappointed he had been unable to comprehend the *Research* and *Northwest Passage*; he could not understand my enjoying Wells, Lawrence, Vera Brittain, *Colin 11*, *N.W. Passage*, and *Blackshirt*. I most emphatically do: he says they are so utterly different and that one person could not embody all those tastes. Well I do. Through Green Park, and finally a row on the good old Serpentine. I rowed first, then Pewsham: my old tie looked liked a rowing blue, or as he said, to my elation, I looked like a young fellow just down from a prep form. The Serp was choppy, windy, grey and chilly, yet I felt neither cold nor hot, but just right. After the row we continued across Hyde Park, (and we imagined an air-raid siren was just about to sound by the tempo of the air) past the gun emplacements, and I was astounded to see the guns had been removed, and so to the Quebec Café. We reposed at ease, and I read an early edition of the *Standard* and discussed the people; the orchestra rattled forth at 4 p.m. much to our joy, and the splendour befitted us two celebrities. I had visualised this moment for a very long time.

I showed A.G.P. (A. G. Pewsham) my journal, and was elated by his enthusiasm; he wishes to start one now. I must say it looked important, and he said it seemed we were two officials in mufti with the Naval Treaty in the bag. The bill came to 2/7d and we hustled out whilst the waitress was absent, for we could ill afford a tip. Down Oxford Street, munching some plums, into Selfridges for a couple of jiffs,[17] then to Oxford Circus. I had previously rang Mother from Marble Arch and learnt to my supreme joy two letters from Binnie awaited me. Also that the under twenties may be called up.

Down Regent Street, Waterloo Place, past what used to be the German Embassy and into St James's Park. Here we walked through very struttingly, my old school tie billowing in the breeze. We sat down by the river, and became engrossed in discussion. A sprinkling of rain shifted us to a more sheltered seat under a beech. St James's was very empty that day, and we revelled in our own importance. Along where we sat all the heads of England had walked, and we were aspiring perhaps for some great episode in the history of England! The trees were, too, very green, yet Autumn had come: the cold grey sky and the blustering wind were glorious. Nature was at her best. How glad I was, for it means our isle is safe. I felt, as I told A.G.P., that we were living in the last war, or years ahead, looking back upon this. Our children will regard the war of 1940 I suppose in the same light as we, in our generation, regard the 1914 affair. I sunk back into the depths of the seat, feeling my hair blowing wildly about my face, lashed by the wind and rain, and my tie, my inevitable tie, billowing forth. My hands were dug deep down into my pockets, as were A.G.P.'s, and my despatch case and *Standard* reposed importantly in our midst. From officers to tramps one and all looked at us. We both had pretty deep furrows knit in our brows.

We took *Homo Sapiens* to pieces, and held forth upon our conceptions of 'ultimate success' which I said was the satisfaction of the mind. Like a man may wish to be a candlestick maker, and he becomes one. That is ultimate success. But if I were to make headlines and achieve world prominence by writing an essay on birds, when my whole being was directed towards the cultivation of Australia, then I should not have achieved 'ultimate success,' which is, as I've said, to do something you want to do. We debated on our age; how safe and secure 16 seems in the light of later years, and how enjoyed and accepted were the ways of life to youth. By 28 we shall be established and think maybe our thoughts of today were childish and impotent; yet I would gladly leave 16–18 years of age behind, for I am one mass of indefinable whims, I feel and see so vastly, yet I cannot pick up my trail. The security of the Standard Oil we exploited explicitly; Pewsham deeply regrets quitting, but as I pointed out there will probably be every opportunity to resume in this Co.

after the war, more especially if he emphasises he joined the A.R.P. directly upon outbreak of hostilities last September on a purely patriotic motive. If we, or I, go to Australia, I at least leave behind a life of security: I leave the safeness of England and the opportunity to settle down and raise a suburban family, own a small family car, and be just ordinary. Yet I believe life should be as one feels moved, for we only pass this way but once, and a life of toil is cheating the body of its desires. I desire to see and understand the world, and I am prepared to quit security. Casocol[18] offers me every scope for foreign progress, yet it's American, and it would not be cultivating my World Order. Of course Churchill may offer U.S.A. the act of union with the British Empire as he offered it to France (how glad I am they refused) but I am hoping he won't. For we are British, and I feel that that is an honoured position, and we should not hold in cheapness our heritage. I would never sign my nationality away. Still if the Yanks enter the war it will mean a lot to my standing with my firm. Yes 18 is truly an enigma to mankind, so profound and unstable in thought and action. I shall undoubtedly be in H.M. Forces within the next 6–9 months, and it will mean I am signing away my uniform of freedom, I shall be organised and impotent. I shall be a machine obeying every command, yet also I feel as if I am made to give the commands. I may change in mannerism and everything. I maintain a man is never the man of his own reckoning if he has served in the forces. His ideals are changed, his whole outlook. Sex is the undercurrent of army life, and I abhor sex. It is all compelling.

Very reluctantly we left that seat after the rain; proceeding to Trafalgar Square I bought another paper, and we adjourned for a cup of coffee.

We read minutely Churchill's speech, and we were unanimous in agreement with the wisdom of his words. Personally I agree the campaigns will open up in '41 and '42, and that the food blockade to the peoples of the continent should be continued without concessions. I do, however, give rise to concern about the ceding to the U.S.A. on a 99-year lease of our western hemisphere colonies. That is liable to cause dispute in 20 years' time. It is increasingly imperative, however, that we secure those 50 obsolete U.S. destroyers, and with that end in view Churchill probably made his gesture. There was also a charming little hint flung to the Soviet as to how they could effectively preoccupy the German Luftwaffe. We stayed in Lyons for nearly an hour, laughing about the antics and warping of George Ivers' mind, laughing about 101 things in general. Discussing at length Binnie, our letters, our ideals, our changes in features, and we were aware of many a look from other customers, but we didn't give a damn for anyone, and I have rarely felt so good, so rollickingly carefree as I did then. We came up to the blackout, and straightway descended to Charing Cross Tube. We laughed about the 'frustrated women' and the office in general, about the exquisite characters, etc. etc. We parted at the Bank, and have agreed to meet a week on Saturday, Hitler permitting. I must say that sometimes I cannot make A.G.P. out. I like him, yet he seems

Colin looks to the skies over Whitehall, 20 August 1940. (*Author*)

so very extraordinary. He seems very sensitive, yet I am more susceptible, appreciative of things and people than he. Yet I tell him most of my intangibilities, and enjoy doing so. I seem to laugh and talk about myself forever, yet he is perfectly content and would not have it otherwise. My aquaintance with him is 'rather indefinable' so it is very befitting. I certainly don't for one moment contemplate I could ever divest myself of so much to anyone else. We have a great deal in common. I don't think I would want anyone else. Yet, yet again, I wonder if ours is a friendship in its truest sense. I love to try daring deeds, and fight etc. but could A.G.P. do it too? No, he is rather a queer mixture, yet I feel I've known him for so long. Well, in conclusion I must say if he had turned out to be a lanky individual I most assuredly would not have continued my lengthy preambles to him. I am very funny about height, and it's rather an inferiority complex with me. However I do hope we can spend some more times together, for I thoroughly enjoyed myself. My one regret is that he seems rather stingy, and I believe if one is really enjoying oneself not to give a rap about money. I don't.

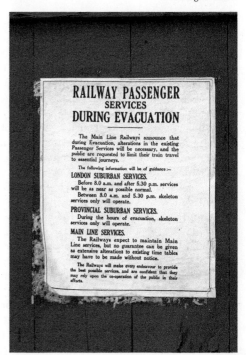

The Blitz resulted in widespread evacuation of London's children, which had a knock-on effect on public transport.

I am churning this out left and right, and Mother has informed me that she must tidy this room up now, so I'll have to cut down.

Arriving home at 10.15 last night, I had a big dinner. Mrs Block 'phoned, and was awfully upset. The dear old soul next door to her had been killed when a bomb fell directly on her Anderson shelter. Her road had been machine-gunned. Her children too were suffering from shock. Their house suffered pretty badly. The old lady was buried the same day. The Blocks are now going down to a village in Gloucestershire to recuperate.

Binnie told me off in her letters – but I really believe she loves me. Gosh I know I do her. I wrote to her 'ah well if Binnie is my destiny I shall meet her, come what may' but I do hope she isn't too tall.

This is positively all today.

Later: I have been writing nearly all day long, and at last have succeeded in completing the notes on *Homo Sapiens*. Wrote to Binnie and Pewsham.

22 August

This afternoon paid a visit to Croydon again. I obtained a splendid view of the whole damage to the scent factory and hangars. One bomb had smashed a huge crater in the airfield just a few feet away, but this of course had been patched up as well as possible. I attained a different angle by investigating the road which ran out into the airfield. Here I saw the inside of the hangars, the wreckage of several of our 'planes (probably 'planes which were being repaired or salvaged) and the enormous amount of ripped roofs, blasted walls and general bashed about atmosphere of all the rest of the buildings around the scent factory.

A number of squadrons of Hurricanes were rolling and twisting in formation overhead, and as I watched they descended in magnificent array, and I pitied any German who may have been contemplating that 'drome. On to Foresters Drive; here a superb panorama is obtainable, and I wandered down to the barbed-wire fencing, just a few feet from rows and rows of fighters. One, camouflaged with a greenish-brown net, had evidently recently been in action, for the rudder and part of the fuselage were shot away. The pilots and ground staff were lounging around their respective charges, some muffled in raincoats, others with just their ordinary uniform carelessly worn over a navy blue polo. It was a very grey, dull, typical Autumn day, and hardly weather to suit the Luftwaffe. To my mind, the windswept 'drome was even more fascinating today in the light of an overcast sky – I thought as I stood there, this time next year I shall be in that uniform, and I hope be in charge of one of those lean, powerful-looking 'planes, which ooze speed and adventure. I remembered the Comet which had broken the record to Australia – not nearly so fast as these birds of prey, nor as elegant or exciting. I suppose the weather was cold, but to me, in my shorts and open shirt, it was the more appealing; it was just 'my sort of weather,' and the mere sight of those 'planes under this Autumn cloak simply made me ache, until I knew that I would not rest until I was actually with those fellows under the wings of those fighters, casually talking and joking when at any moment the call may come for action, and they soar into the air on an adventure which must be the greatest on earth. There exists that spirit of 'supreme friendship' enjoyed only by those who live with death by their side. I can imagine nothing I would like better in this world than to be a fully-fledged fighter pilot awaiting a gigantic air offensive, lounging on the rough grass talking with Pete and Steve and A.G.P. by the side of our aircraft as we awaited the signal to scramble.

At the top of Foresters Drive and at the turning of Highfield Road I was amazed to see windows boarded up, and slates in the garden. Next moment I saw the demolition squads (at last earning their money) 'tidying up' a house, I remember in peacetime as one of extreme beauty, which had suffered the direct hit of a Nazi bomb. The bath was in the front garden, the stairs were holding on dejectedly to their upstairs storey, and the actual house, at least what was left of it, had burst from its foundations. Literally it had been blown sky-high. I watched the tragic removal of the wardrobe, and as the drawers were removed I saw all the little personal odds and ends which but a few short days ago had meant so much to someone. A workman (all the workmen were enjoying this clearing up business and I wondered at their joviality since I assumed the occupants had been killed instantaneously) rummaged out a whisky bottle and to the envy of his workmates he there and then polished off its entire contents, which were quite considerable, with the remark 'it tasted all right so I suppose it was' to the amusement of everyone. I ventured to enquire of a warden how many were killed. To my utter astonishment he replied, 'Nobody at all, they were all untouched' and I think my belief in 'fate' is justified beyond dispute. I looked with new and increasing interest at that utterly destroyed house; you can't tell me it was luck that its occupants were unharmed.

The top end of Purley Way was also police-guarded, so taking the alternative route I disposed of any scheme I had for getting through the cordon. However I soon found myself faced with a road upon which only a notice stood forbidding entry. Although a good half mile from the 'drome I knew it should bring me to the council estate which had been bombed. I explored, found another police guard, but evading them managed to get into the estate. I knew an alley to Purley Way existed here, so ruffling my hair, dirtying my shoes and making my shirt hang out, which was in keeping with the neighbourhood, I calmly hiked my bike along the footpath from Bates Crescent, whistling and slouching, and thus as a member of the 'Casey's Court Community' I fooled the police who thought I was a resident. Once in Purley Way it was plain sailing, and I loitered (to keep up appearances) casually up Purley Way and to the aerodrome. They seemed to have scored another direct hit on the hangars, and although things were pretty well tidied up the damage appeared worse. Personally I can see no reason for another visit of the Luftwaffe yet, unless the temptation of the factories prove too much. Outside the hangar was a notice 'Constipation cured here' which was apt. A bomb also seemed to have fallen on the soldiers' encampment, and I thought of those jolly fellows who chalked on their tents 'Itsabuga' and 'We can take it' which appeared after the raid of last week. Evidently renewed damage had been caused on Sunday.

I'm glad I've seen absolutely everything in conjunction with this Croydon raid. Speculation is rife about the total number of deaths in the scent factory – the morale is superb. I would mention one bomb fell on the Southern Railway Sports Ground, just missing several large houses. Removals are few from the vicinity – one elderly woman in Bates Crescent I heard say: 'It's not worth moving, nowhere's safe really is it?' with a look for confirmation in her neighbour's eye. Indomitable.

23 August

I was awakened in the early hours of the 23rd by the pom-pom-pom-pom of anti-aircraft fire. I lay as if in a far-off existence, snuggling down in my bed;

half-consciously I remember thinking 'I suppose the sirens will go soon' and they did within the next minute. Instantly my drowsy brain cleared, and I recalled with clarity that it was the 23rd, and my prophesied date for invasion seemed quite plausible. The moon was magnificent, silvery and shimmering, and looking about me I saw the dark, sharp contrast of the houses of London. As the sirens rose and fell, I thought how queer, how unreal, how like a vivid novel portraying in wild, fantastic form events to come it all was. And as I watched the houses drain themselves of people, like water going down a sink, and as the dull, vibrating noise of 'planes became audible in the distance I knew it was real. In this perspective I saw how cheap, how frail our life is. Just a puff, and a life, perhaps of a great man or an ordinary person who liked his pint of beer and his pipe, was snuffed out, for ever, just like that. And I wondered exceedingly about that 'ever.' The gunfire had ceased now, and it was cold outside, so I went into the warm, sticky atmosphere of the shelter. It was one constant hub of noise, of old women and squeaking babies, and men in their ridiculously long, overstriped pyjamas. Somehow I fitted myself in but only for a few minutes. I was back again with Dad indoors making tea when the 'All Clear' went about 4 a.m.

It was evident as the day developed that the raid was not serious, and I learned from Dad at 9.30 that several bombs had been dropped near Wealdstone, so I concluded the Kodak Works had been the objective, but only four bombs… so half-hearted.

I was for very personal reasons in an angry mood today so I took myself out to Clapham Common, after riding to London Bridge back to S. Wimbledon and again back to Clapham South on the Underground, deeply engrossed in *I Shall Not Want* by Norman Collins, a Book Club selection which had reposed for some time in my bookcase as I had considered to all appearances it was dry, but which I chanced upon this morning, having completed *Ah King* by Somerset Maugham (a sticky book of the Malay States) and within a few seconds I found myself deep within its covers, content. On Clapham Common (I sat on the first green near C. South tube) the wind played havoc, and sang along as if rejoicing in escape from its summer captivity. It held a cold grudge, too, and it prevented me from settling down as I very much wanted to. Finally I could tolerate it no longer; I was in no frame of mind for a brisk, invigorating walk; I desired nothing more than my book. As a consequence I spent nearly an hour over a coffee in Balham ABC. I made my way slowly in the direction of Tooting Bec Common. As I wandered up Bedford Hill engrossed in the *Standard* the cold became less intent, and when I reached the common the sun was shining on a scene typical of Autumn. The smell of the decaying leaves, of the hard earth, seemed, somehow, to remind me of Kate. I found a clearing upon the far Streatham end, and sprawling full length on the ground I once more found solace in my book. The book was just the type I wanted at that moment, and Kate came the more clearly. The sun shone so peacefully through the heavy green oaks, and filtered actoss the yellow, coarse blades of grass, and ran over my face. At last it was dusk, so I dug one hand deep into my trousers pocket, grasped my despatch case and *Standard* with the other, allowed my tie to blow at random, let my hair resort to its will, and with eyes on the ground I struck for home.

24 *August*

I awoke and was just going to have a cup of tea when the air-raid alarm smashed the early morning air. I had my tea, dressed unhurriedly, did my hair, opened the windows and breathed in, then collecting an early edition of the *Telegraph* I followed Mother and Alan to the shelter. I never entered the shelter except to take Mother some tea. I then realised that a letter from Pewsham was waiting for me, so I got it and spent some time reading it through in the warm sunshine on the steps. I am glad he enjoyed Tuesday. I went for a walk round the flats, went indoors, sat in the sun. At last the 'All Clear' sounded, and I settled down to bacon and eggs and my book. I sat the whole morning in the sandpit reading, and I finished off the most excellent *I Shall Not Want* but found myself wishing the book had been longer, and that Mary's daughter and John's son had met and thus made the balance even and complete. I was very disappointed this did not occur.

This afternoon I again sun-bathed, stripped to the waist, olive-oiled, in the sandpit. At 3.40 a patrol of our fighters went over, the balloons were high, so I anticipated a raid.

Sure enough at 3.50 the alarm was given. I went indoors, dressed more presentably, then went once round the flats, and so to the top of No.1 block, which is my favourite, unchallenged viewpoint.

Over Croydon I followed the track of a fighter patrol. Then in the west I saw a large, formidable-looking formation of big black 'planes. At first I thought they were Jerry, but as the second patrol swung round and temporarily joined with the first squadron I knew this was not the case. Two wardens joined me, but at that moment two 'planes were making straight for us, and the wardens, to my amusement, remembered an urgent appointment about seeing two old ladies into a shelter. As they ran down the stairs I sang out – 'It's alright, they're ours' but they weren't taking chances. The Hurricanes roared over me some 5,000 feet up, circled, and tore off to the south. The clouds were now at a very low level, and the sun had disappeared.

At 4.40 I got rather tired of keeping watch over Croydon, and I began to think that the reason for the sirens were to be on the safe side and not to risk another 'Croydon.' So I went down the shelter, and sitting myself down in a chair I became aware of a quite pretty girl. I spoke to Tom C's sister, Judy and discussed *N.W. Passage* with her. When the 'All Clear' went at 4.50, Judy said to me 'What was the attraction; I guess you had your eye on somebody to stay down here' and I could not help bursting out into a loud peal of laughter. 'Oh Judy...' I said, to which she retorted 'Perhaps it was me?' but I replied

'I'll put that in my diary' and I have. Tom[19] is now a Sergeant, and being in the War Office (a job any C.3 conscript could well do) admits to having an exceptionally easy time. How a fellow can rest on his conscience like he does is beyond me; to think he was time-serving in the regular army and then as his battalion crossed to France to be annihilated he stayed here in safety. I couldn't do it: the principle is wrong to blazes.

German long-range guns have been shelling convoys and the South East coast from France. Dover damaged I gather badly. Bombs were dropped in a London suburb this afternoon. Waves of 'planes attack Ramsgate.

Sunday, 25 August

Last night I played darts in the shelter, and had just won a game of scrub when we were startled to see a female robed in a blue dressing-gown descend upon us. 'Sirens' she said. The time was then about 11.10 p.m. I rushed upstairs to the flat and Mother and Alan were on their way to the shelter. I got an apple and then went downstairs. It was a simply heavenly night. Overhead we heard the roar of a German bomber, and myriads of searchlights scanned the sky for a trace of her. This bomber to my mind seemed intent on circling around our neighbourhood, though I recall reading articles how bombers never circle, but drop and run. I went to the top of No.1 block after I had heard three whooshes signifying explosions, but all Surrey and South London seemed quiet. Coming down I wandered around outside, and could not make up my mind whether this was some futuristic novel or the stone age; everyone appeared to emerge from shadows below the ground and merge into the inky blackness of the buildings. The bomber went round and round and the 'All Clear' went at 1.50 a.m. or thereabouts. Two hours!

About 3 a.m. I was awakened by another hellish German, and as I listened to him drawing nearer I heard him drop a heavy bomb, and the explosion seemed close. I listened... nearer... now the guns were in action... no sirens... like waiting for the luck of the draw. I poked my head out of the window; the searchlights were still up though I considered them much less powerful than ordinary peacetime practices, but of course the moonlight was brilliant. I debated things, remembered the instructions we were given, and that on hearing the sounds of guns we were to take cover irrespective of whether or not the sirens went. The sirens are not to be sounded if the raid is not a massed affair... the civilian population must take risks if we are to win this war, as Sir John Anderson said. Anyhow I thought it high time to call my people, which I did. We went down the shelter, as did many more. The bomber came right over our heads... I stayed on top... three more terrific explosions, guns or bombs I could not say... however they were certainly businesslike.

We got back into bed about 3.30 a.m. I omitted to mention during the air raid at 11.10 we saw a gigantic red glow in the sky Citywards, and I groped my way to the roof of No.3 block and surveyed the scene. But I could not

A recent picture of Lothbury, where Colin worked in 1940. (*Author*)

get a good view. This morning Dad tells me, on the authority of a People traveller, that a bomb set fire to Rylands in Gresham St and Fore St and razed it to the ground. And this only a few minutes from Lothbury and the office. Barbican had a bomb. Two sugar storehouses were set on fire. Ford's works at Dagenham also sustained damage. On the whole the Germans had a busy night, and Mother says why don't we bomb Berlin?

Thank goodness my last week's hol. is up, and that I'll be back in the middle of things tomorrow.

25 August, 10.30 p.m.
Due to the air raid alarms of last night and in the early hours of this morning I am very much fatigued. I spent the latter part of this afternoon reading the opening chapters of *Marriage* by H. G. Wells, and after only 40-odd pages I actually fell asleep but awoke suddenly owing to pins and needles in my right leg which I had been holding in one position for a very long time. After this I simply could not continue and went indoors meaning to sleep, but there was a lovely fire so I decided not to turn in until 9.15 p.m. after the news.

I reckoned, however, without the Luftwaffe. Dad came into my room and told me just as I was undressing that the trams were running in darkness, the radio was off the air, and G.65 has a 'purple' up. I re-dressed and went outside. Seeing searchlights to the south I mounted the stairs to the top of No.1 block, and I beheld an amazing spectacle. Floating, almost hovering in the sky, were two beautifully bright stars such as I have never seen the like of before. Searchlights played incessantly, and the heavens this cloudy night presented the most fascinating of all pictures. As I watched I saw another star slowly mature until finally in all five such lights were in view. I then realised their origin – parachute flares dropped by German raiders. I knew then at any moment we could expect the warning. Everyone in Holmbury Court seemed aware of this impending danger and all had made their preparation for a hasty exit to the shelter. The flares have been mainly in the Kingston vicinity, and two appeared over Croydon. Another night I would have relished the excitement, but tonight I was too over-poweringly tired.

Since I have written the above the sirens have been sounded and all are in their shelters. I stayed indoors after a preliminary survey to satisfy myself all was quiet. As I stood alone, fully composed, listening to the waves of sound, the whistles of police and wardens, the noise attributable to people hurrying to take cover, and gazed heavenwards the warning sirens wailed southwards seemingly over all England. I returned to our flat. I enjoyed the feeling of writing this front line report. My eyes were aching and my body demanded rest. However the warden came along and informed me it would not be possible for me to remain indoors due to an inferior black-out which I could not repair. In consequence, I have retired to the shelter, where I am writing this. I am glad I managed to snatch up my ink, although I have limited myself

Sleeping accommodation was primitive yet effective for those waiting to hear the 'all clear'.

to the space of a solitary sheet of paper. Despite my fatigue, I will fill this page with impressions and generalities:

I think this is London's fourteenth raid warning. Recently we in the capital of world freedom have spent valuable hours of rest in air-raid shelters. Obviously this will affect morale. The outcry will be 'Bomb Berlin' and it will be increasingly difficult for our Government to ignore it. By sending, as I believe Hitler does, sparse raiders over the enemy's capital we shall seriously affect the Nazi morale, and the undernourished German will weaken the quicker. It will develop into raids of tremendous proportions on London in retaliation – but the British, better and more ably fortified, will withstand the tornado. Thus I hope the more speedy conclusion of this war will be achieved.

A statue of the Poet Milton, knocked off its pedestal at St Giles' church, Cripplegate.

I am now going 'up top' as I have heard raiders are about over Croydon. My impetuous nature! I had no sooner taken my pen from the above paragraph than the 'All Clear' sounded.

However once again at 12.45 a.m. (26 August) the sirens went and we were in the shelters for another 15 minutes. One raider passed directly overhead.

Monday, 26 August: 1.15 p.m.
Have just returned to the office from the scene of the City raid. It is only a three minutes' walk away.

At the corner of Wood Street and Fore Street a large block of commercial property has been entirely destroyed. St Giles Church, Cripplegate, sustained heavy damage; the statue of Milton (buried in this church) has been blown clean off its pedestal, but I am glad to see that the actual figure is undamaged. All the large and beautiful stained glass windows have been broken beyond repair. There is something tragic about this sight; my mind raced back to the days of the stage coach and the *Ghost of Moorfields*. The eerie atmosphere of those ancient novels clings to this wrecked church. The firm of Henry & Hitchcock suffered most, and only the bare skeleton of the building remains.

Thousands of windows were shattered, but those of the L.C.C. Fire Brigade Station – fortunately opposite – being of the small pane type were intact. A clock on the building of the Fore Street Warehousing Co. (?) has been deprived of its entire centre, yet somehow it contrived to keep correct time. Glass and hats (this being the centre of hosiery and millinery) lay everywhere, but the authorities had made a magnificent job of clearing the debris up. Ironically enough on one corner of the wrecked property reposed a City of London plaque of the kind erected on sites of historical importance. This particular one read 'Site of Cripplegate demolished by Fire in 1706.' Perhaps they will place another by its side. The ancient walls of the Romans in St Alphage were gutted too. Oh well it could have been much worse.

The barrage balloons are extraordinarily high, and the radio has closed down. So I suppose we shall have the sixteenth raid soon. Thank God we've started bombing Berlin.

Further to my story written during last night's raid the sirens went again about 1 a.m. and a raider passed right overhead. I cannot see the reason for sounding the sirens for these lone birds, for they are continually passing over, and the sirens rarely sound. After the 'All Clear' on Saturday they came over and dropped stuff.

28 August

The air-raid warning of the night of 26th-27th lasted 6 hours, during which time I was mainly indoors vainly trying to go to sleep. The guns on Clapham Common brought me into the Court once. The 'All Clear' was sounded at about 3.35 a.m.

Yesterday I arrived home early and went to bed at 7 p.m. and managed to secure a long-awaited hour's sleep before the sirens went again. The warning lasted till midnight, and then half-an-hour later we had another lasting forty minutes. People cannot hope to continue in this strain, and Hitler causes more damage by robbing Londoners of their sleep than if he destroyed factories. The trouble is we must take the risk and sleep, although Jerry's system is obvious, he drops one or two bombs here and there in the suburbs so that people take cover as they can never be quite certain. On the 26th-27th German planes came over Holmbury Court every ten minutes. Of course people are now beginning to ignore warnings with the consequence that one night we will awake to a siren and it will be no unnecessary alarm. (Indeed they are not anyhow.) The 'yellow' warning has been on all this morning so I suppose the twentieth alarm will shortly come. This morning after I had actually got to sleep, and was dreaming about crashed German bombers and bombs, of Pewsham and I racing for shelter and capturing Nazi airmen, a terrific growl awoke me, and in the greying dawn a German bomber flew right overhead. His noise was terrific – proved to wake me up – and I really thought he would drop something. It was a typical German drone – like a bee buzzing to its hive. Definitely the Forces are better off than us, for they at least are not disturbed in a warning if they are off duty and on duty they can see and take part in

retaliation. Henderson who lives in the flats and is attached to anti-aircraft,
saw a Heinkel shot down near Caterham the night before last.

I have not had a peaceful sleep since Friday. I am past fatigue. One cannot
even settle down to sleep in a warning for the continuous drone of enemy
planes overhead makes it distracting, disturbing. However, I spoke to Miss
Spindler and Miss Mann for a time yesterday about my rise. They are all most
indignant and think, as they have long done, that I richly deserve one. I like
both Miss Spindler and Miss Mann very much indeed.

Miss Spindler has very kindly given me her Kodak camera, which is a little
beaut. I shall give her 2/6d though to contribute to her local 'Spitfire' fund, in
which cause it was originally to have been sold.

The girl in the ABC looks very nice, but I guess she is not in the slightest
interested in me. Oh Binnie darling!

Wednesday, 28 August (night)
I cannot say how tired I am. I have never known how much sleep means.
Since the early hours of Friday morning the Nazi bombers have been over
continuously, in consequence we have had warning after warning. It is now
9.45 p.m. – the warning went at 9 sharp. I will indulge in a brief resume of
the whole raids.

During the first few warnings on Friday and Saturday every-one was alert,
prepared. Prepared for intensive bombing raids. We took cover. I only did so
when circumstances forced me – i.e. in the office where it is compulsory to
evacuate to the basement. At home, however, I always went to the top floor
to view the south. But during the last few nights single German raiders have
been systematically crossing the Metropolitan area. These lone raiders have
occasionally dropped bombs, deliberately on the suburban districts, with the
result that now every time a raider is reported the sirens have to be sounded.
It is obvious that these raiders are only sent to affect our nerves, and try to
shake our morale. They are termed in the Press as 'nuisance' raiders, and
indeed that is the most fitting title for them; It is these that are responsible
for keeping all Londoners awake and in their shelters for hours every night.
Many people are now taking the risk of staying in bed when they come over.
Sooner or later this will materialise into the 'Wolf, Wolf' parable. I mostly stay
in bed, although my people have remained in the shelter. It was impossible
during the early hours of Tuesday to do so, however, as every ten minutes or
so for 6 hours the German raiders passed right over our flat. I have expanded
my impressions, of the searchlights, the guns, and the parachute flares in my
diary, so I'll stick to my original purpose – a resumé. Last night the raiders
were more infrequent and I vainly struggled to get to sleep in bed, but I must
admit I found it pretty well impossible, for my mind was alert, and the drone
of German machines every so often became exacting. It was certainly not
comfortable to lie in bed with the knowledge that everyone else was safely

installed in the shelter and I was stuck on the first floor of a block of flats which, to quote an old lady in the local newsagent's – 'With their wireless aerials and decorative top must look from above like a military objective,' and she continued 'I wish I did not live so near to them.' My reply had been 'well I live in them' but in bed in a raid it seemed not quite so funny or heroic. I stayed half in bed and half out in the Court, scanning the sky, following the searchlights, and listening to the Nazis.

Everyone now anticipates the nightly warning, and it always sounds at 9 to 9.30. Everyone is hopelessly tired, but somehow one can always see the funny side, and it is a source of great mirth to be looking at your fellow compatriot and find yourselves both yawning heartily.

This is being typed during an air-raid alarm. I find this is the only way of keeping my journal up-to-date. In the daytime I am too exhausted, and in the evening (no one is expected to arrive at business until 10 a.m. and all leave at 5 p.m.) I dash off my evening meal and go straight to bed, and manage to sleep for an hour or so before the sirens go at 9-ish. I now type so much, then go outside and watch the searchlights as another German comes over, come in again, type a little more, then if the guns go I cross over to the shelter until it gets too hot when I may find it necessary to go below, but this rarely happens. I left this just five minutes ago as an aeroplane passed over – the searchlights found it but it frantically signalled down in morse, and dropped two extremely pretty red Very lights, proving its identity as British. This kind of thing frequently occurs. Here is another. He went right overhead droning like hell, but the myriads of searchlights failed to show him up.

I am wondering, not anxiously, just how we intend counteracting these 'Nuisance' raiders, for sleep is imperative and it looks as though we are to have another sleepless night. I am (another German – two came over then and I can still hear their drone dying over London) dark-eyed, have a terrible head, and long for Hell's own blizzard which would keep these damn infernal droning machines away for a night. I may be tired and somewhat depressed, but by God all this only makes me the more determined to smash blasted Hitler once and for all. The whole of Britain is now more fiercely determined than ever. I wonder in view of my recent air-raid experiences just how Helsinki and Madrid, to say nothing of Tientsin, Shanghai, etc. held on for so long. When the epic of London is written it will ring down through the ages, and I am most thankful I shall be able to say I knew that epic. (Another blasted Hun – two. One heading south, the other S.W. which is unusual, and makes me believe they must be returning from a job.) The awful thing is when an 'All Clear' has been sounded it is with only a remote degree of certainty that you can retire with a feeling of safety. Invariably they come over soon afterwards. It is only towards dawn they begin to sheer off, for they dread the R.A.F. Yesterday morning one woke me from a very deep slumber and the vibration of his engine literally caused my window-panes to hum. We had no siren for him.

People in the office say that it is confirmed Kenton and Harrow had bombs again last night, (Hun again just approaching – five in all, and I counted 41 searchlights in two concentrations) mostly incendiary. Very little damage resulted. It is rumoured that enemy agents are suspected to be guiding the bombers to their targets. It is true that the route of these Germans appears very persistent. Apparently they cross the south coast, come over Surrey to Staines, follow the river, and then cross North London. I assume Northolt and Hendon aerodromes are their prime concern, but so far – touch wood neither has been hit. For my part it seems as though the Nazis consistently approach by way of S.W. London, for they constantly cross right over our block of flats. It is also amazing the way they seem to steer clear of the balloon barrage – it was withdrawn from our immediate neighbourhood, but I believe, judging by the activities at the Tooting Bec balloon barrage station, that it will very shortly consist of its old proportions.

I cannot remember, it is nearly midnight, just what I really wanted to say, my mind and body are so completely in need of rest. I will close therefore with a brief observation.

As one German bomber passed overhead tonight I was near some A.R.P. Wardens, and all they were talking about was, 'What (Another Hun – powerful close – sheered off) chance does my greyhound card stand?'

As I have written so intermittently about the Jerry coming over I think it would be a good idea to jot down what kind of night it is. It is beautifully clear, cloudless, one mass of stars. There is no moon, but I think it rises later. (And here, would you credit it? comes yet one more German bomber as a matter of fact there were another two, one sounded extremely big and was fairly low.) Clouds too are forming, and the searchlights look really jolly. As they went over I started talking to a 'figure' who turned out to be an extremely nice nurse, who has just arrived from Blackpool – she has missed no sleep except for now. I was becoming really interested in her (that was another) when Dad came bellowing along wondering where on earth I had got to. A Jerry is circling about us now – and a low murky cloud has suddenly descended and blotted out all the stars.

In conclusion I had my photo taken on the roof of 6 Lothbury today – I am glad I have at last got a camera and perhaps now I'll be able to shoot some off to Binnie. Snaps are so much better, so informal, natural.

It's 12.15 a.m. and Jerry is still circling around and the raid is still on. The midnight news came over the air – so the raids cannot be too extensive.

Friday, 30 August: Noon
The 'All Clear' went the other morning at 4 a.m. thus it had been a seven-hour raid warning, the longest to date. I did not once go to the shelter, but prowled around outside. My people came in and went to bed at 1.30 a.m. but no sooner had they done so than we heard guns or bombs thudding in the

distance. I got off to sleep and never heard the 'All Clear' but my mother vows never again to quit the shelter before the 'All Clear' has been sounded, as she found it rather trying to rest comfortably with the Jerries constantly roaring overhead.

Yesterday the *Evening Standard* man whom I always buy my paper from in Princes Street, had chalked up on his lime black-board 'Black Out 8.22 p.m. – Dug Out 9.22 p.m.' which shows an intelligent wit and the Englishman's unrivalled sense of humour.

Last night everyone anticipated the warning would sound at 9.30 approx, but all were doomed to disappointment. It's funny how accepted, expected this has got to be. I noticed before I went to bed (at 6 p.m.) that the balloons were not up – but at 10 p.m. a Jerry went over. At 11 p.m. we heard the distant thud of guns – but we went to sleep and found to our surprise no warnings had been sounded that night. Unbelievable, delightful. At least we had another good night's rest, although I could do with many more before I could hope to catch up on myself. Some say the absence of 'planes last night was due to the smashing success of the R.A.F. over Berlin; if so I say on no account stop going over there, for I am positive that constant warnings in Berlin would seriously impair the Nazi morale, cause Hitler headaches for his beautiful city, and shorten the war considerably. I later learnt we had the 'purple' up until 2.10 this morning. During the 7-hour raid bombs were dropped at Cricklewood, Ilford and Loughborough Junction – which must have been the distant thudding we heard. The *Express* this morning says we should stay put in bed during raids if we cannot sleep in our shelters, as it's a 1,000 to one chance of your place being hit, and constant loss of sleep in the long run proves more disastrous than the possibility of being wounded in a raid.

It is now 12.15 p.m. and the sirens went at 12 sharp to echo their twenty-first warning. It's a beautiful day, cloudless, perfect. I suppose they are over the Thames Estuary again.

Took some photos on the office roof yesterday. Meet Pewsham tomorrow – good. I am the only one left in our office now – the rest are installed below. I've locked my *Seven Pillars* in a fire-proof cupboard. In view of the excellent broadcast by some men last night about 'putting that odd money in the wallet' into a Post Office Savings Bank made up my mind to do so, which I have just done. I deposited £3 and my Book No. is 7313 opened in King Street E.C.2. (And I didn't really want '13' but it was given me.) A very charming girl served me and spoke to her assistant of a girl named Anne – excellent. The warning was cleared at 12.35.

30 August – continued

Just 12 hours ago the sirens sounded their warning. I wrote up a page of my journal during that alarm. Now, nearly Saturday, I am again writing up the latest developments. I outline the happenings. After the 1st alarm today – the

Colin's Post Office book from 30 August 1940, showing an account to the value of £7 8s 9d. (*Author*)

21st alarm in the bombing of London – I opened up my P.O. a/c and purchased a camera case. The second alarm sounded at 3.17 p.m. and lasted only until 3.22 p.m. The third occurred at about 4.15 and lasted until 5.35. I was just going home in the rain when the 'All Clear' sounded. A mad rush took place for the tube; I fought my way through but encountered a setback near the Northern Line platform, where a pimply-faced porter was slamming the gates and shouting the platform was too crowded. The mutt – I said I intended going to Blackfriars whereupon without even demanding my ticket he passed me. If the rest of the crowd had only thought they too could have caught the first train.

I spent half an hour gazing from the top window of No.1 block this evening. As I saw this war in its true perspective I outdistanced the fate of Londoners and Berliners, rose above the internationalism into space and eternity and our war did not seem so terrible but a very tiny phase in man's history. The smoke from the factory chimneys died down as night closed in; a squadron of Hurricanes disappeared into the evening sky. A solitary Croydon searchlight pointed its finger sternly heavenwards.

The alarm came at about 9.30-ish sure enough. It is now past 12 and Saturday morning. I am sitting in the hall, surrounded by my bags of papers, books and newly-acquired camera. A German bomber has just passed right overhead – as I listened I felt how easy it would be for him to drop a bomb at the precise moment and destroy me. I am engrossed during raids in analysing Wells' *Rights of Man* and already class it along with my *Research*, *Sapiens* and T. E.'s *Letters*.

Saturday, 31 August

During the raid which lasted until the early hours of this morning, Mother and Alan came up to the flat at about 1 a.m., but within fifteen minutes Jerry was over again and four very loud reports echoed from the back of my room. I decided they were bombs. Mother and Alan returned to the shelter. Dad and I remained in the flat. About twenty minutes later several Huns came over and we stood in the hall. I must admit as I counted the reports coming nearer and nearer that it appeared as if any moment might be our last. Surely this war had always been upon us? There was a crescendo of noise. Yes, but somehow I felt much better whilst this action was upon us. It was not nearly so remote as the tension built up in the interlude between the meanderings of the Luftwaffe. For what seemed an age the Huns hovered overhead. After the howl of one bomber's engines, at first so regularly irregular, it increased to a high pitched mur-mur-mur like a marathon runner calling upon his last reserve of breath, as the pilot successfully outflanked the searchlight and the more material sting of the anti-aircraft guns. So he passed, and Dad and I looked at each other – in ridiculous remnants of night attire and he said 'It's a bugger.' I agreed.

31 August (written 1 Sept.)

After that German had passed Dad and I went to bed. Within ten minutes, however, over the sleeping City came a thunderous roar, like gigantic, rolling claps of thunder. Gunfire? Bombs? Another German passed over, and apparently he must have been caught in the glare of the searchlights for he too revved up, then shut off his engine, and glided – an ominous sign. The guns opened up from Clapham to a deafening rolling retort. The cannonade from the distance still rumbled incessantly. Dad and I decided then to go outside and if necessary to the shelter. We both thought the invasion had begun and were listening for the church bells. About 2 a.m. I was standing in the entrance to the shelter and I heard Jerry dive-bomb (it appeared) the gun-position on Clapham Common. To the right, Brixton way, there were tremendous, window-shaking thumps. No gunfire – heavy 500 lb salvoes of bombs. Definitely Jerry was busy. The guns and bombs became monotonous so I endeavoured to turn in on some chairs down in the shelter, but could not get off to sleep. However the 'All Clear' rang out at approximately 4 a.m. so I did manage to get some real sleep in until I was awakened by the sirens howling again at 8.27 a.m. They woke me up from a deep slumber. Mother and Alan went to cover but I wandered twice to the top of No. I block and finally retired to bed again. The 'All Clear' sounded at 9.5 a.m. I stayed in bed and listened to another warning given at 10.40 and lasting until 11.20 a.m. Yet a third was given when I was dressing to meet Pewsham at 1.5 p.m., but we had had dinner so we all stayed indoors. I was ready, complete with camera, at 1.58 p.m. to hear the 'All Clear,' and I straightway started for the tube to meet Pewsham at the Bank; I was of course already late as I was to have met him at 2 p.m.

It had been an extremely busy morning for the siren sounders... the shoppers in Tooting took very little notice of the sirens, and went on with their daily shopping routine in those shops which did remain open. I arrived at the Bank at 2.50 p.m. having taken the wrong train to Waterloo. I had to wait some minutes for A.G.P. and I did not think he would turn up. It proved, however, that he had done the waiting and had been to 'phone me... and Dad was sleeping! We discussed all the raids, and it was evident very little visiting of the Luftwaffe to his district (Dagenham) had been done. We took the tube to Marble Arch and strolled across Hyde Park to the Serpentine. It was a most perfect, gorgeous, hot summer's day. We took out scullers and rowed away... delicious... and we envied the bathers in the Serpentine Lido... why hadn't we brought our costumes?... at the far, more exclusive, Kensington end we took snaps of one another rowing, and I hope mine comes up to scratch to send to Binnie. We turned in the boats upon the expiration of our time period at 4.30 p.m. and feeling greatly refreshed walked along to Hyde Park Corner. In the Park on this most glorious day, the day of untold sirens, we came to the band stand at the opportune moment. The band of the Royal Marines was just playing *God Save the King*.

It is correct to say this was one of the most impressive moments in an eventful day. As the anthem rang out, all London seemed aware of its significance. Sailors from South Africa, French sailors with their bright red pom poms and pierrot appearance (another siren just gone as I write – about 11.14 a.m. 1 September and I've only seen a smoke trail high in the south), bronzed, carefree fellows from Australia, Canadians, New Zealanders, officers from various continental countries, and a host of civilians, pretty glamorous girls and children all stood silently, resolutely, to attention. It was a most magnificent spectacle indeed, and one would have imagined it to be the most triumphant moment of the British Empire instead of its most anxious. Continuing, two officer horsemen, Czech I think, galloped down Rotten Row;

one, young, had his head bandaged. So this was England at war. This was the gathering of her sons, this was her most motherly moment. It was one mass of colour, gaiety, calm, confidence, victory.

Down Constitution Hill and so to Buckingham Palace. Here a splendid mass of geraniums spread out in a glorious red carpet, and even rivalled the stately majesty of those superb, velvet red tulips of May. I took Pewsham's photo here, with the statue of Victoria and the distant tower of the Houses of Parliament as background. I had mine taken on the steps of Victoria's statue, with Apollo and the Lion, the red geraniums and the luxurious, fine expanse of The Mall stretching away behind me to the Admiralty. This was surely the most fitting view to send to Binnie. Even so the taking of these photos caused one or two suspicious glances to be cast in our direction.

The above were all events of 31 August. I learn today (1 September) that we brought down 86 German planes on the 31st. Croydon too was dive-bombed on the 31st and no sirens were sounded until after the raid was over. Casualties were many I fear.

German Bombers over Westminster

1 September

Last evening after leaving St James's Park with A.G.P., we made our way across Whitehall to the Lyons teashop in the shade of Big Ben, and next to Westminster Underground Station. We were especially thirsty on such a hot and beautiful day. We had, fortunately, the table by the open window overlooking the Houses of Parliament. The time was approximately 5.40 p.m. We had previously decided that it was the wise procedure to secure our much-wanted pot of tea before the sirens went, for everyone anticipated they would howl out again before the nightly warning. As the cafes close upon receipt of a warning we hated to chance postponing our tea, and as one can stay in the shop during the period between sirens we knew at any rate our tea, if the sirens went, would be enjoyed.

We discussed the news of the previous air battles of the morning, and turned to more personal, inconsequential items. At 5.55 I said to Pewsham 'wouldn't it be funny if the sirens went now, here in the shadow of the seat of the British Government, and not five seconds from Winston Churchill,' to which he replied, jokingly, 'Think of it, if they bombed Westminster, why we're right in the centre of it. I can see the headlines "Nazi 'planes Bomb Westminster" – definitely *our* names would be in the papers.' And as we laughed at our absurdities the sirens went. We looked at one another in astonished silence; we both laughed. Amazing, providential coincidence! I sprang to the window and gazed across Westminster Bridge – if only I had a mike. 'This is London at war, this is London in 1940. People are calmly going to their shelters, taxis are whirling around and buses, packed, speeding to the suburbs'; but I didn't have a mike and I wasn't broadcasting to America.

We finished our tea. Only a clergyman and a Home Guard left the tea room. We went out into the brilliant sunshine. We walked to the middle of Westminster Bridge and surveyed the Thames, the balloon barrage. I let my *Evening Standard* flutter into the murky depths to the remark from A.G.P. 'I

Despite constant disruption from air raids, public transport continued in true 'blitz spirit' style. (*Jeffery Pain*)

suppose a German submarine will find that and read the Englander's news.' It was swiftly whisked out of sight and under Waterloo Bridge. Suddenly we thought we heard gunfire. Gunfire? Surely the trams going over their cross-points? No. We slowly wandered back to the shade of Big Ben and seeing a policeman gazing skywards I too looked up. By God – an air battle? There about three miles above central London three tiny specks, silvery white, dotted the blueness. Jerry? Spitfires patrolling? No! More dots. As they circled, now seven in all I counted, I knew instinctively they were the Germans. So – here was the realisation of all those far-seeing, imaginative authors, those day-dreamers and Yankee newsmen. At last they had their bombers over London. It needed only the poison gas to complete their novelish plots. No – I didn't like that. We carried no mask – never had done – but I wouldn't say never will. Now a crowd of sightseers had collected, and soldiers, sailors, policemen, cab drivers, civilians were all blocking the pathway of Westminster to see the twirlings of the Luftwaffe. The glare caused my eyes to ache, the height was so intense, and the specks constantly disappeared as they turned into the sun's eye. Big Ben struck the hour, 6 o'clock. How many times I had heard that in earlier years after the Children's Hour – now I suppose I'll always remember its striking, so majestically, on 31 August, 1940. The newspaper-seller, oblivious of the news above placidly counted out his quires. How many times that old man had displayed placards of events in far-off lands; of the German bombers over Poland, Norway, France and now the news was coming to him first hand. The Huns were still high above, still circling, and two bursts of anti-aircraft fire exploded about them. I could not hear their engines, or their bombs – if bombs they dropped. It got boring. We went on down Whitehall. Government officials stood, helmeted, on the steps of their offices. London under cover? Hardly. We passed the Cenotaph, ironical. By the Horse Guards I looked up again. I shouted excitedly. No longer were those 'planes circling with impunity. Hurling earthwards in a steep, vertical dive was a long, lean silver streak. Dive-bombing? But it was near, and I could hear no engines whining. Crashing? but I could see no smoke or flames pouring from the fuselage. Still high above two minute dots were descending, as if gloating over their prey. Spitfires? The plane was now hurtling at a terrific speed, it must have been 700 m.p.h. I have never seen anything so fast. It literally fell like a meteor. It disappeared behind the offices of Whitehall, and then I knew, I had seen a Jerry crash and its crew killed. We walked on; the birds were singing. Just before reaching Trafalgar Square I again scanned the sky. There came another. This 'plane, a fighter I thought, was falling like a leaf, like the cockpit seat which fell on to our school in 1935. It, too, fell behind the rooftops. Far above it came another, small, fluffy white cloud. The pilot had baled out. I watched him for five minutes, until he drifted out of sight. A number of people joined me, stoppped, made some incoherent comment, and walked unconcernedly onwards. I could not help thinking that that German, even then dangling on the end of a parachute, must have been supreme. There he was, falling, presumably safe, into the heart of the British Empire. I could picture the story he will have to tell his children after the war, and how he was captured by the Home Guard. A last look up – three white dots were scurrying hell for leather towards the sea as if all the devils in hell were on their tails. I thought though that it was the angels of God chasing the devils.

Trafalgar Square was as usual. The pigeons, sparrows, all chirping merrily away. Buses and cars chased one another round Nelson's Column. The fountains, long since superseded by shelters, were thronged with Anzacs, Canadians, South Africans. No one was troubling about the raid. It was rather wonderfully inspiring there, looking down Whitehall, the Houses of Parliament, to the Strand: at the barrage balloons, the green trees and the setting sun. The sons of the Empire certainly were enjoying their Motherland.

We sat on the fountains until the 'All Clear' sounded at 7.15 p.m. talking to a Canadian Air Force man, and debating Wells and the air-raids.

Soldiers were on every roof top, armed with rifles, bayonets, gas-capes, masks, etc. South Africa House was swarming with Grenadier Guards, who indeed, frequented every pill box in and around Whitehall. We were prepared for the invasion. After the 'All Clear' we walked to the Bank, via St Paul's and Cheapside, and so departed for our respective homes. We had air-raid alarms twice before midnight, and a few 'planes went over. After the second

An aircraft spotter of the observer corps on the roof of a London building, looking out for enemy aircraft, 1940. St Pauls is in the background. (*Jonathan Reeve*)

'All Clear' about midnight we came up to the flat. The third alarm sounded again almost immediately and we heard bombs, guns and 'planes. The family debated. The *Standard* said we must cheat Hitler, we must take the risk of bombs, we must not lose sleep. As the bombers circle we must take courage and stick it out – we must not take shelter for a few bombers. We didn't. As the warning rang out we undressed, and as the whistles shrilled we got into bed. Silence. More bombs. Guns. I fell asleep, a deep, satisfying, oblivious sleep. I awoke at 9.5 this morning, and learnt that the 'All Clear' had not sounded until 4 a.m. Thank God I had slept, otherwise I should have been a wreck today. The 'All Clear' had apparently been extraordinarily loud – but the devil wouldn't have awakened me.

Sunday, 1 September
Firstly I want to record an incident of last night, about 8.55 and before the sirens went. Scene – outside the public shelter at the bottom of Holmbury Court. Characters; an air-raid warden, an old man of eighty, and his wife, some twenty years younger.

The old man, evidently childish, was pleading to be allowed to spend the night in the shelter. The warden emphasised the fact that the Home Office did not allow public shelters to be opened except upon receipt of a warning. In any case people who were able to reach their homes had to do so. The old man, who wheezily retorted to the warden that he was still young, was scared of these sirens. Apparently, I learnt afterwards, he persisted on going out into the garden after the sirens had sounded to look for the Germans with a torch, and he tried to catch them. The old lady said 'You heard what the gentl'm'n said, you can't go in the shelter until the *sireens* go.' Somehow, although on paper this does not convey much, to me at that moment it seemed very tragic.

As I wrote the preceding page this morning, this corresponding weekend of the anniversary of war, the sirens howled. As far as I can remember exactly the same time as they did on the day war was declared. The alarm lasted about 35 minutes, during which time I tried to catch up on this journal and was looking through binoculars, kindly lent, out over Surrey and Croydon. The day too is identical to that first day of war. Patrols of fighters droned overhead, and smoke trails appeared everywhere. At first I thought they were Nazis drawing their question-marks. Three trails spread right across the sky over our flats reaching in several directions. The sirens are sounding again; I have lost count of the warnings now; it's 1.55 p.m. Just been on top of No.3 block and seen Jerry bomb Croydon again and the 'All Clear' is sounding – 2.30 approx. It's hopeless to keep pace with this journal these days, but I must record the Croydon bombing just taken place. I rushed to top of No. 3 block and with the glasses surveyed Croydon Airport. Our boys were up. The thud of bombs and rattle of machine-guns came ever louder. Then I saw a 'plane, heard its whine, and concluded Jerry was power-diving. A fire started up apparently in Foresters Drive – a house(s)? This was under control in thirty minutes. Then all hell was let loose. Jerry must have decided to get to hell out of it, and jettison his load of death as he did so – for there unfolded before my gaze a proper Western Front bombardment. In all, twelve bombs were dropped in a line about a mile long. Terrific whooshes and craters were blasted. Just as one would imagine. Dull black clouds ascended on the horizon and it was possible to trace the blast and explosions.

I shouted down to the people four storeys below, 'Take cover,' for I had spotted an anti-aircraft barrage thrown up just half a mile to the south of us. A stray Jerry I suppose. A moment later a Hurricane roared overhead. Looking back to Croydon I heard fresh machine gunning and bombs, but within a few minutes all the line of fires was out, and everything appeared undisturbed. From what I know of the country and the row of bombs (definitely very heavy explosives from the blast and height of their columns of debris) all fell on open country, probably Merstham, Reigate and Epsom way. Our fighters are still patrolling around. It's a perfect day for bombing, the sun so brilliant and a terrific haze. Where was I? yes – the smoke trails of this morning. Well there is little else to say, except this one, most symbolic, significant, amazing thing.

Shortly after the 'All Clear' I chanced to glance at a bank of fleecy white clouds practically overhead. I was stunned. There imprinted on those clouds were the colours – red, white and blue. Identical to the French tricolour. I pointed this out to a warden who concluded it was the sun shining at a peculiar angle on the exhaust of a 'plane. To me it appeared as a vision, something like Joan of Arc must have beheld. It represented the emblem of Britain, freedom, and as it faded away it conveyed the impression that the supernatural, God, was fighting with us in our cause. It made me feel very sure. Perhaps it was one of these ordinary commonplace unusual things – but I preferred to think of it otherwise, especially as a moment before battles had taken place overhead. A salute to the brave.

Well by dint of much concentration I have, I think, caught up with myself. But I don't suppose it will be for long – I feel very good about these raids. At first I was a little anxious for my people, for Holmbury Court seems such a big target, but now I can sleep peacefully through the roar of German bombers and feel remote. I would rather be in Town during a raid though – the air of nonchalance prevails.

It's increasingly true – we in London are now in more dangerous positions than the dug-outs on the Western Front of 1916. Incredible.

Monday, 2 September

Last night we sat outside on the steps waiting for the sirens to go. It was like waiting for a train. The wardens had got a 'red' up, which is never given unless the sirens are imminent. Out towards Streatham we watched anti-aircraft shells bursting or they may have been tracer bullets – but I don't think so. The searchlights (why are they so weak? so as not to light up the ground? Is it because they are awaiting a mass attack? Are they more efficient weak?) swung round in a huge semi-circle, to warn their fellow batteries to be on the alert. Then we heard the far-off drone; now for the sirens, we thought. But no; by midnight we were all safely tucked up in bed, and I didn't wake properly until the sirens sounded this morning at about 8 a.m. The peaceful night was a most delightful treat, although the news is Jerry was persistently around all the time.

The sirens at 8 meant nothing more than drones, which I thought were our fighters. The haze was too intense over Croydon for me to see anything. Got to work at 9.50, and what a crush on the tube – but how jovial. We were astounded in the office that no sirens created a diversion until 4.20 p.m. The staff went down to the shelter, but I hung perilously out of the third floor window, and finally managed to persuade the warden to allow me on to the roof. I saw several smoke trails over the Thames Estuary. Ten fighters roared placidly across. Nothing more until 5.25 when 12 more went over. I do not think one solitary Jerry penetrated the actual City area. The anti-aircraft barrage was intense over the Westminster Bank direction. I left the office

North Woolwich station was put out of action by enemy bombs on 7 September 1940.

whilst the raid was still in progress, and caught a bus across London Bridge, to pick up the tube, as the tunnel under the Thames is closed upon receipt of a warning. London streets were swarming, and scarcely anyone took to the shelters. I certainly had no intention of doing so, but scrammed off home before the crowd. I heard the porters at Kennington shout that the 'All Clear' had come through.

There is nothing glamorous about this war. It is not a war. It's a mass butchery. In the olden days the civilian population were far removed from the scene of battle, they were respected by both sides. Now the Germans think fit to rain down their loads of death on harmless, defenceless civilians. Thank God Churchill is firm enough to refrain from ordering a retaliation bombing on the German civilians. I fear I shouldn't be.

I suppose one day the sirens will cease to wail – but I cannot imagine it. It was wonderful coming home in the tube tonight during the raid and reading the *Standard's* most uplifting leader. 'London' it was entitled. I looked at the people around me as I read it – yes, they would uphold, with their smiling faces, the future of mankind.

3 September

A year ago today war was declared on Germany.

At the precise hour that momentous announcement was whipped round the world the sirens sounded their first warning. Now today we have the sirens sounding at precisely the same moment of the day just as last year. Obviously Hitler intends, or so I imagine, to celebrate his anniversary.

The sirens went this morning and kept the clerks etc. in their shelters for about an hour. I remained mostly on the roof.

This afternoon the sirens went again – and the raid is still on. To my indignation, I have not been allowed on the roof – we interfere with the efficiency of the A.R.P. – indeed! I am typing this in the office, alone, again.

Bomb damage being assessed
by the ARP.

The men on the Bank of England still wear their gas equipment. So far I have neither seen nor heard a thing.

Last night we remained indoors throughout the long night warning. I awoke occasionally but slept through the 'All Clear.' Constantly Germans went overhead, and last night and in the early hours of this morning gunfire was predominant. The Germans to my mind used far heavier, far dronier machines like the dentist's drill. Our fighters also appeared to be up and doing – a new system. I have also learnt that searchlights are on quarter strength and do not switch over to full until they have tracked the marauder down – jolly splendid idea. Alan is absolutely impervious to their potency – so are we all. I have got used to lying in bed and hearing the bombs drop – what if they do come on our place? The hall is pretty safe – and I believe in Fate! No other parts of London seem to get the Germans over so persistently as us, and indeed over our flats seems to be their turning point – perhaps because of the balloons. They cross over our flats nightly; by the law of averages they must drop bombs sooner or later.

Paula Starkie has a boy in the Bank who is very keen on her. However she seems to still like me – a little. I think I'll pop down to the shelter now and see what she is doing.

4-5 September
Last night I cycled all round S. Wimbledon and Morden and Malden. Morden I had heard had been badly bashed – I found it untouched. The mess around Wimbledon had been pretty well cleared up and I found I could get all through these areas without conflict with the authorities. Malden Station had been dive-bombed. I found, when I went on to the platform, not nearly so much havoc as I had anticipated. But the shops, especially the pub, in the immediate vicinity had suffered heavily. If this is a sample of Hitler's bombing it is nothing to be feared.

Many homes were destroyed during the Blitz, including ones shown here in Mortlake Road, Canning Town, on 6 September 1940.

I got home and the sirens went about 10 p.m. The anti-aircraft was terrific. We were ringed in by steel. It was magnificent. I counted 41 searchlights in one tiny area alone. It seemed the barrage completely encircled London. The Nazis must have made a go. Dad gave me a clip round the ear for remaining in the open, but I remained. I had waited ever since I can remember for something like this, and I always thought I should have to be in the army to see it. One Nazi burst through and came right over us. A fire was started somewhere. Flares were cascading down and the magnesium lit up the whole place. The fire was quickly under control. It seemed only a minute of time before at least some more Nazis penetrated the defences: but none did. I saw through the glasses several Huns caught in the beams and by hell did they get it. Nothing could have survived the intense barrage. It was like a great firework display.

7 September
The night before last the bombers kept us up for some time. Bombs fell in Balham. Literally they fell all around us.

Last night we had the warning at 8.55 p.m. but all was quiet for some time. I stayed indoors reading H. G. Wells's *Marriage* and I find it very much to my liking. A stray bomber or two went over and I watched off-handed several rounds of anti-aircraft fire. About midnight Mother and Alan were turned in. We had been discussing whether Alan should sleep in the hall or in bed when I just went outside to see if all was comparatively clear, as a German had just passed over; when what should I see but the whole of Tooting lit up so brilliantly that I could have read my book in the street. I yelled to Mother and Alan, for when a Nazi drops his flares it is usually followed by systematic bombing, machine-gunning, or maybe it was to take a picture and come back tonight and bomb us; or again he may merely have been trying to find his bearings. As Mother and Alan ran across to the shelter in that unreal glow I watched the sky and flares through my glasses – there

Newspaper seller
7 September 1940.

were three altogether, and each was on a parachute. It was quite uncanny. No searchlight could penetrate the glare. At any moment we expected to be blasted to smithereens.

The papers describe the dropping of three flares as a new Nazi technique – just what they mean I shudder to contemplate.

Weekend: 7-8 September
This is the most momentous weekend. Yesterday I lived my most momentous day – so far.

I set out on my old bike yesterday afternoon and pedalled through Carshalton, Burgh Heath, and on to Collie Hill – that great viewpoint overlooking all Surrey and Sussex to the south coast. I took a pair of prismatic binoculars – for my intention was to scan the horizon and await the attempts of the Luftwaffe to penetrate the London defences. As I lazed on the brow of the hill, sunning myself, I watched several aircraft flying around the Sussex Downs. Nothing exciting. I tired of waiting for something to happen so I turned my tracks to the summit of Reigate Hill. I watched through my glasses the activities at Gatwick Airport some 10 miles off, and decided that it was quite likely that a bombardment of it would materialise before my eyes. But no. I took to sun-bathing. It seemed funny we had had no visit from Hitler that fine day. But my thought was premature. The banshee warning of the sirens went out over the countryside, and I watched Reigate far below, and all the outlying districts, and was most fascinated. The many people also lazing on the top of Reigate Hill did not stir, and it was not until several squadrons of our fighters went over, and the Lewis Gun team of Canadians took up position on the open hilltop, ready to frustrate any dive-machine-gunning, and the Civil Defence people asked everyone to take cover under the trees and thus give the gun crew firing space that anyone budged. I managed to secure a grandstand post on the small footbridge over the main road, and from here I observed for half-an-hour the antics of our fighters – but there were no Jerries. I tired of this, and mounting my bike cycled along the deserted roads, past the Home Guards and their barriers, and along the country lane in the direction of Chipstead. All along this lovely lane alive with the beauty of summer, every field seemed to have its squadron of British fighters high above it. I have never seen so many 'planes. The sky was full of these 'Birds of Freedom.' Here and there people on foot, in cars, on bikes, had deposited themselves under the screen of trees, away from the eyes of Messerschmitts. One and all remembered the Nazis' machine-gunning zest. I continued, binoculars at the ready. An hour after the warning found me at the top of Chipstead Hill, lying full length in the thick grass, binoculars glued to my eyes, watching the many 'planes, and their landing on and off at a field some miles away. Suddenly I thought to make Croydon, and remembered a marvellous viewpoint overlooking the 'drome from a hilltop some miles distant. I got every ounce of speed from the old bike, and simply flew down Chipstead Hill. I kept skidding to a standstill every so often as I picked out fresh tangles of aircraft, but they were always British. I had just passed the bottom of the deep valley between Chipstead and Woodmansterne when from a hole in the ground an air-raid warden told me to take cover. I conveniently ignored him, and bent hard on my pedals to climb the very steep hill. I was no more than half way up, and already overlooking the whole of the district south of Croydon, when masses of 'planes roared above me. British I thought, and concentrated on climbing the hill – one solitary figure on an expanse of road. Suddenly to my astonished ears the thud, the crunch of bombs came ever nearer. I looked out over the country – but pressed more eagerly to get to the top of the hill, from where I knew a better view was obtainable. I had no chance though to progress more than three-quarters of the distance. Pandemonium broke loose right above me. I jumped off my bike and looked up. It was the most amazing, impressive, riveting sight. Directly above me were literally hundreds of 'planes, Germans! The sky was full of them. Bombers hemmed in with fighters, like bees around their queen, like destroyers round the battleship, so came Jerry. My ears were deafened by bombs, machine-gun fire, the colossal inferno of machine after machine zooming in the blue sky. As I watched, spellbound, too impressed to use my glasses, a voice bellowed out 'Take cover' and I realised then that it was the only sane thing to do. I jumped under a large and spreading oak, but no sooner was I under its protecting leaves than I realised the ridiculousness of my cover, and anyhow I could not control my burning desire to see what was going on, and as the noise became yet more intense I rushed out – twisting, twirling, spinning, zooming, the universe was alive with lean silver shapes. It came home to me that in all probability it was the greatest mass raid the country had ever known, and I guessed they would be after Croydon. I remembered my viewpoint for the airport was only another mile away, so under the cloud of death I cycled furiously – but had got no more than into the village of Woodmansteme when I was compelled to dismount. Looking up – squadron after squadron of Spitfires and Hurricanes tore out of the blue, one by one they tore the Nazi formations into shreds. 'planes scattered left and right, and the terrible battle came lower. As I stood on the neat grass verge of the row of suburban houses, transfixed, I saw one fighter (I very much fear ours) rush earthwards. With ever increasing speed it fell, silently, to its last resting ground, amongst the green of Surrey. I had no time to dwell upon the fate of that man – I could not look up – I just stood, and machine after machine rushed frantically, screaming, it seemed, at me. I had no cover, I held my glasses; I don't know what I felt, but I was proving my theory – that in danger one knows no fear, only a supreme, feeling, indescribable. I would not disown those minutes for Life itself. Zooommmmmm, eeeoooohh-hhhoooowwww, rururururururrr – engine after engine, machine-gun after machine-gun, boump after boump, and I could scarcely see a thing so hazy was the sky, so brilliant the sun. Somehow in search of yet higher excitement I mounted my bike, tore headlong past Home Guards and police of this tiny village, one and all of whom cried 'Take cover' to which I shouted above the inferno 'Just going to – down the road,' but 'Down the road' was my outlook over the airport.

My good fortune held. I came across a tumbled-down, rat-infested, one-time cottage, and clambered up its rickety stairs, tripping over debris of every description, to meet with a rebuff – there was no upstairs window overlooking the distant airport. I pelted down, ripped my way through weeds, hedges, trees, to the 'garden.' I focussed on Croydon – bombs I still heard – machines I still heard deafeningly. Above it all I discerned a babble of excited, jolly voices. I ran to the front – into the farm across the way. A group of suntanned, laughing farm labourers met me. Together we shared my glasses and scanned the numerous British machines, with which the air seemed infested, some came low, others so high even the glasses failed to locate them. 'Planes continuously kept landing and taking off from Croydon – so I concluded the airport was not the main objective. Then men said they had seen smoke on the horizon, and as we looked so it happened – the densest, biggest cloud of smoke I have ever seen formed itself on the skyline of London. A smaller one ranged itself alongside. We all stood, silent, quietly wondrous, to be joined by the men's family: two little girls from the depths of their shelter hewn out of the thick clay-like soil; by their mother who left her cooking; by an old man who screwed up his wrinkled-brown face and said, 'Oy, they must be over the East End.' I thought it was London Bridge station. Fifteen' minutes later I was just going to continue my journey when a mass staccato of machine-guns rent the air. Like thousands of saws out of time. We scanned everywhere until our eyes ached, but could only hear, and not see. Finally I got moving. Down Carshalton Beeches and the 'planes so low I felt

London Docklands
at the beginning
of the Blitz,
7 September 1940.

I might have touched them, on under the shadow of that ever increasing fire, and so to Carshalton proper. As I rode over the pond the 'All Clear' blared forth. I meditated. I had commenced that alarm at the top of Reigate Hill, I had cycled along deserted roads the seven miles to Carshalton by the time of the 'All Clear'; with my stops it had taken me over two hours – during which I had spent one hour and thirty minutes under the clouds of fighters and bombers. I pressed on, and made home by 7.10 p.m.

I had longed for a cup of tea – and was disturbed by an excited cluster of neighbours outside. I looked up over the balloon barrage and through my glasses saw a tiny white puff. At first I thought it was a parachute – then a balloon broke free: the Press this morning says it was a parachute.

Before 9 the sirens went, but earlier in the dusk I had been on the top floor watching the enormous glow which lit up the whole of London, bigger even than the Crystal Palace blaze I remembered so well in 1936, and I knew that whatever the Germans had hit had been their target. I knew too it had been totally demolished. Speculation was rife – Woolwich, the Docks, Surrey Commercial, London Bridge – but finally it was the Docks that awaited confirmation. This glow I had thought at first was caused by flares dropped by raiders – but I soon knew otherwise. I simply could not comprehend it was the same one I had witnessed started some hours before from the top of the Woodmanstane countryside. As I said the sirens went – we knew it would be Jerry's busiest night, for with a beacon the world could see signifying London what enemy would miss his opportunity. Certainly not Hitler.

I stood outside, the fire and the reflection in the windows of the flats as my companions. The balloon barrage stood out gaunt over the glow. Yes, the fire would give the Nazi fliers confidence that night. Things happened immediately – Jerry went over, almost gleefully I could imagine, rubbing his hands by the warmth of that fire which did his coldblooded heart good.

One 'plane became centralised in the searchlights – very ineffective tonight thanks to 'Jerry's Fire.' The beams held him – shells burst all around, his tail very nearly shot away – then overboard two red lights floated to the ground – British? the signal, yes – but him? a trick? Anyhow the guns still fired, more lights came down. The guns ceased. His engine spelt, to me, Hun; however he passed over and out of sight with the searchlights still clinging tenaciously to him.

Two incendiary bombs fell in the next road to us, but the wardens speedily put out the small fires. Bombs fell everywhere. Midnight and we were all indoors, undressed. Practically everyone else was installed in their shelters, but we went to bed. As I lay asleep, rather half-and-half, I listened to the roar of hundreds of 'planes. Three or four bombs fell just near us with deafening explosions, like a firework – Bang! and the shsssing and hissing of sparks. A fire? I went outside with my glasses – stabs of searchlights, the glow, so steady and consistent, seemed brighter than ever. Evidently we had another fire yet nearer. I believe the fire was from gas – so does everyone. A person from the flat above us, the only other besides ourselves who 'stayed put,' crept down the stairs, and said she was going to sit in the concrete hall. I don't blame her. This was Hitler's big attempt, and I knew that the 'planes I had seen in the afternoon, was hearing now, constituted part of the greatest air-battle of mankind. I went back to bed, guns, guns, guns, thud, thud, thud. London was worse than the trenches of 1914-18. I listened to three screamers, meoooowwwwwheeeellll – they went. About a mile away I think. I preferred the screaming bomb, it at least gave, however brief, a warning. How those outside the shelters dived for cover. Not a word said, but one impulsive, automatic dive. The screech certainly was rather ghostly.

Amongst this inferno Alan lay serenely asleep, as did Mother and Dad. Me? I was afraid I was missing something, so kept both eyes skinned. As those bombs fell I did not, on the first storey of our flats, feel one jot scared. I knew no fear. I felt in the midst of the battle, yet remote, as if nothing could touch us. Ten thousand times I would rather take my chance up here than down in that shelter. Anyhow I could so easily have been pipped this afternoon that I felt it would be silly just preserving me for the night.

As I sit here in my room, 11 o'clock on Sunday morning, I hear the constant drone of 'planes, have my binoculars ready to hand, and wear my flannels, white shirt with rolled sleeves, blue sports tie and walking shoes. I expect everyone else is in bed, fast asleep, in the other flats. I hope the clattering of this typewriter doesn't disturb them. The 'All Clear' sounded at 5 a.m. It awoke me, damn it, it was unusually long, and I thought 'unsure.' But I did not know what time it was. Despite the worst air-raid in history I secured a good night's sleep, and shall continue to do so.

A special News came over the radio at 10.15 this morning, regarding the casualties and damage of the raids. 400 people, at least, were killed in these

Fire-fighters attempt to control the bomb damage. (*Jonathan Reeve*)

few hours of air-attacks. It is estimated 1,300–1,400 are seriously injured. (Nothing about 'ordinary' casualties.) London's Dockland is on fire. Houses galore in the East End are no more. Thousands of refugees from the smitten quarters were bombed as they fled. Mothers lay protectingly over their children in the gutters under the glow of the fires as the Nazi bombers rained down death. Fire-fighters worked through hell.

All those sights of pitiful Spain, China, Finland are left behind compared with this tragedy of London. This is a City beleaguered. Bombs, it is announced, fell very near to us last night and this morning. Schools and churches (how they suffer) seem to have got it again. The Elephant and Castle (the area actually announced on the radio) and Balham suffered, although the damage to the Elephant is not so awful as one would imagine. So it goes on, and Hitler, realising his huge 'success,' perhaps fanned by our people giving so much real information away, may be inclined to attempt bigger, even yet vaster things. He lost some 86 planes, compared with our 22 fighters. He sent over some 500 'planes – I saw over 100 of his flock.

It rained this morning for the first time for so long. Will the weather break? A respite? But I fear the sun is coming out again. In any case Jerry was over this morning, feeding his bonfire probably, in the rain. Bolding rang Dad from the East and all the East of London is without gas, unable to cook any meals. The gasworks are on fire. Undoubtedly Hitler intends to follow up on this, so we are prepared. The damage in the last two days was how I, how all London, (there go the sirens) imagined the war would commence. So – the sirens scream again, as I write this page, but we stand firm.

Binnie: As I end this entry amidst the sirens I think of you, and Australia.

Monday, 9 September
London, my London, is wounded, bloody.

After a night unprecedented, of screaming bombs on the local common, of guns roaring continuously, of German bombers droning with impunity overhead, dropping death by the ton, the building shaking and rocking on its very foundations, I survive to come this morning to the office, an office robbed of windows, a City smoking.

To write in order – the sirens sounded last night at 7.59 and straightway 'planes were diving and booming overhead. We could hear the thud of bombs and guns. I saw a whole ring of anti-aircraft fire mark out Clapham Common high in the sky. With it came the night, and the great fire in the East End was telescoped until the glow was as ruddy as the previous night. Becton gasworks had been hit, and with it all the gas and public utility services of the East End suspended. We stayed in the shelter for a while, but I kept rushing around with my binoculars. At one period the firing was so intense I dare not risk the 18 yards' run to the shelter, and stood against a concrete wall, flat. Another fire started, nearer, and the glow outbid the other. By 10 p.m. Mother and Alan, Alan being flu-ish, came indoors. Alan sent straightway to bed, fortunately fell off to sleep. We crouched in the hall, and screamer after screaming bomb pounded around us. Every moment we thought our last. The guns shook the ceilings, and earth spattered my window. Finally at 11 I turned in amongst that inferno. I was awakened throughout the night with crashing guns, zooming 'planes, bomb after bomb. Somehow we survived the night, and I was awakened again this morning at 8 by guns, and the noise of Jerry, whose engine seems to throb in my brain. We anticipated the sirens, but they never went. The sirens kept people up for nearly 10 hours last night, ten hours of hell! Somehow I did get about six hours' sleep in – so feel fresh, comparatively speaking. The 'All Clear,' for what it is worth, sounded at 5.30 a.m.

I came up by Tube to the Bank, and had to queue up for a long time in the subway. I suspected a bomb had fallen, and we should have to produce identity cards. I came up in Princes Street, a Princes Street hitherto unknown to me. Cars packed the roads, people rushed here and there, calm and collected, fire services, ambulances. Refugees from the East End, cars and bikes, luggage and babies, all poured from Aldgate direction. I crossed and surveyed the front of the Bank of England – a high explosive bomb had fallen clean in the middle

Bank of England, 8 September 1940.

of Threadneedle Street, just missing the Bank's main entrance, and somehow missing the old, ancient, traditional Royal Exchange. A notice 'No Smoking – Danger – Gas Escape' set off the cordoned thoroughfare. Here in the heart of the City, the City of Gold, next door to my office, always considered by me as untouchable, had descended the cold and bloody stab of Hitler. I walked down Princes St and so to the office. In the office windows were cracked and smashed in Mr Spry's and Lane's rooms. Dust and earth covered my chair. The office boy told me that our crocks were broken, and when I asked him how he had come to break them he answered cheekily, 'Don't be silly, it's, shrapnel' and then I beheld the third floor. No windows – debris, dirt. I was staggered as I beheld the spectacle. I took myself to the roof with my binoculars, and saw the most appalling sights. All over the heart of the City fires were burning, hoses playing. Moorgate, behind St Paul's, smoke! ruin! I cannot describe my feelings, they were all too dumbfounded, and I was incredulous.

A typical view of 1940s London.

Since writing the last page I have been touring around the City. Every solitary window in the head office of the Westminster Bank is smashed. Glass in piles litters every street within a mile radius of here. I hear a time bomb exploded in the Kingsway this morning. The Bank is teeming with millions and millions of beings, cars, soldiers, police, fire-engines, gas men. I have seen practically every kind of excitement in the City during the past three years, but this – it is unparalleled. There is no panic; no worry; absolutely no feeling of fear, of anticipation of death, of the feeling that after all we may lose this war. Over all prevails the serene, all supreme, air of victory, nonchalance. It is amazing. The bomb crater just outside the Bank of England is terrific. Concrete blocks weighing tons are littered over the roadway, as if they were pieces of paper. Three huge concrete boulders, once part of the gutterway, are reposing precariously on top of a clock some twenty feet above the ground. That bomb must have been THE highest explosive possible.

In the excitement and haste of this note I am jumping like a cat on hot bricks from one story to another. I cannot hope in my breathless typing to form any kind of grammatical, clear report. I merely jabber incoherently, but at least the facts are all true, and they will serve as interest in later, peaceful times. Dad's office has been bombed, and he cannot get within 300 yards of it for broken glass – the office is the *Daily Herald* in Long Acre – what a 'success' for Hitler! All papers are terribly late today. There is no hot food obtainable in the City. I had a bar of chocolate. I am afraid Dad is awfully upset about the ruins of London. Flats, houses, commercial property, all of no consequence whatsoever to Hitler, have been remorselessly bombed. Stockwell, Kennington, Clapham, Balham – houses pulverised. I never dreamt, nor even did those fantastic authors, of such a bombardment. It breaks my heart to see London so defaced, however temporarily and as I hear the reports of the wreckage coming in – Leicester Square, Central, Suburbs – I feel myself burn, and not one atom of anxiety penetrates my heart, not one feeling of 'Should we submit?' (such as Paris) but I feel, indeed all London is alive and glowing with the feeling, that we will resist even amongst smouldering ashes, and everyone is the more fiercely determined, if one can be more so, to smash the Nazis to exterminate them from the earth, and the strength and hugeness of our task makes us glow the much more exultingly.

As I stood, just a few minutes ago, on the Bank crossing, surveying the broken windows of the Mansion House, the bomb crater, listened to the newspaper men crying their news, the noise of exhausts of thousands of cars and lorries and buses, the smatterings of conversation from the passers-by, the smiles and laughter of City clerks and girl typists, it was to superb to see the courage and greatness of it all. One most pathetic, pitiful touch of the hardness of the war came home vividly. I stood on the traffic island in the middle of Threadneedle St, and watched the constant stream of lorries, cars, all carrying babes in arms, mothers, children and old men away from the inhumanity of the smitten East End.

I knew then that my diary is not 'exciting' reading of happenings to be envied, it does not really show the spirit of glamour which I take from these raids, but it shows simply the callousness, the futility of war. It depicts bloody people, smashed bodies, tragedy, the breaking up of homes and families. BUT above all, high above this appalling crime the Nazis perpetrate, there is something shining, radiating warmth above all these dead and useless bodies, it is the SPIRIT, the will to endure, which prevails. We are not English for nothing, and as one looks back upon all the perseverance of the past, feels the tingling of the blood, one sees now why we are the greatest nation on this earth, and one is lost in the greatness of it all. Surely the education of no man is complete unless he has experienced the hard reality of war, war as waged today.

Yesterday I walked all round the shattered suburban homes of Balham. The torrent of water from burst mains was still flowing down the streets. In this particular neighbourhood there was no military objective, only residential houses. Yet here the Nazis wilfully released their eggs and wrought havoc in the homes of ordinary common folk. As I walked back across Tooting Bec common I lay in the grass and followed a 'plane with my binoculars (always to hand these days) and as I focussed them, I knew instinctively it was a German. My suspicion was confirmed later. Undoubtedly he was on reconnaissance this cloudy day.

Last night we drove Mother round New Malden to see the destruction there – while passing gun emplacements we saw the troops getting ready for firing, and we guessed Jerry was around. Mother was glad to get out of that district, especially after seeing the total destruction of clusters of suburban shops, houses, churches. The Germans flew low over Malden and callously dropped all their bombs on these harmless civilians.

I bluffed my way past police and Home Guard cordons to view the damage in Balham.

Just spoken to Dad on the 'phone – damage all over London, terrific. The person upstairs at home, a hairdresser, went to his shop this morning and one of his assistants was missing; it turns out her home was bombed last night and nothing has been seen of her, her sister or mother yet. People simply cannot comprehend how we slept last night – I don't know whether we will tonight.

During the raid last night I spoke to a warden from Westminster, who was on the scene of the bomb which fell on No.2 platform on Victoria Station, and outside the *Windsor Castle*. His descriptions were horrifying to the ladies – van labelled 'Dead Only' passed, the mobile amputation unit worked all the time. People were lying around in bits and pieces. One soldier had only his jaw left intact with the rest of his body – the rest of his bead had been blown away.

I obtained two pieces of a German bomb on the office roof this morning. I write this to the tune of tinkling glass from offices nearby, all of which are being fitted with fibre windows.

I can write indefinitely now about the raid havoc – but I must draw the line. Probably, God forbid, the Nazis will rain more sticks of death on London tonight.

The City of London

9 September: 3.30 p.m.

I look out of my window, down on Lothbury, across to the Bank of England. I see the beginning of Moorgate, Princes Street, and Gresham Street and Old Jewry. I look up into the sky – dull, cloudy, grey; I listen; the noise which is echoing in my ears is of a strange origin; it is banging and hammering, tinkling and squeaking. Lorries pass under my window laden with timber, cars stream by into Moorgate, great vans and powerful motor-cycles. Buses grate their gears, cars vomit huge clouds of exhaust. People surge through the streets, hurrying, dragging great parcels, gas-masks strapped round their bodies; this is London today – a London industrious, dutiful, a City of calm, of confidence, a City licking its hideous wounds in the lull of the storm, a storm of machines which fly through the air with the buzz of the bee, the sting of the wasp. They come by night, they come by day. They rain death upon the citizens of this, the greatest, most learned, foremost City of the World, the Civilised World!

How great an irony that strikes. Civilised indeed. Nightly London buries its head into the ground, turns out its lights, and sticks out its claws. Its long, tapering, accusing fingers of light prick the universe, probe the darkness. They search for the birds of prey, the hawks of massacre who frequent our skies these September nights. The bark, the spit of her lungs echo across the starlit heavens and, turning yellow, orange, they flicker and dance and pierce the armour of those birds. And as the morning comes, as the people set forth into the light of another day, they survey the sting of the hawks, weigh up the damage showered upon their great, free City, note with hardened brow the bloody mess which once was their fellow man; this, these thoughts and sights are stored, locked away in their deepest cell, until, one day, in God's good time, they may without mercy exact from the nests of the prowlers of the night full and lasting revenge and fulfil that old and wisened proverb: 'An eye for an eye, a tooth for a tooth, a life for a life.'

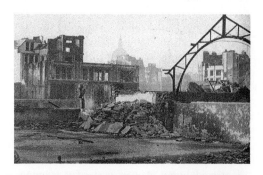

Right: Moorgate station was totally destroyed following an air raid on 24 December 1940. (*K. A. Scholey*)

Below: St Pauls through the smoke of the great fire raid of Sunday 29 December 1940 (*Jonathan Reeve*)

So life goes on. As the clatter, the pounding of the labourer's tool becomes more incessant, I take leave of my meditation, I return once more into that which is London, Freedom, and I sigh, and breathe in the smoke, the smell of petrol fumes; I look at St Paul's and the figure of Justice, and I see myself looking back upon these long, dark, unreal days, when all the world seems mad, and lustful and sinful.

I look back from a garden green, the sweet fragrance of red roses, roses of a New England, and I bear different noises – the sound of children playing, so gay and happy, and the yap of a spaniel and the meow of a kitten, and as I sit there, so content, so utterly happy, I find I hold the hand of a woman, a very beautiful, good and keen woman, and I see the son of my blood, and hers, set forth upon a clean, straight trail and he, righteous, shall make his mark upon the world until he is acclaimed by mankind as the advocator of a free and noble world, in which all mankind lives and works in peace.

But I have memories…

10 September, a.m.

I write this with the smell of burning London in my nostrils. The smoke sweeps past my window. It is with a blank feeling I pen down my notes of the past hours.

I arrived home at 4.30 yesterday evening, and had no sooner started my dinner than the sirens went. I took no notice, until the roar of aircraft was overhead. Even then I did not take notice until the scream of zooming engines and the brrr of machine guns cut into me: the whistle of a bomb and the thud as it smashed its way into the ground just at the back of the flats. Yet another – this time a dive-bombing attack, and as Mother, Dad, Alan and myself crouched against the wall of the hall the thud and explosion shook the building like a terrier would a rat. Doors, windows, foundations, all shook and wobbled. As the 'planes still screamed and zoomed and dived we waited for the blow which would fall upon us. Bomb after bomb – Mother shouted 'Oh my God' and clasped Alan. The noise abated slightly, and grabbing my binoculars I went outside. I was just in time to see the beginning and end of a dog-fight – three white trails racing across the sky, now two, now one – one long white smokey trail. I saw in detail the spinning of the machine as it crashed, saw the pilot bale out, and 'plane and 'chute dropped to the ground. Guns were in action, and the 'planes, staccato like, cut the sky to pieces.

After this alarm I went out on my bike to Clapham, where I imagined a 'plane had been shot down. But no – I saw several roads roped off due to unexploded bombs, the Nelson pub was completely demolished, along with the row of small, dingy slum houses at its back. It was complete devastation. Back to Tooting Bec common, where I endeavoured to see the bomb damage which I heard the previous night. I found part of the common, where the day before I had lain in the grass, roped off, and police guarded the area with a notice which read: 'Unexploded Bomb.' I was told I could cross the area at my own risk, which I did, but saw little. Going home I saw many more houses at the back of Trinity Road Tube station, a few minutes away from us, smashed, finished, wiped out.

Last night we sheltered until 1 a:m. and all the time German bombers were roaring overhead. Guns barked until their sting almost crashed in the flats. Bombs dropped with tremendous repercussions within a few hundred yards of us. To offset it all, the people in the air-raid shelter got out of hand. A fight threatened, and I had my coat off ready to smash the daylights out of Walters. He is the disturbing influence every time. Dad politely asked him to refrain from talking (he protested about the lights being darkened at midnight) and

Victims of a raid gather their few reamaining possessions.

he turned round with 'You shut up shoving your nose in' – I was all stripped ready for a fight, and my God I would have smashed him. Miller, the porter, fetched the police and Walters ran off. Lines, the sneaking rat, ran after him to inform him of the arrival of the police. Anyhow he threatens to 'belt' Dad today – if he does I'll smash him, and get him summoned for assault.

Many London hospitals have been hit, including St Thomas's. The rest of this news I'll make into another 'chapter' during the lunch hour today.

The Heart of a Great Nation

It is 1.10 p.m. on Tuesday, 10 September, 1940. I am sitting in my office on the second floor of the Royal Bank of Canada building in Lothbury. An air-raid siren sounded ten minutes ago. As I write under a grey sky, under a pall of acidy' smoke, within a few seconds walk of wrecked and burning buildings, I take heart from the news I am to record.

I left the office this lunch hour at 12 precisely. I walked to the corner of King Street and Cheapside. My ABC was closed. Cheapside was a mass of charred debris; of firemen on ladders, hoses pouring jets of water into the charred and burning remains of elegant buildings of yesterday. Fire units, engines, troops in steel helmets move in the dense, choking clouds of smoke. Until the police move me along I stay and watch. The smoke rises high above St Paul's, obliterated the dome for minutes on end. Cheapside, in the heart of London, was stabbed. I moved along...

I saw a crowd, milling, cheering, near the Mansion House Station. More people rushed to the spot... I tore headfirst. What a crowd. Throbbing with anticipation, I fought my way through, jumped a police barrier, and heading off the crowd found the core of the excitement. Winston Churchill! I cheered, I yelled. I fought harder, and finally established myself in between Winston and his escort of the Commissioner of Police and an Officer of the Army. The crowd pressed on either side, but whether they mistook me for one of the party or not I cannot say; the fact remains I kept next to Churchill the whole route from the Mansion House Station to the Bank. I had my photograph taken countless times, and once had my hand on Churchill's coat. He looked invincible, which he is. Tough, bulldogged, piercing. His hair was wispy, wiry, tinted gingery. As he made his way through the smoke, through the City workers all crying 'Good old Winston' – 'Give 'em socks' 'Good Luck' – and the culminating cry of 'Are we downhearted?' to the heaven rising response of 'Nooooooo' which echoed round the City, round the world indeed, and warmed the 'cockles of our British hearts' and of all the free men in the

The interior of a retort house at Beckton gasworks, 10 September 1940. The Germans had chosen Beckton gasworks as one of its major targets, dropping bombs and incendiaries on it throughout the Blitz.

world. It was magnificent, tremulous, stirring, dramatic. Amongst the 'ashes of London' stepped the man, his people, acclaimed, assured, and fulfilling the declaration that we will fight in the streets, in the fields, on the seas, in the air – that we should rather see London in ashes, but free and ours, than standing under the will of Hitler. Churchill bought a flag outside the broken-windowed Mansion House, and I squeezed myself into the photo. He mounted the Mansion House steps and shook hands, presumably with the Lord Mayor; the people stood cheering themselves hoarse below, and we all stuck our thumbs up and yelled louder than ever for the Press photographers – and I guess I am in every one of their pictures. Next, Winston crossed to the bomb crater outside the Bank of England, and threw his cigar down upon the notice 'No Smoking – Danger Escaping Gas.' I could easily have retrieved the butt, but I had no desire to acquire such a souvenir – the sight, the memory is sufficient, and, I hope, the pictures. Winston stood on the bomb crater, waved, took off his bowlerish hat (how typical of the Churchill of the Sidney

Street siege), sported his walking-stick, dug his left hand deep in his overcoat pocket. Approaching once again the crowds a young boy dashed up with an autograph album – Churchill signed. As he did so I had my hand on his sleeve, indeed I could not help myself, the crowd's pressure and enthusiasm was so terrific. Into his car and away – my hat, I certainly do seem to wangle my way into things – right by his side throughout his tour, the records of which will find space in every future book of history.

Churchill left to the roars, cheers and greetings of Londoners, Londoners under bombardment of the Nazi bombers.

I walked back prancingly to King Street and deposited ten shillings in my savings account. I bought a snack at Lyons and came back, full of jubilation to the office, and retired to eat it on the third floor. I had just got through a bun and butter when the air-raid sirens sounded. I crossed to the window and heard the staccato of machine-guns, the zoom of 'planes. 'Hullo, something doing,' I thought. The sky was too overcast for me to see anything, but I listened intently, and waited. I came down to the second-floor and the typists were all going to the shelters. They asked if I was coming – I said 'presently,' but with no intention of doing so. I looked out of my window – the streets were literally teeming with people, more than I've ever seen before. I wondered where Churchill had got to. Princes Street was alive with vehicles, honking, crawling; a taxi laden with sailors and their kit dashed by towards Liverpool Street, and one sailor, fair and touslehaired, poked his head incredulously out of the window. People under the smoke of the night's bombs made calmly, but a trifle more efficiently, for the shelters. Everywhere was alive with humans – and I wondered if the machine-gunning had been from a German into the streets. It was all very absorbing, but the purpose which caused this movement was terrible to the nth degree.

I stayed typing this during the alarm. The 'All Clear' sounded some fifteen minutes ago. It's now about 1.40 p.m. – not that I've spent that amount of time typing this.

Just spoken to Dad on the 'phone. A time bomb fell in Ansell Road, next to us, in the small hours. That was the whistler which I had thought to be a 'dud' shell. If it had been an explosive of immediate detonation all our windows, doors, and perhaps wall would have been blown out. Or of course a little nearer…

Well I must buy all the papers for the next few days, and if I am lucky enough to have come out O.K. I will buy the plates and send one to Binnie… with my friend Winston!

11 September
The Channel is No Man's Land; the advanced posts are the big guns battering one another from the French coast and the southern shores of England; the front lines are London and Berlin.

Yes, at least one angle of the war has materialised according to prophecy – i.e. the bombing of London and Berlin, the visions of smoking ruins, maimed people and stacks of dead.

After the sirens yesterday afternoon, about 4 p.m., the crush of home-going City workers was so great I thought I would save time by walking across London Bridge. But a horrible shock – King William Street, Monument, Billingsgate were a mass of ruins, smoking, charred. Aerial torpedoes had smashed them to pulp. I have never seen a scene so dreadful, so vivid of air-warfare. Pieces of shells, metal, every conceivable thing was embedded in the nearby buildings. Thank God at least the Monument itself has survived. I always considered this building – 6 Lothbury – in which I now write, as safe, even from direct hit – but now I know differently; and as I viewed with incredulity the havoc, with buildings of eight storeys razed to the ground, I realise that no building is safe. I remember writing a little while back after seeing the Kent damage, how impotent the German bombs appeared to be – but I have now beheld the most potent bombing of the age. As the sun streamed down on that scene I recalled again those visions of a year ago when I read Gibbs and Wells, and how I had imagined the bombing of London would be. But then it was all very vivid imagining – now it is real, present.

I made my way back to the Bank and somehow succeeded in catching the first train after being right at the back of a crowd six deep. Arriving home three more alarms were sounded.

Last night, bearing in mind the devastation of London, Dad and I went to the shelter, although I came back indoors until 11 p.m. when Jerry seemed only to be playing around; but 1 a.m. found me awake, excited, in the warden's post. I stood outside as the Germans went over – then Humphreys shouted 'In' and we all rushed inside the concrete walls, bent low on our knees, tucked our heads down, and waited. I thought 'This seems really businesslike.' Then a shrill whistle, nearer and I heard the salvo of bombs crash down some hundreds of yards away. The wardens told me you could never be sure just where these bombs were going to fall, but I certainly give them credit for knowing just when they had been released. But I too had learnt the 'knack' within another five minutes. Ten times we threw ourselves low in the post, ten times we heard the nearby thud of bombs. I could, can, only compare the scene with those stories of life in France in 1914. Now and again terrific, blinding flashes would light the sky, but unless they were balloons crashing down I cannot think of their origin.

I was going to turn in at 1.30 a.m. when I suddenly spied the flashing of lights across the way as a Jerry passed menacingly overhead. Dad agreed it looked remarkably like a signal to the raiders, so did the wardens and everyone who saw them. Miller and I, under the roar of the Hun, dashed along the blacked-out main road, lit with a dim moon and into back gardens. The spy proved to be nothing more than sparks from a bakehouse chimney.

An eyewitness to history, Colin Perry recorded everything he could about the London Blitz. He is shown here with Winston Churchill. (*The Daily Telegraph,* 11 September 1940)

But even so those sparks constituted a definite danger to our locality, and furthermore may yet prove to be signals.

Another fire started up in the East End (poor souls) and yet more bombs. It's – I cannot express my mind – to use aerial torpedoes on houses: they're meant for sea warfare, not to bomb residential districts. One torpedo and a row of houses slide down like a pack of cards. One usually reckons, according to the ideas of humanity, that a bomb employed for civilian bombing will, at the most, destroy two houses.

I contrived to get an hour's sleep in the shelter in the small hours, but the guns kept me awake, and keen to be up and doing. However we in the office now work a day in and a day out alternatively, thus making up for lost sleep. A very excellent, very considerate arrangement.

Cheers! I am on the front page of the *Daily Telegraph* today along with Churchill. Oh boy – and the *Telegraph* of all papers – wow, all the Cabinet Ministers, all the society, all the intelligentsia will see me! but above all so will Binnie, I hope... I never thought I would be able to send her my photo in such a romantic manner. I have ordered a picture of it from the Fleet Street office. The *Sketch* too would have had me in the 'Thumbs Up' crowd outside the Mansion House only they superimposed Winston himself over me – thus giving him a crowd background at my expense. I must endeavour to trace what happened to all those other pictures, as many were taken. Probably the *Illustrated London News*, the *Tatler*, etc. have them. Pity the *Telegraph* picture was not a few minutes later when I was on the inside of the Police Commissioner, and next to Churchill.

Saw the terrible devastation in Watling Street, and Cheapside this morning. The whole of a block of commercial property in Cheapside was demolished, and only the skeleton of the walls, very precariously placed, was left. Hoses still played on the smoking remains. Of course it may be something to do with the fact that these old buildings are composed entirely of brick, and have no steel girders etc. that causes them to be destroyed so utterly.

As I left home this morning the sky was overcast with a pall of thick black smoke from the East End: the sun silvered its edges. I wondered if we had bombed Berlin and, therefore, was delighted to read an hour ago that the Reichstag, the Unter den Linden etc. have felt the sting of our bombs too.

I should like to put under Churchill's picture in the press 'Present – Future'.

11 September, 4–7 p.m.
An air-raid alarm was sounded in the City area shortly before 4 o'clock this afternoon. We in the office did not take cover. We heard the blowing of whistles, and the crash of gunfire. We knew the whistles signified to the banks and other City workers that the raiders were in the immediate vicinity and that it was time to take cover immediately. The office all hastened to the vaults, but Mr Spry called to me. Looking out of his window over the Westminster Bank we saw a dogfight. It appeared as if some five enemy aircraft had penetrated to the heart of the City. We watched, fascinated. Slowly those silver shapes veered off – one fighter hurtled earthwards in his last dive – until I wondered why they had not at least dropped their eggs whilst they were in the vicinity of the City. We had thought them remote, when suddenly the white clouds of anti-aircraft smoke drifted across the blue; then we saw a number of machines – some, presumably the German bombers, continuing in a straight line, until suddenly – boomp – finis. Our fighters rushed in amongst their hordes, flashes of machine gun fire shone out, the cannonade of anti-aircraft batteries. Then five bombers seemed to make a bee-line for the Bank of England, and remembering those wrecked City buildings both Spry and I made for the shelter.

I had my leg pulled quite a lot by the Bank staff about my *Telegraph* photograph – and Paula too seemed interested. We came up from the shelter some 20 minutes later, and going straightway up on the roof beheld a big fire raging over Aldgate. I gather a bomber had crashed there. Obviously the object of the Nazis was to start fires for the raid tonight. I left the office and joined in the hellish long queue of homegoing City workers at the Bank tube. As I queued I could but help wonder if the sirens would sound again and they did instantly. Several people left the queue and went to cover; I made my way on to an island in the centre of the Bank crossing. The sun streamed down Cheapside. I took in the black buildings of Cheapside, to the left those of the Monument area; I turned and saw the bomb crater outside the Bank of England. This was the war in the air, these the panic-stricken citizens rushing for cover – oh Gibbs, shame on you; the citizens still thronged the streets, millions of them. So vast a crowd even for London, all black and laughing, gay, absorbed, making for home. Fire-units tore past, auxiliaries, swaying dizzily, dashed along King William Street with a clanging of bells, taxis, cars, lorries, buses; London was swarming with life, and I still stood transfixed, in the shadow of the Mansion House, watching all this amazing scene; and to think everyone of those millions knew that a squadron or squadrons of aircraft were set to tear out their hearts, that for nights on end the Germans had been trying, and tonight again, they knew they would have to spend in shelters. But no fear, panic, alarm, entered their being; they, we, were Londoners! We were the soldiers of the very front line, and no ties of uniform need bind us. Yet a further alarm sounded, and I was jammed in the subway for an hour or more waiting for my train, and was packed like a sardine for the whole journey. 3 hours to get home when it usually takes 30 minutes.

12 September.
The sirens blasted at 8.34 last night, and straightway an intense anti-aircraft barrage was thrown up. The raiders, lone ones, had evidently anticipated a coursing over the Metropolitan area in calm, bothered only a little with searchlights and an occasional gun. Instead they met an entirely different opposition. It was impossible to cross from the shelter to the flat (only at the most 18 yards) for fear of shrapnel. In one lull I did achieve the crossing, but was marooned in the hall for twenty minutes whilst our guns fired. As I stood there, binoculars at the ready, I became spellbound. Flash, flash bruh brup – and a Jerry passed over the suburbs without searchlights, but pursued by every available gun. I'll warrant those Germans breathed a sigh of relief when, if ever, they reached their bases. Everyone in the flats was in the shelter; and even the shelter itself rocked and groaned under the bangs of our guns. I would keep coming up the shelter steps on my stomach, my eyes glued to a ruddy glowing sky (a fire started by Jerry), the blinding flash of guns, and the firework effect of the bursting shells. I found myself saying 'B Company over' and we rushed over the German lines – all the old salts agreed it was just like 1914.

After midnight I tried to get to sleep. The guns crashed incessantly – but it was sweet music, and already it did us good to feel we were hitting back in earnest. Few, if any, raiders penetrated the actual City area this time. As I tried to sleep the pitter-patter of falling shrapnel (great jagged pieces of iron flung through the air with the energy to kill a man) disturbed my dreams, and when some came in the shelter doorway I wanted to rush and secure a red-hot souvenir, but to have stood in the doorway would have been suicidal. The 'All Clear' went at about 6 a.m. and having today free (the first under the new office scheme) I slept until midday.

A few stories: A notice outside a very popular City cafe yesterday: 'NO GAS. NO WATER. SODA AND MILK ONLY.' On the tube: It was packed like sardines with workers endeavouring to get home after the sirens, and before the 'all night' affair. Someone said: 'if only Hitler could see us now, wouldn't he be surprised,' to the retort 'he just wouldn't believe it.' Indeed he wouldn't for one and all of us Londoners are anything but like besieged people. From Germany: 'We might send 10,000 'planes nightly to raid London.' Joke over.

12 September (later)
Dad driving home from the City today during an air-raid alarm had a bomb dropped two minutes in front of him. He drove through the still smoking debris near Cavendish Rd, Clapham before the fire-fighters arrived. Invasion becomes more threatening daily. The War Office stood by last week for the event. Gas, too, is expected to be used, and I have now started to carry my mask. I really feel gas is 'on the menu.' Extracts from a cable sent to New York by Raymond Daniell, published in tonight's *Evening Standard*.

> On Londoners – Their suffering was reflected by their drawn, tired faces as they trekked homeward tonight, afoot, packed in tramcars and buses, past wrecked buildings, making detours around roped-off areas.
>
> 'They are a tired, nerve-worn people who have clung unshaken through it all to their belief in the power of their ideal. Their beloved City is toppling about them, but their chins are up and, so far as I can observe, they have just begun to fight.
>
> Life after dark, however is stilled, and, moving about the deserted streets at night, one gets the creepy, eerie feeling that one is living in a doomed, abandoned city.
>
> However when dawn comes the raiders flee from the defending forces and life begins to teem once more through the city streets. The nightmare passes and sanity returns to those who still breathe.
>
> Unless something happens to divert the German air force to more vulnerable targets than London's millions of helpless civilians, the world is witnessing the beginning of an era of ruthless destruction and mass murder.
>
> Britain was ready to repel any seaborne attack, as the people of London have withstood the most cruel, most trying bombardment from the air that any people have yet been subjected to.

As I write this the sirens will sound any moment signifying another all night air attack. The tube by which I travel to work is disorganised, bombs have fallen all around us. Persistently South London seems to suffer worst. It is true that unless Mother and Alan evacuate soon (perhaps to St Albans) they will lose their chance, for to travel in and out of London will soon be nigh impossible. I would mention that Buckingham Palace has been hit, and beloved St Paul's is in danger from a time bomb which may explode. The 'phones were hopeless today. I live that 'impossible' moment – life in a besieged city. The sirens sounded today when I was in the pictures seeing *Night Train to Munich* – the commencement of the German invasion of Czechoslovakia was on at the time, and as I watched German bombers on the screen, so I heard them. overhead. Extraordinary. We – Alan and I – did not come out (of the cinema). How on earth I am to get to and from work tomorrow is a mystery.

Friday, 13 September
I got to the office in between raids this morning after a night of terrific gunfire. Dad and I slept in the hall, and once, about 1 a.m., Jerry jettisoned his load over Tooting. I slept till 6 and then had a couple of hours in bed, in pyjamas. I also slept sub-consciously through another alarm.

The alarm sounded this morning at 9.40 and has kept on all the time – it's still on, now 12.45. Jerry circled seemingly over the Stock Exchange a few seconds ago, very low, and the clouds also were extremely low. It has been raining. I must say he circled with impunity and had he been of the mind I am convinced he could have bombed any City objective. I watched him from the second-floor. Constantly the sky is spattered with little black puffs of anti-aircraft smoke. That Jerry, though, must be, to give credit where credit's due, a very cool customer. He side-slipped the fire, and streaked southwards.

Maybe at this precise moment the Germans are invading the south-east coast, or attempting to, and that may have been a stray who succeeded in breaking through our lines. Whether he was reconnoitering or no, he met very little opposition, and in daylight that is remarkable. Moreover one solitary plane would not be allowed the satisfaction of paralysing the whole of the London organisation. Our anti-aircraft would never have shelled him if our boys had been to hand, and why weren't they? Usually they mincemeat any Hun in daylight, especially over the City. What is rushing at London as I write here? The men on the Bank of England keep fingering their rattles – Gas? It's Friday the 13th. I could not but help thinking last night how absurd it seemed to pen so many homegoing travellers down the Tubes etc. marooning them in the City: and I thought how many millions of working hours had been and are being lost, cheated.

All this talk of living at the office. Fine, but how about food, and cooking facilities, to say nothing of laundry. Soon London will be isolated, I fear. Should Mother and Alan go to St Albans? It's difficult times, and I can no longer visualise the feeling that I could go home tonight, eat my dinner in peace, read a book by a roaring fire, and knew that I had not to spend the night in a shelter or rather under fire.

I had a letter from Ivers in Wales today. He certainly is fortunate to have escaped the crisis of London, but I would not quit London, my beloved City, the greatest in the world, in her hour of darkness for life itself. I am proud, glad to have the privilege of sharing her suffering in this, her most glorious, most bloody hour. The Epic of London will ring down through the ages, and people will marvel at the tenacity of the Londoner. I had thought him degenerate – but now I know that he is more resilient, resolute, tough and fierce than any other of mankind. Thank God I am a Londoner, and thank God that the freedom of the world rests on such able shoulders as those of my fellow man. This is a City, now, uncanny, as if the devil incarnate is descending on her borders. It is queer, unreal, eerie. It is a London hitherto unknown in history, a City in which every citizen represents the spirit to endure, the symbol of freedom, the castle of fortitude. What is coming? What is threatening this ancient and magnificent City? You read novels, of the unknown, like H. G. Wells and his Martian invasions, and you feel we must be one too.

14 September

A deliberate cold-blooded attack by a dive-bomber was made on Buckingham Palace yesterday. A Nazi swooped out of the sky and pounded five bombs on and around the Palace, and the King and Queen were in residence. Well, the effect on the British is to spur them into hate, until soon we are angered so much we shall kill all the Nazi airmen who bale out. There will be no sympathy. I always, as I have so often written, admired the Duke of Windsor, and always wished him our King. I have changed my mind; our King and Queen are contending with war magnificently, carrying on here in their capital when they could be miles away in safety. They visit bombed and devastated areas seeking to relieve worry. They shelter with commoners whilst the bombers roar overhead. This is the King and Queen of whom we are so proud. Yet Hitler has only cemented public feeling until we think of nothing else but his extermination.

I hear from Lancaster in the flats, who has just been to Wickham Market in Suffolk, that on Saturday night and again on Tuesday invasion was attempted. Not one Nazi returned. Their bodies are still being washed up along our shores. That is the end of all Nazis who seek to molest our freedom – death.

Downing Street and the House of Lords also had incendiary bombs on them yesterday – but very little damage. I wonder if I shall see Buckingham Palace in so much glory next year or whether the bombers will have wiped it out. They may wipe the building out – but certainly not the people. Units of the British Fleet are anchored in the Thames, and can throw up an anti-aircraft barrage over many miles.

Last night Germans came over and the barrage was even more intense. We really could not cross from flat to shelter for fear of shrapnel, which rained down all around us. One minute piece could kill a person. Bombs were also

The King and Queen
viewing a bomb crater.

dropped all around our flat, and today more roads are barricaded off. They
were all Delayed Actions.

Gave my binoculars back today – they were only lent me. Damn.

Of course many more sirens today.

15 September

We drove through the arteries of this, my native town, today, round small
and dingy by-ways, diverted due to time bombs; I saw houses mere heaps
of crumbling ruins, and furniture, beds, personal belongings peeping from
beneath the pressure of masonry; I saw a shelter in Chelsea in which fifty
persons took cover during a raid, in which fifty persons were wiped from
this earth when a bomb from Nazi Germany fell upon them – just a hollow
tomb in the ground, under lofty, tinted autumn trees, and already partly
covered from the gaze of mankind by dried and shrivelled leaves. We drove
through my beloved Kensington Gardens, past the Serpentine; the exquisite
splendour of the green, the autumn flowers rich in colour; the sky patched
in blue and wispy trails of grey and white. The river ran so merrily, so
twinkingly beneath the intermittent golden sun. The whole scene was one to

Holles Street, 18 September 1940. (*Brian Girling*)

draw the lovers of London, the aristocrats, the sweethearts, it captivated the imagination. Yet this scene was pathetic, lacking. It lacked the people. It was devoid of life. No small boats drifted by, no hardy swimmers, no children. Kensington was uncanny. To Paddington Station – here a little more life was evident, reminiscent of the carefree holiday life. But this time the incentive was evacuation, to quit a London pounded day and night by the wrath of the Nazis, to achieve respite from aerial combat. I was glad to leave Paddington. We drove along, past the ruins of Madame Tussaud's and the area near King's Cross, and down Tottenham Court Road, the cosmopolitan quarter of London. The sirens screeched as we approached Oxford Street.

The few people abroad hurried to shelter. We accelerated and found shelter in the Herald offices, in the basement under the printing machines. I settled down to *Thirteen in a Fog* by Bruce Graeme, an author I always enjoy in relaxation, and this novel was most gripping. My attention was distracted by a flickering red light – indicating the presence of enemy aircraft overhead. I left my novel and went to street level Damn! I had just missed seeing a German bomber literally shot clean to pieces in the air – one of the crew had baled out. This bomber had been set upon first by a solitary Hurricane and, in seconds, more of our fighters had simply fallen out of the blue and shot him up. The Hurricane executed the familiar Victory Roll.

I stood there amongst that crowd of rough printers. 'That'll make my pint taste sweeter,' roared one old timer. 'Gor lummy, that's the blimin' best sight I've seen for ages, that is an' all,' his mate replied. We all stood there excited as a pack of school-kids, and I found myself speaking to a Turk who could not get back to his own country – and in the shadow of shattered buildings which once were tenement flats of Covent Gardens' workers, we talked about Turkey and the war.

Soon we made our way homewards, heartened by the news two Germans had been shot down, one in Victoria – a *Herald* photographer had rushed to secure pictures. The streets, bar for A.F.S. and A.R.P. personnel, were practically deserted. Through Trafalgar Square, down Whitehall (little evidence of material damage to Government property), across Westminster Bridge and past the tragic, cruel sight of wrecked St Thomas's Hospital. On past bombed residences in Lambeth, Stockwell, past the huge crater near Kennington Oval where a tram had been blown skyhigh, and so to Clapham.

The 'All Clear' sounded. At Clapham we beheld excitement. Yes Sir! Just near the tram depot one German bomber had crashed, and an ordinary, everyday dwelling house was burning fiercely. Firemen were temporarily playing stirrup-pumps on the blaze, but as we were diverted fire-fighting appliances dashed to the scene, accompanied by ambulances. We were diverted all round Clapham Common and, as we drove across, it became obvious that Jerry had shoved his load overboard before crashing – burst water mains, scattered debris, small fires and craters marked his path. The top of St Barnabas Church had been knocked clean off by its wing. I could not help thinking that that bomber had crashed upon an unsuspecting household, perhaps killing some persons, in the midst of their Sunday dinner. To think – two hours before, the Nazi crewmen were breakfasting in France and that London mother was putting her dinner in the oven.

This afternoon we had yet another alarm. I saw formations of heavy German bombers circling Clapham as if to peel off. They soon disappeared. Within ten minutes I saw approaching from the south-east a dark cloud. A huge, tightly-wedged cloud, almost like a plague of locusts descending upon their prey – Germans. I thought of those pictures of German bombers sweeping across the Lowlands. The bombers came on, in a dead straight line. One menacing, speeding line of death, roaring ever nearer – like an express train bearing

Tram car damaged in a daylight raid in Blackfriars, London 1940. (*Associated Press*)

down on you. I told the sky-gazers to take cover; no second bidding was necessary. Citywards a huge black cloud loomed. I counted with no feeling seventeen bombers, but I knew there were more. No fighters surrounded them – just that avalanche of bombers. I was about to take cover when they veered around towards Victoria. They were bent upon a set mission, that was sure, therefore I didn't suppose, unless molested, they would tarry with Tooting.

I thought, and I think quite correctly, that high above this cloud of Huns I discerned the fleeting glimpse of a silver wing, the tip of a Spitfire. I had the feeling our boys were up there, ready, gloating over their prey before the meal. And as time progressed I heard no bombs, and if that squadron had reached London proper they would have unleashed. The 'All Clear' soon sounded and then I knew they must have been our boys – waiting.

Tonight, another warning, probably all night, is on, and the moon is brilliant. But as I think of the heartening news which has just come over the radio, of 165 (165! I repeat) Jerries down my joy knows no bounds. We have also smashed the daylight out of Hitler's invasion ports, and blown the hell clean out of Antwerp. I know we shall hear more Jerries are down today for during an alarm a few hours ago I saw a Spitfire chase a German bomber and could see his machine-guns blazing away like billy-oh.

Which reminds me. Yesterday about 6 p.m. during a raid I saw a massive swarm of Nazi bombers fly directly overhead, to be followed within seconds by another, more powerful force of 'planes. These flew in rigid formation, forming a series of small V's together forming one V. As these swarmed through the dull grey clouds, I became struck – were they British or German? One burst from Clapham guns greeted them, followed by a rattle of machine-guns. If they had been German I am confident our anti-aircraft barrage would have opened up on them, for they would have brought a host down. As it was the ground defences remained comparatively inactive. I recall they all appeared to be the same standard size machine – i.e. no large ones ringed with what could possibly be fighters – I am convinced that the following 'planes *must* have been ours in hot pursuit of Jerry. If they were British it was a great sight – the air was dark with *British* 'planes. Of course should, God forbid, they have been Jerry things are not so good, for that number looked as though they could wipe out almost anything whenever they wanted to. However they didn't and London seems to be contending with the usual damage.

Priestley was most excellent on the postscript.[20] 'We Londoners,' he said 'are living in probably the biggest battle of this war. We civilians, we Londoners whom the provinces imagined were getting soft, are now the soldiers of the war fighting the greatest battle.' As I write this at midnight the battle of London is waging over my head, the pom-pom of naval shells, the crump of anti-aircraft pounds incessantly. Yet I have just been talking here in the flat with Miller and Dad all about the last war and what we think will be the outcome of this.

To conclude. I happened upon a man in our shelter yesterday who lives in the Causeway, Carshalton. Jean Doville and two sisters have been evacuated to Canada. I am glad.

Thank God the 500 lb time bomb which had been threatening St Paul's has been safely removed. The man who did it deserves the V.C. as do any men who remove such menaces. Anyhow the whole of London raises their hats to him.

Buckingham Palace has received its third bombing.

GOD SAVE THE KING!

16 September

At long last a letter from Binnie, posted in Sydney by the airmail service on 6 August before our raids started, so I cannot judge her thoughts about what is happening. Undoubtedly this is Hitler's big effort. All through the night his bombers passed over our capital, every few seconds they came. Our barrage of fire was all enveloping in its proportions, and I watched the bursting of shells high in the starlit sky, listened to the deafening crump crump of guns, and stood spellbound, absorbed in the most utterly fantastic scene, of a London under the soft caress of a most heavenly moon, and red hot and reddened with wounds caused by the enemy bombers.

Shell caps screamed overhead, crashes, rumbles, bangs, crumps and thuds – all night long the din went on. It was like an elaborate firework display in which the whole of London joined.

A terrific fire started near Clapham. I heard the Junction had been hit. Another in the City – fire-engines clanged by in the Shrapnel-riddled streets, tore along the deserted, moon-bathed roads, on into the centre of the marked city.

But although everyone was in their shelters, Dad and I kipped down in the hall. We asked for trouble, really, and perhaps in view of the appalling damage we had witnessed in the day we were foolish. But if so we were aware of it, and took the philosophical outlook if we are going to get it then we will.

At first, when Jerry used to stray over, I became perturbed, and was annoyed to think that my 'ideals' were not materialising as I had intended. But now I am in full command, and have won. There is no fear. As I watched the bombers, saw one caught, held in the searchlights, mere silent weak beams of light in the moonlit universe, saw the flash of bursting shells, saw the trail of flaming onions, saw the bomber nose down, crash, and as I heard too the insistent boom of guns I felt all-supreme, and felt such a spirit of elation as I cannot hope to explain.

Thank God and Lieutenant Davies[21] St Paul's is not razed to the ground. They removed a 500 lb bomb, so fused and dangerous that but for the sacrifice would never have been attempted, and Davies drove it through cleared London streets to Hackney Marshes where it was exploded. It made a crater over 100 ft in width. Thank God St Paul's is intact, my own beloved cathedral of such significant memories. Thank you, Davies.

We shot down 189 'planes yesterday. We only lost 25 fighters. Magnificent.

16 September (later)

Again I write amidst the hail of guns, the drone of bombers, the thud of bombs. Oh boy – tonight I left the office at 5 p.m. during a raid which had been on for at least a couple of hours. Indeed we have had four lengthy raids in the course of the day. I legged it over London Bridge in a damp, muggy atmosphere, as naturally it was useless attempting to catch the Tube at the

The Monument,
16 September 1940.

Bank as the Northern Line is closed during raids on account of its passage under the Thames. In any case a vast crowd was already waiting. I walked past the huge bomb crater outside the Monument, peering down into its jagged depths, and so across the bridge.

The crowd was enormous, it choked the whole roadway (of course traffic is no longer permitted to cross the bridge due to the bombing) as it surged towards London Bridge Station. I glanced at the clouds, so low, and bearing in mind the many treacherous assaults upon civilians in daytime I could well imagine how much a German would have given to have bombed London Bridge with all those countless numbers of people on it. I reached the Station – the crowd was stretching as far as I could see, milling and jostling. I did not line up, but jumped a lorry, and another, finally making the Borough. Here I found a Hackbridge Cable Company lorry, and I jumped on to its back. The driver was a sport and in a few minutes the lorry was chock-a-block with homegoing Londoners. We passed the bombed Elephant and Castle (negligible damage compared with other districts) past the Oval and so to Clapham. I thoroughly enjoyed the ride, it was a novelty, and the road was a river of cars and lorries and vehicles giving lifts. We came to Clapham – which since yesterday had been bombed to hell. A whole block of flats above shops had been divested of their sides – it was like a doll's house with a movable back – I could see tables and chairs, beds, bookcases, pictures, and every conceivable domestic dressing on every floor. Clapham was a wreck. Passing the guns I saw three craters where bombs had fallen, indicating Jerry's aim was primarily to silence these guns. I was glad to get across the Common, although the muzzles of the guns were lowered; I finally arrived home at 5.45 approx. and was in the middle of dinner when the 'All Clear' went. If I had not got that lorry I wouldn't have been home until at least 8.30 – but then people say I am 'fly' and indeed if I put my mind to it I can work anything.

Once down the Royal Bank basement shelter this afternoon I had a good look at Paula Starkie – but somehow I always get Kate tied up. I feel I shall marry Kate – her presence comforts me – certainly she is not voluptuous, but I don't mean it in that way. Somehow Kate feels embedded within me. As I have not seen Binnie, I cannot think of her with any 'real' feeling. But Kate's face – oh, her very being – it must be love! But only time and Kate can tell me.

Again today the R.A.F. advertises for volunteers for Flying Duties. No longer 'school certif' required; but with an expanding air force the requirements are: 'Qualifications: Applicants must be fit, intelligent, and possess dash and initiative' and if I haven't got a whole lot of those qualities then neither has anyone. Now I am sure I shall join the air force, but I will first see the Battle of London out, this phase, the worst, at least.

The guns swell into crescendos of power, they roll and rumble like waves at sea. The roar wobbles into the heart of England. London, England, Freedom speaks – it rattles my doors as I write, shakes the windows, but I am firm.

I believe *now* Hitler's invasion attempt is being frustrated. Maybe we shall wake in the morning and find all is won; but somehow I feel I shall be in the final punch to outsmash Hitler.

Ever more the guns roar, guardians of the night.

17 *September*

Last night was one of the heaviest London barrages of anti-aircraft fire I have yet witnessed. German bombers came over about 8.30 and roared low overhead for a solid three hours. I did not go down the shelter but stayed indoors typing up my journal and generally reading through my files.

As I listened to the rumble, the crash and wobble of our guns, watched the moon rise and become set amongst a hive of bursting red and orange lights, I realised how magnificent an age I am living in. The moon glistened down on a wet and shiny suburb, illuminating all the tiny pools of rain water, threw into relief the mass of buildings and small suburban homes, and over it all was the retort, the fierce and deafening growl of naval guns, pom-poms and guns of all sorts and sizes. Yet still the bombers flew low, and the whistle of shells became more intense.

I stood in the concrete hallway of the flats with Miller, the only two above ground. As we listened and watched we suddenly heard a shrill scream – we threw ourselves flat in the hall, waiting. The bomb fell 200 yards away. I tore through a hail of shrapnel to the A.R.P. post and with the wardens we rushed along the deserted moonlit streets of this London suburb to the affected spot. I was the first to reach there. I saw a tiny front garden in which a shell or a bomb (I cannot say which) had fallen and exploded. Very little damage had been done – the front merely blown in and windows broken and glass scattered. The stink was putrid. So acid.

The guns and bombers still roared like hell at midnight so, dressed in my old bags and sports, I kipped down in the hall on cushions, throwing an eiderdown over me. I fell right off to sleep to the tune of incessant gunfire, which does not disturb me, and did not wake until Mother stepped on me coming into the flat upon the 'All Clear' at 3 something in the morning.

I viewed Cheapside today – Gamages and shops I used only last week are down – a direct hit wrecking Gamages completely. In fact Cheapside is a shambles, but traditional Bow Church still rises unperturbed. Perhaps I mourn most of all the loss of the ABC and with its going losing all contact, however remote, with the 'Girl in the ABC.' I wonder if she thinks – 'it was only a moment ago'? I've written a lot about her – is this the Finis? I don't think I mind if it is.

19 September

Last night, after another day of numerous air-raids, when I saw a large number of our fighter aircraft and smoke trails high in the sky, was quite eventful. But before I mention that I cycled (it being my day off) to Carshalton and visited the Howarths, but they were out or away for I could get no reply. I noticed that they had their beds downstairs, and a surface concrete shelter in their garden. But the house looked deserted. In our old house in the back garden is an ungainly white cement air-raid shelter. I saw no trace of any such shelter in the Williams's. Of course I could write to Kate and inquire if she were O.K. but I know she is – so I find no reason to. My purpose for visiting Carshalton was to verify the story told me in the H.C. shelter some nights ago by a man who lives near the Dovilles that factories in Mill Lane and houses in the Wrythe had been gutted. After a careful scrutiny all I saw were two houses in Mill Lane partly demolished; the factories were untouched. As for the Wrythe – it's true I'll admit I didn't go right the way along in Hamsie's direction but the main part, where I had been led to believe the damage existed, i.e. near the Central School, I found completely untouched. So much for that story – and as I wandered down the Causeway and by the river I stopped and thought: Les was in Winnipeg; the Doville children (and Jean liked me) were evacuated to somewhere in Canada; Kate has become a complete stranger to me and goes to work in a bank. Robert too had gone – where I knew not. Martha no longer looked from

Evacuees. Note the cardboard boxes carrying the gas masks that the entire population was issued with.

her window and saw Bob and I paddle our way, boyishly self-conscious upon a tree trunk, down the Wandle. Oh I think of so many reminiscences and am full of regrets – yet I look forward indeed to my destiny and the R.A.F. I cycled back to Tooting, so strange to me and unreal, and reached the Broadway as the sirens sounded. But there were two more raids before nightfall.

This night, the 18th, I stayed indoors endeavouring to read *Revelations* in the Moffatt translation but when a German bomber swooped low a neighbour came in the flat, and she remained for two hours, and then I was too tired for *Revelations*. The guns of course were as loud and incessant as ever. About 11.45 I undressed and went to bed, for I had decided I would not kip in the hall. However I acted too soon. A naval mobile gun was stationed just a few yards from my window, hidden behind trees in Scotia's scrap yard, and as Jerry came over it fired suddenly, and I was nearly knocked from my bed. I went out on to the landing – two more such retorts from our friend the naval mobile and the blast literally hurled me back a yard or two. Then came a penetrating scream, and in anticipation I held myself against the wall. It plomped down somewhere out the back, and I concluded it was either a shell or light explosive. As the shrapnel rained down (I found a huge piece) Miller hailed me, and in my pyjamas I stood in the roadway looking towards Clapham and saw one of the now familiar red glows which spring up for seconds to an intense brightness and then subside. As we watched we saw a great clutter of falling debris all red hot, flaring, smouldering and smoking. We cheered for we thought it to be a Jerry but this morning the Press described it as a 'fire leaf' which is a new invention of the Hun. I do not imagine it will be as awful as an aerial torpedo. Then the shrapnel drove us in – and I went to bed and slept like a log until 8, when three letters from Binnie and my *Telegraph* photo greeted me. I cannot imagine why the Press tries to reason with all the people who seek shelter in the Tubes, and also tries to smooth over the fears of all the millions of Londoners who nightly camp in air-raid shelters. I have all the time slept through the raids in our flat – and this on the first storey of a block four high. I am not frightened in the least degree – why should I be? If I get it then I do.

Binnie wrote pages and displayed an intelligent knowledge of world affairs and a keen sense of humour. She also mentioned a friend of her father's who has sailed to England twice since the outbreak of war – he's a Captain on a freighter I gather. Sometimes I feel I might make a name for myself in the war and although I should love the publicity I do not want any such thing to affect people's, and esp. girls', opinion of me, and perhaps be led away with glamour. I do not desire that. So maybe I'll assume a name until I have pocketed my ideal female. Yes, Binnie, you seem quite fitted to my mind. The *Telegraph* photo of me with Churchill touring the bombed area of the City appears as good as can be expected of me.

The West End which I love and enjoy so much is very badly battered. John Lewis, Bourne & Hollingsworth and D. H. Evans all gutted more or less. A bomb scored a direct hit on the subway under the Oxford Street part of the Marble Arch Tube and killed fourteen. It was only a little while ago I was there, and I wonder if Lise in Germany is thinking of me as she reads, if she does, of St Paul's and the Marble Arch where we tea'ed and of Oxford St which we went along on the top of a bus admiring the gay lights. How things have changed.

John Lewis' department store, London, 18 September 1940 (*Associated Press*)

19 September (afternoon)

I am sitting at my desk in the office with very little to do. I think therefore I will jot down this odd note or two by way of keeping up on this now rather voluminous journal. Incidentally I am beginning to wonder if the word 'journal' applies to this – but anyhow it sounds alright.

A few minutes ago I had just completed typing the Imperial Airways Rebate and was poking in the biscuit tin when all of a sudden I heard a colossal explosion. 'Time bombs' Miss Spindler yelled. I made a dive for Lane's room, but he met me in the doorway with his A.F.S. tin-hat on and said: 'Get everyone downstairs' and simultaneously the Bank's alarm-bell added to the commotion. Two more explosions followed in quick succession, to my annoyance, for I felt I was missing the fun in dashing round and telling the staff to go below. However I finally got into Spry's room and together we watched a pall of smoke disappear into the clouds. It was obvious – a stray German bomber had somehow contrived to penetrate into the heart of the City amongst the low grey clouds, and notoriously fulfilled the Nazi practice of dropping his bombs and machine-gunning. I suppose Liverpool Street Station was the object of this unsuspecting attack. The sirens did not sound, and along with the Bank's the only other alarms to be given were those of the roof-spotters, whose whistles blared forth.

Today I think we had the hundredth alarm. Good Lord. I arrived at the office this morning by way of the Borough, from where I walked in the pouring rain. Still I had saved my fare by getting a lift in a Ford saloon. This 'lift' business is particularly suited to me, as besides being a trifle more out of routine it saves me money, in consequence my aim of £25 comes nearer daily. I deposited £1.1.3 in my account this morning. My financial status is now:

Saving Certs	£1.10.0
Coins	£1.0.0
Dad owes	£12.10.0
Savings A/c	£5.16.3
Total	£20.16.3

considering I only get 30/- per week is most splendid, and just goes to prove what one can do if one tries.

Places known intimately to me and damaged terribly in raids are: Oxford Street, Marble Arch, Regent Street, Strand, Trafalgar Square, St Thomas's, Stockwell, Kennington, Brixton, Clapham, Wimbledon, Malden, Shannon Corner, Hammersmith, Shepherds Bush, Chelsea, Threadneedle St, Monument area, Minories, Cheapside, Wood Street, Cripplegate, Inner Temple (I hate to think of damage in the Temple), Long Acre, and of course locally. These areas are what I've seen in the main, and which react strangely upon me. I cannot even now credit the amazing era in which I am living.

Oh yes, the ABC in Cheapside which I mentioned yesterday seems to be thinking of re-opening, and actually served a few customers with bread and cheese etc. today. I wonder if through that broken glass and brickwork the Girl will tread? I do not think anyhow I care two hoots, in fact I know I don't.

Mother and Alan, Dad has decided, are to spend a few nights away from the Metropolis; how I'll miss not having a hot meal awaiting me when I get home.

What a bloody war!

21 *September*

The night of the 19th I again travelled home from the office by lorry, packed chock-a-block with City and factory workers. I picked it up at the Borough. Along the route I was struck by the enormous number of old women and children lining up like a cinema crowd to enter the Tube stations for the night. It was then only 5 p.m.

We were diverted south of Balham and we had to go round by Tooting Bec Common. Just opposite the balloon-barrage station here (devoid of balloons for some months) a house had been completely shattered by a bomb the previous night. Four persons had lost their lives. Barely one other house was affected except for broken windows.

Before dusk fell the sirens wailed their nightly warning. My people went down to the shelter, but comfortably installed by a cosy fire I stayed put. I typed a letter to Binnie. However the guns, 'planes and bombs seemed to me extraordinarily intense, maybe due to low clouds carrying the echo. I again fulfilled my boyish dream – standing alone amongst an inferno of flashes, bursting shells, roar upon rumble of guns, the thud of bombs, the crumple of houses falling, and the rain glistening upon London's roof-tops. As the flashes showed up every minute detail, illuminated every tiny pool of rainwater; as the whistle of jagged great pieces of shrapnel flew through the air and three bombs screamed down around me shaking the building I felt strangely indifferent, elated.

Once a 'plane zoomed over me with such a noise that it was as a car accelerating. I learned later it was a German bomber which had crashed just near the Nelson Hospital, Merton.

So the night of the 19th wore on, and by midnight it quietened down and I fell asleep, the guns echoing a lullaby in my ear, but I was awakened in the early hours by terrific gunfire and bombs but I soon dropped off again.

Yesterday evening I cycled round Tooting Bec Common through Balham and so to Clapham: perhaps the worst hit district in London, except for the East End. The Chase had numerous bomb craters in the middle of the road, and the old mansions stood defiantly, chipped, minus windows, minus bricks. It was a wrecked road – but I can visualise it tomorrow repaired and forgotten. I came back by way of Wandsworth Common – it was saddening, the number

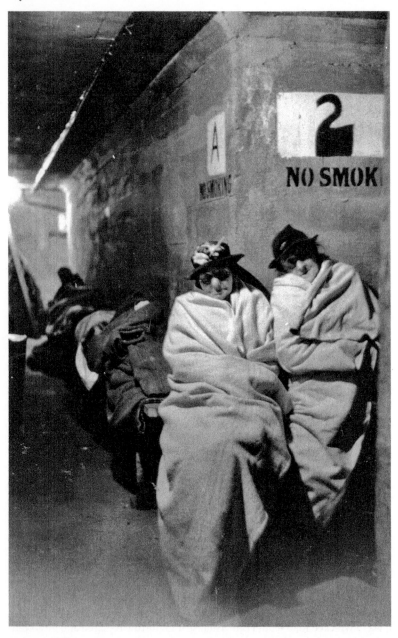

Sheltering from an air raid could last all night, and blankets were advisable to keep warm.

of men, women and children, all laden with large mattresses and blankets, cushions and pillows, bags and cases, who trudged cheerfully to the public shelters where they wished to stay the night. Even old men and women of eighty-odd made their way – why I cannot comprehend for if I were eighty I wouldn't care a bugger what happened to my aged carcase. I went down one underground shelter – tiny cooped passages, airless, stuffy and stifling hot, and I glanced at the type of people who sought refuge there. I could not understand where their courage was, for staying nightly in a living coffin was not my idea of dodging bombs; they stood to become exceedingly unhealthy, and indeed they were. I was glad to get out into the clear crisp evening air.

As I cycled past the Clapham guns I thought how each night those who man them have to fight for their lives, fire like merry hell – but soon the troops will know worse. I thought too of Kate, perhaps because it was an evening which typified my idea of her personality; I gave myself to thinking of her, my lost opportunity, and of how nice it would be to feel that someone other than my family really cared for my welfare, really could be happy from a word from me. It seemed funny that way. I don't suppose I'll ever have a girl. But the increasing numbers of people at the shelter entrances soon made me forget what might be a childish fancy – why did all these people seek refuge from the night raiders? The sensitive, well-versed people make our pilots the best in the world, the same material constitutes the unruffled Londoner. Personally, Dad and I have slept in the flat and often in bed, through nearly all these raids which are classed as the worst the world has known. I am. regarding these raids as mere thunderstorms.

Last night I saw a fire over the Central London area and watched the dropping of a Molotov Breadbasket and 'firesplashes.' The universe was lit for seconds by an intense orange glow. The raiders sheered off and surprisingly enough we had the 'All Clear' on midnight – but I was in bed. Another warning followed an hour later but I slept on; but one exceptionally heavy burst of gunfire near dawn disturbed me for a few minutes, until the guns' usual stanza lulled me off again.

Today, a misty morning, we are to visit St Albans for one night.

Monday, 23 September (Early Morning)
Oh boy, what a weekend.

On Saturday afternoon at 3.15 we motored to St Albans. We viewed a lot of the damage in London on the way. King's Cross had copped a packet on the Potato Market. North of King's Cross we came upon a roped-off road, an officer and private of the bomb disposal squad were just hastening from the area, and police and troops were stopping traffic; we guessed a time bomb was about to blow up. Dad drove a little way away, but I got out of the car and hung in the very near vicinity. Booooom booom it went. And that was another timer out of the way. Continuing through Barnet we were struck how peaceful

Extensive bomb
damage at
Newham Docks,
23 September 1940.

and normal the whole scene was. London is so huge a City that at least a half isn't touched. Certainly, but for the roar of aircraft, war hadn't yet come to North London. It is us in the South who catch it. I'm glad anyhow I am not out of it. On the Gt North Road outside Barnet a field had been converted into a temporary airfield, I assumed mainly for the defence of Hendon. The day was warm and sunny and I availed myself of the opportunity to snap my people. As I did so Alan spotted a 'plane and said it was a German; it dropped a white something or other which he said was a bomb. We also imagined Hatfield aerodrome was being bombed but it turned out to be nothing more than our own machines practising. Reaching St Albans we went straight to Dorie's and Ted's. How John and Jennifer grow. Jen is now 4 and John 7 years old. They are dear little children. St Albans is certainly 'behind the lines' and accordingly our journey to and from was most interesting.

Dad slept on the rug in the drawing-room and me on the settee. Ted was out on A.F.S. duty. We had two raid alarms in the night, but in St Albans they are but alarms.

Next day I went for a walk in the direction of Batchwood and quite by chance encountered Steven Milne. How glad we were to meet, and how fine a fellow he has got to be. We were once best friends and are still. Steve was waiting for a girl, and she came, shyly, to be introduced. Her name is Susan and I immediately fell in love with her charming personality – I'm so pleased she has Steve. I talked over many an old time with him, for after just one meeting in about three years there is an awful lot to speak of. Steve is 19 in November and works in the research dept of de Havillands. He is exempt from military service. I surmised Steve would be damn keen to get in the R.A.F. but when he learned I intended to go he advised me not to be such a damn fool; he said the 'planes, esp. bomber command, are nothing but flying coffins.

In St Albans, unlike Tooting, the air seems all good and pure, and as I write this today I feel utterly cleansed, refreshed and deliciously clean. I always thought St Albans dull and boring, but I know better now. Ah well, after a

Oxford Street bearing the after-effects of a raid, 18 September 1940. (*Brian Girling*)

very complete talk with Steve's parents (Steve saw my picture in the *Telegraph* – such a lot of people have) I had to go back. But first let me continue the morning's walk. Steve was anxious for Susan so we departed laughingly and arranged to meet the following Sat. when we are to fetch Alan and Mother back. I continued across the fields in which Hooker and gamekeepers in the days of old terrorised our life, and we theirs, but oh what glorious fun. Along the wet and dewy pathway to Chillick, through Solly Joel's estate, and then bang slap into Steve and Susan again. How distinctly envious I am of him; if only I too lived in St Albans again, and Kate too... what a foursome, Susan and Steve and Kate and me... Steve had his arm round Susan – who wore a channing dark green coat, whilst Steve wore a splendid tweed sports coat and flannels, along with his old school tie. Well we 'passed in the night,' and now I cannot await next Saturday. But I am now up 'in the line' again and the atmosphere of this great City is wholly changed.

We entered London from Barnet and Golder's Green. Our route took us past Wimpole Street, Baker Street (where a bomb had fallen and left the house standing but blown the basement clean in), Oxford Street (still closed),

Marble Arch (where the bomb fell on the subway), Buckingham Palace (damage indistinguishable), Queen Anne's Mansions and the West End in general. When crossing Hampstead Heath we had seen a Messerschmitt 109 belonging to Goering's Yellow Nose Squadron (Goering's old squadron of the last war) and a powerful, compact, complete machine it looked too. Very wicked to an air-gunner…!

Arriving home we had no sooner got indoors than the sirens went. As the hour was early, even for Hitler, I guessed the alarm was not the nightly affair, but it proved so. I understand there were at least two alarms, but I slept solidly, hearing gunfire to lull me off. However I am jumping ahead. All London, as we travelled from the north to the south, appeared to be trekking pathetically, tragically, to the shelters. Mothers, children, men – laden with beds and blankets, all flocked to the Tubes. As I say, they are, I think, without intelligence (blunt as it may seem) but on second thoughts I learn they refuse to leave their London homes, and consequently inhabit the Tubes nightly. One cannot blame them, I suppose, and indeed it seems only me in the whole of London who carries on normally, getting into bed at the usual hour despite the guns and alarms. Momington Crescent Tube had a stack of perambulators outside, and I loathe to think of the pitiful conditions below – hot air, dirty bodies, filth – why must humans exist under such degradation? The *Pictorial* carried an excellent, outspoken article on 'The hotels refusing shelter to passers-by in raids,' and Claridge's, the Berkeley, and the Ritz were heavily criticised.

Before I went to bed I became a bachelor – and I confess I rather like the novelty. I tried to cook some porridge, but made an unholy liquid which filled a large basin completely. However I 'drank' the porridge. I cleared up the house, swept, made beds etc. and of course washed up. So much. And today after cooking myself a boiled egg for breakfast (for quickness's sake) making beds, tea, etc. I feel really jolly, and it's fine to think Mother and Alan are safe out of this hellish mire.

24 September (later)

At St Albans in 1934 I met Steven Milne; we became friends, best friends. We shared everything. We had great fun. Then I moved, and Steve and I lost touch with one another. However I met him again, accidentally, on Sunday last. Boy how I wish we were back in the good old days, or better still together now. Steve has a charming girl by the name of Susan, and I bet I too would have had some such companion if I still lived in St Albans along with Steve. But that does not really worry me, although I confess I can imagine nothing more delightful than Steve and me, with our two girls having the best of times. Steve was loyal, decent, just the fellow I want. I think of Pewsham, who is not nearly so down to earth. Pete was a very good friend, as was Brian in Southampton, and several others – but Steve is best. How we used to scrump from Batchwood House, eat spuds with gipsies over on the golf-course amongst snow drifts. I

An interior view of the
damage at Newham docks,
23 September 1940.

think of the air-guns and shooting the copper's kid in the leg, and above all of
the gamekeepers, and Hooker with a hook for a hand. By George they were
splendid times. And in any scrape we always went together, inseparable.

I hoped in a way Steve and I would be able to join up together but that is
unfortunately squashed on the head with him being in the Research Dept of
de Havillands.

Well, I just wanted to write about Steve and my hopes, but I guess they may
yet come true.

23–24 September

Last night coming home I was surprised, disgusted, and horrified, as I
came home by Tube. It was my first Tube journey for about a week, having
achieved lifts by road. All the Bank underground station was crawling with
fat old women, filthy kids, louts of men, all with packs of food, dirty-looking
blankets, and oranges. They lined all the Central platfonns, the subway to the
Northern Line, and the Northern Line to District platforms. I squeezed my
way on to the train at last, and was jammed in – by God it stank like hell, of
sweating bodies and body odour. Every single station all down the line was
filled with these 'refugees' from the Luftwaffe. At last I reached Trinity Road
and as I did so the sirens went and the flood gates were closed. How damn
silly it seems to maroon the passengers on the wrong side. Well, I snorted
and shouted but to no good, so I took myself to another entrance – here I
bluffed my way out by pretending I had to get to my factory – thank goodness
I escaped that tunnel of disease. I got home in time to hear the King's speech[22]
– how I must try for the George Cross.

But those people in the Tubes. They arrive there at 3 in the afternoon and
rise at 7–7.30 the next morning. Well if that isn't asking for trouble. I can
foresee disease will be rife amongst the people who shelter in this way. It is
the ignorant people who flock to the depths. It does make one think, and even

I thought surely I too should take cover if thousands rush down the Tubes so early. But I wouldn't for all the bombs in the world. As I have said Dad and I are the only two people I know of in the whole of London who carry on in the normal way – i.e. going to bed etc. etc. But I am of the opinion that if anything is to happen I shall get a premonition, an impulse; I have before! But whatever befalls us I would rather take my chance in comfort than risk disease in the unhealthy air-raid shelters. But as Dad says – it is a gamble. So it is today – we ride with death at our elbow. This is comparable with the front line in the last war. I see my next door neighbour – here today – but, maybe, gone tomorrow. Such is life and I don't think even I can say it is boring now in Tooting; the guns are all around us, and our flats seem to stand directly in the line of the Luftwaffe.

General de Gaulle has gone to Dakar, with a Free French Force supported by a British contingent. Fireworks? You bet.

The *Evening Standard* seller outside Cooks in Cheapside displayed the following composition yesterday:

Hitler ex painter and now chief Town-Crier
is trying hard to set London afire;
If in this effort he still does persist
then Hamburg and Berlin will cease to exist.

I am viewing this war more and more with the eye of a chess player, watching critically every move in this terrific game – and after all it literallly does seem a battle of wits.

Tuesday, 24 September

Dad and I are on our own this week, Mother and Alan being in St Albans. I am more or less in the same position as over a year ago when my people went to Cornwall and I kept house for ten days. Yes siree, I am the housekeeper. What fun!

Arriving home last night I set to work and made my tea, then swept up the rooms, tidied all up, washed up the crocks, tidied dirty corners. The sirens went at about 7.50 signifying the nightly air-raid. But I stayed in as I always do and got on with the housework. I cleaned out Joey, our canary, and fed the goldfish. I washed handkerchiefs and pyjamas and my favourite white shirt. As I washed these articles guns were howling all around me, and just as I had put the kettle on for my cocoa three bombs screamed down, shook the building which swayed distinctly, and blew up. German bombers roared overhead, searchlights lit the sky. Oh boy – I wonder what Lebkicher or even Kate would have said if they could have seen me – in my dirty old flannels, rolled-up blue open-neck shirt, hair ruffled, and washing clothes amongst those eggs of whistling death. I hung the clothes to dry in the bathroom, and

Bomb damage,
West End, London,
24 September 1940.

as it is not blacked out I had to grope my way to hang the clothes, and my path was lit by constant gun flashes, flaming onions, and bursting shells. Phew. But I must say I did enjoy myself, and I am extremely fond of housework, and if ever I get married, then my wife'll have to work like a Trojan to clean every nook and cranny in the place, for I cannot bear untidiness. Anyhow the German bombers did great damage last night, and over seven bombs were dropped in our immediate vicinity, and I hear Wandsworth Common Station has been hit and busted up.

Dad and I went to bed in the ordinary way – well what are the odds if the shelter was to catch it? I suppose the whole lot would cave in but the flats escape – and vice versa. However I am a fatalist. The apartments Lebkicher had in Dolphin Square are said to be gutted.

This morning I have washed up, cooked breakfast – eggs and fried bread – washed up, washed kitchen floor, and bathroom, made beds, tidied up in general, washed walls in bathroom and again put things in ship-shape order. Ironed (I love ironing) handkerchiefs.

Am lunching in Town with Dad at the Sussex in Long Acre.

25 September
Last night and in the early hours of this morning we experienced our worst aerial bombardment. We anticipated this in view of the R.A.F.'s extensive four-hour raid on Berlin the other day.

The alarm was given early, and until 10.30 we had a great deal of gunfire and bombs, in which period some fell exceedingly close. After 10.30 we had a comparative quiet period and Dad and I retired to bed. I was awakened by Dad calling at me to go in the hall at a quarter-to-one this morning. Above, an enormous number of enemy 'planes were roaring; our guns spoke I don't know how many times to the second. Great powerful guns just near us. Suddenly there came a whistle, shrill, followed by another nearer, yet

Bomb damage on the Broadway, 25 September 1940. (*Wimbledon Museum*)

a third, this time seemingly on top of us. Bombs! As they thudded down, whistling, and then sudden silence, another salvo descended, and the fourth fell the other side of our flat, so did a fifth and sixth. In other words a stick of bombs had straddled our building. Well, we got back into bed, and without exaggeration it was undoubtedly our busiest night. I was awakened almost hourly, and lay listening to the roar of jockeying 'planes, the scream of bombs,' and the terrific noise of our guns which vibrated in my ears. I looked out – fires, searchlights, shells – a pandemonium.

Looking back this morning I am elated. Yes, elated. Last night Wandsworth had its very worst raid. History will prove that the area in which we live is the most frequently bombed of all London, including the East End. Every other area at least has its off and on nights, but we – well, every night is an on. (I write this during a raid. The alert was given ten minutes ago, but now the whistles telling of the immediate presence of hostile aircraft has warned all London to take cover. But my journal comes first. London doesn't all take cover – and I am not in the least degree perturbed, merely curious, indifferent.)

Yesterday afternoon we (Dad and me) went all round Victoria etc. in the car. It is a fallacy to say Dolphin Square has been bombed, it hasn't. Lebkicher's flat which I had expected to see in ruins was standing complete with windows. What appears to have been a house in the very near proximity had been stripped of its floors. I also saw Wandsworth Common station which had been hit whilst I did the washing the other evening. Later I took a snap of Dad by the side of a Mercedes looking like Churchill. In St Albans at the weekend John certainly tickled me by saying that Jennifer had said upon seeing my photo in the *Telegraph* 'Look there's Uncle Bert and Colin, Mummy' – I must say Dad looks like Winston, and how he likes to think he is!

In concluding this entry I must emphasise that last night saw the most terrific air-raid, and it seems impossible Dad and I could possibly remain indoors through it – but we did and will. Uncle Ted rang this morning from St Albans inquiring if we were all right as Mother was worried. I guess all the people out of London must be concerned. I hear, least the *Standard* says, that over 800 time-bombs have been reported in our district. Gosh.

The Tubes stank this morning. Filth and litter of every description, including the common sight of piss which fouled the air. I foresee pestilence. We have the balloon barrage all round home again, similar to what it was in September, 1939. Five balloons in an absolute straight line stand convincingly from Clapham to us. yesterday I did some ironing, and after taking much care brought my favourite white shirt up beautifully, I had only the collar to do – and tragedy! I scorched the damn thing. I have bought a new one, also a pair of socks.

I meant to state this morning 'planes dive-bombed all round us, zooming and accelerating like hell's angels. One bomb screamed down like a car going round Brooklands, and suddenly braked so to speak. A dull crunch followed. De Gaulle has withdrawn his forces from Dakar as he does not wish to be a party to a fight against his own countrymen. But the episode is far from finished.

27 September, 11.45 a.m.
Quite a day for the Luftwaffe.

Woke this moining, after a very good night's sleep, to learn that bombs had fallen all around me as I had slept, including one in Beechcraft Road. Did the housework, washed, all in haste as I was rather late, and just as I was leaving home the sirens went. Of course I took no notice; so stepping out crisply this beautiful nippy September morn I made my way to Trinity Road where I hoped to get a lift to town. Whilst waiting, the rumble of gunfire became audible, nearer; the people quickly vacated the roadway and sprang to the shelters. I stood out in the middle of Upper Tooting Road, bang in the centre of the tram-lines, and stared up at the sky; there sailing directly overhead were twenty German bombers, huge great shapes, and they literally ploughed their way as a battleship through the Bay of Biscay in anti-aircraft fire. Enemy or no there was something remarkably fine, proud about those bombers, as disdaining, ignoring absolutely the gunfire, they flew on in stately manner, all keeping splendid formation. Two hours before I could picture their crews all keen and alert, eating and washing at their French base, and as they took the air I could see the real life version of 'Dawn Patrol.'

Anti-aircraft first burst in front, to the sides and seemingly in their midst, but they paid no heed. I did think though that they veered slightly from the actual City direction; I thought they were bent on Battersea or Lotts Road. I passed these areas last night in getting a lift from Blackfriars to Wandsworth, and found myself rather non-plussed as I had to walk all across Clapham Common – and I thought I was being so clever getting a lift. A lot of damage was round there. However these bombers disappeared and catching a bus I made my route to Blackfriars. The bus had net glued to the windows to prevent blast. Across Clapham Common the guns pointed menacingly skywards. Stockwell, where evidently bombs had just fallen, amidst a mass of smoking debris I saw A.R.P. personnel presumably trying to extricate casualties. In a back street a house was on fire. Past Kennington Church, which had been hit the previous night and was badly damaged, and past the repair squads relaying the tram-lines outside the Oval Underground station which had been torn up. I arrived in the office at 10.

London is beautiful today, and with the green trees and red buses looks as peaceful as anywhere, and lovelier than anywhere else in the world. Yet as I write, the alert is in progress. A few minutes ago, before the sirens, the guns of the City opened up at white smoke trails lying across the sky over the Bank. The crashing rumbles were impelling. Miss Spindler (the girls all rushed to the shelter) came back, almost stamped her foot and said something to the effect that I was to go down the shelter. Quite matronly she was. I went instead to the third floor and looked out over the Bank. I can write so much about what has been bombed, but I will control my zeal and just say that Epsom Grandstand was bombed. As I write, smoke trails are being formed high above my head by marauding bombers and the guns and whistles are blasting forth. Lane came into my office (I suppose because Miss Spindler reported me) and ordered me to the shelter, saying we couldn't take chances. Well I've sneaked up another floor higher to our empty offices from where I write this. Shelter indeed! Cannot they understand my philosophy? The 'Spurs F.C. ground was blasted; there were 200 corpses there from Bruce

Grove awaiting identification, so I am told; one typist in Seymour, Pierce & Co., has been cut by shrapnel and her fiancé had had his jugular vein cut. On being taken to hospital the ambulance in which they were travelling fell down a bomb crater, and when they finally reached the hospital two incendiary bombs fell just outside and they had to spend the night in a receiving ward.

Today is evidently a 'field day' for the Luftwaffe. For German squadrons were seen over Liverpool St Station, Paddington etc. – and all these must have been in addition to those I saw at 9.20 a.m. Hitler apparently likes Fridays.

Dad said last night that London is worse than France in the last war. Good Lord – and he is an 'Old Contemptible!'

Saturday, 28 September (Morning)

Yesterday afternoon, for the third time that day, I again beheld a thrilling spectacle. Some minutes after the alert the whistles shrilled. Lane came in again and said everyone below; I again sneaked up a floor higher. Guns were pounding away, until I was convinced the whole of the London ack-ack defences were in action. High over the Bank I saw a squadron or two of Jerries, but as for keeping in any formation – why they were hopeless, flying this way, that way in their effort to dodge the terrific anti-aircraft barrage. The whole sky seemed a huge black and white spotted cloud due to the unprecedented daylight barrage we shot up. Jerry soon dispersed, but within a few minutes another squadron in perfect formation went over; one shell burst in their rear. I am sure they were ours. I saw several more stray Jerries hovering around, but it was the same droll tale. The heartening thing to me whenever I see Jerry over the City in daytime is the fact that that night we shall read of at least 80 Hun down. For they are the scattered remnants which have snooped through our coastal defences, and we know when they do head back they'll be pretty well marked down. So much – the *Express* this morning (again delightful, sunny and Septemberish) compares the soldier of the Great War with the one of today. 'Now the soldier rushing to the colours to defend his home hears in camp how all the valour of the battlefield is being displayed down his alley... There is no base, no down-the-line for the Londoner or for other citizens whose ordeal is exemplified by the attacks on the capital' etc. etc. Consequently I find that the glamour is somewhat removed, I mean, after all, finding the war on your own doorstep, upon your own people. But I guess a Spitfire or Hurricane will do me fine. Incidentally, it was announced last night that the V.C. has been awarded to a wireless-operator of one of our bombers over there; he is only 18 years of age. He put out a fire inside the plane – but how I look upon it is like this. He had no parachute with which to bale out, consequently he had to do something if he hoped to save his life. Of course I do not begrudge him his award, God forbid, but the V.C... no not quite so high a distinction, surely?

Last night I cleaned up the flat, which was really dirty. I scrubbed out the kitchen, washed out a couple of shirts and a half-dozen hankies, polished all the dining-room furniture, and cleaned everything generally, including a vain attempt to clean and press my flannels. Too bad. Still they're not scorched.

I started reading *Midnight on the Desert* by Priestley last night. I rather like his dreamy, flat style, and I can almost hear him lazily drawling out the words over the radio.

Going to St Albans today, and, boy, I have great hopes of a great day with a great friend.

Sunday, 29 September

I have just returned from St Albans and am bursting to write up my log of the weekend among my old haunts; I feel, however, precedence is to be given to the momentous happenings of the war. I intend, therefore, to write of my actual interlude 'behind the lines' in St Albans entirely separately. Consequently I will write of the war since Saturday midday.

We drove to St Albans yesterday, just after the alert had been sounded. We took the Harrow–Radlett route as we thus avoided the thousand-and-one time-bomb diversions in Central London. Taking the Beechcroft Road (next to us) and just past Alan's old school (the Bec) we saw three houses completely down, not fired, and knew that the bomb responsible had been one of the stick which had straddled us the previous night. Shepherd's Bush had an enormous number of windowless buildings, an air of desertion. One huge wing of the Fulham Hospital was absolutely no more. Just one huge pile of rubble, worse than any picture I have ever seen of Ypres, or conjured up by tales from Grandad; stretchers remained ledged on bare framework walls, and iron bedsteads littered the scene. Past White City (here people were flocking to see a dog race – indomitable) along Western Way, in which a big church had been pretty well destroyed, through the factory belt of Park Royal, and so on to St Albans. We did not hear the 'All Clear,' and St A had not had the warning.

Today we came back the same route. Just on the fringe of the Park Royal factory belt we saw the factory of Browns, engaged in important munition or Governmental work, which last night had received a direct hit: 'Here today – gone tomorrow.'

I do not think a tremendous amount of significant damage had been achieved by the Nazi bomber. We drove over glass still littered in the roadway. The sirens went to greet us upon our return home and as I looked out over industrial London my thoughts were very vivid, very proud, and a lump rose in my throat. The fat, lazy, rolling barrage balloons appeared so ridiculously like overfed elephants littering the sky. We had just got back to Holmbury Court as the 'All Clear' sounded and were greeted with the news that a gigantic bomb had fallen just a hundred yards or so away. But that is another page of my journal, a very delightful, peculiar, very angry, tragic, sorrowful one. One moreover I should not term 'delightful' but I have to believe: 'What is done is done, and past; we must look to the future' and I do. In fact the 'future' as I see it from these daily scenes of havoc and death is one of immense comfort to me; I feel the physical inhumanities now temporarily being inflicted on London enables me to see my life in a totally new perspective, which is something I have always yearned for.

Outside it is a grey, dull night. Dusk is falling quickly, and with it the raiders come again, and something here now in this City will tomorrow be gone. Into this Octobery weather at any minute now the citizens will quickly run, and in some underground hovel spend the night in dampness and discomfort, but safe from the pirate country's bombs. I sit here at Dad's typewriter, in white shirt and 'old school tie,' with 'slomiky' but comfortable grey flannels, and brown, trail-worn shoes; my head is a mass of ruffled fair hair. I am supremely comfortable in front of a roaring winter's fire, drinking a cup of soup. Tonight finds my mother and brother back, so I am relieved of housework, and it is perhaps with regret. Also I much prefer to think that my family are in the safe walls of St Albans, but as Mother just remarked to Alan who enquired if 'Colin is going down the shelter' to which I replied in the negative, 'Colin trusts in the Lord, and when our time comes we shall just have to go, that's all.' So instead of sitting here for the night and then going to a lovely warm bed, Mother and Alan, maybe Dad too, will have to trek into the atmosphere of the air-raid shelter. But I – I simply ache to write of St Albans and the episode of but an hour ago. In fact although at 6 o'clock my whole end was directed to St Albans, to comparison with Kate (and of Kate I seemed full), by 7 my whole outlook was firmly moved to one side; for the better, most certainly. Further I think the 'episode of an hour ago' takes precedence, but somehow I am not exactly in the mood to tackle either with the style I wish or with the command of thought which I had just a while ago. If I did now write this I should have my regrets in the knowledge that 'it could have been better, more explicit,' but the fire, the comfort, the wanting is there. Oh I ramble, am dreamy, it's the fire! So tomorrow, and it's more homely to me in the type of an office machine.

8.10 p.m. The sirens!

Sunday night, 29 September
Around me the Nazi bombers drone; the crash of our guns echoes across the skies above my City; and the toppling – like the sea washing over pebbles on the seashore – of property makes itself heard as it is split apart under the bombs.

In this convulsion, this phase of human massacre, Dad and I have once again been talking over matters of greater values. When one commences the undertaking, say, of a diary, one is at first imbued with the craze, then perhaps there is the lull, boring, until finally the long strived-for transition when the diary becomes an obsession and one will exert every sinew into fulfilling its requirements.

Hitler is bombing London. What does he hope to achieve? He can only hope to undermine the morale of the Britisher, and hope to throw the efficiency of our organisation into chaos. He fails totally to grasp the morale of our people. We are no continental race. Go to our bombed areas, see the bombed homes, see the bombed and hear their talk. By God if London, if England, was over-run by Nazis there would still be a band somewhere, undaunted, fighting. We will never surrender. Never! Our people grumble and groan, the world think us disunited. Aha! The Englishman would not be English if he did not grumble. Oh, no, Adolf – whatever you do there will be Englishmen to beat you in the end. Not an inch of England will be yielded. Thank God I'm English – how good it feels, is.

This is only additional.

I wonder sometimes at the history behind medal ribbons.

The Bomb Crater

I learned at approximately 6 p.m., soon after arriving home from St Albans, that at 11.40 last night an aerial torpedo or land mine had fallen on Chetwode Road, demolishing seven houses and killing three people. I became exceedingly curious, and after a quick meal I made my way to Chetwode Road; as it was spitting with rain I put my raincoat on.

Chetwode Road is approximately 200 yards away from us as the crow flies. It is the first turning on the right past Trinity Road tube going in the Wandsworth direction. The road consists of very run-down houses; they are old, some thirty years at least. Its inhabitants are what I would call typical Cockney. To me it has always symbolised dull, routine Tooting, a place in which no sparkle of the untoward is to be found. However now, in 1940, the whole aspect of my neighbourhood is changed, as it is now, supposedly, the area traversed regularly by the Luftwaffe. Indeed that much is definitely true. Also the City, of which this suburb constitutes a part, is (dare I again say supposedly?) the most battered, heroic, capital in the world, and air-attacks daily rained upon it cannot be compared with anything hitherto known in history. However tonight I walked along my usual three-minute walk from home to the Tube, taking in the now familiar sight of shops minus windows; turning left up Trinity Road I finally came to Chetwode. A crowd of sightseers flocked in front of the barriers, but exerting a little strategy I positioned myself in the front. What a sight! A huge, gigantic crater, bigger than any I have yet seen, bigger even than the Monument crater, spread from the middle of the road (where the bomb had fallen) sprawling itself over houses and property like an uncompromising giant. Above this scene of havoc floated supremely, splendidly, the Union Jack, fluttering on the chill October wind. I viewed with indifference the mass of A.R.P. and Home Guard busy as ants clearing the remaining battered residences of furniture, personal belongings, treasured possessions.

Above left: Destruction caused by a land mine – high explosive delivered by parachute, on 24 November 1940. (*Joan Schwitzer*)

Above right: A bomb incident in South Molton Road, Canning Town. The emergency services have been called and a member of the Home Guard is on duty.

After a few minutes I took myself along the corresponding road running parallel to Chetwode. I noted all the calm, gossiping women, the little child busy as ever chalking unintelligible signs in the middle of the street. I saw cumbersome women, and ungainly men struggling to erect suitable protection for the night in their rooms, all robbed of glass. The other entrance to Chetwode was also barricaded off, and I glimpsed nothing more of enlightening interest. So, feeling I had seen all I could, I followed the road, past the little child, still chalking, back. I had walked half-way along. Suddenly I stopped. I felt a funny, peculiar little feeling run round my heart. There walking towards me was a girl, a small girl, no taller than me, dressed in smart, well-cut blue coat, kid gloves, no stockings but ankle socks and soft rubber shoes of good quality. Her hair was dark, like Binnie's photograph, and short; her skin, I noted with a side-glance as she passed, was milk pure, soft and clear, glowing in health. Her eyes were dark brown. Her whole stature was erect, proud, and she bore herself along that poor, devastated street like Joan of Arc going to meet her death – oblivious, but aware. I turned, I followed her, stunned, down the street. I made no effort to conceal what it was I was looking at. I, too, commenced walking back along the street.

Perhaps it was Providence. Perhaps just coincidence. Just luck perhaps. Anyhow 'the Girl' took me back (figuratively speaking, of course) to Chetwode. The wardens had vacated the scene, and I found myself following her (fancy me following a girl – and moreover into a prohibited bombed area – Good God) under the barrier and to the bomb crater. A crater so deep, so vast, so engulfing, so tremendous in its proportions I had never seen. It was at least 25 yards across. I surmounted its sides, stepping over great lumps of clay, rock and debris. I found myself standing on what twenty-four hours before had been a bedroom. Now I stood there amongst all the wreckage of home life. I looked down; my feet stood on a torn and scattered child's paint-book, upon a peculiar shaped cornflower, beside which reposed the mark seven out of ten.

That page, that painting of some child's treasured possession, struck deep into my heart. I surveyed the mere skeleton walls, the baths, the beds, the litter of vases and clothes, the mirrors and pictures which peeped appealingly out from under the rich soft earth, the pile of metal and bricks and timber. I looked down into the looming depths of the crater on to muddy, runny little patches of rain water. I stood upright, feeling the full significance of the Union Jack; I took in the one remaining picture upon the one remaining wall, of a soldier smoking a pipe, a warrior of old, and its faded colouring roared defiance, revenge at the Nazi bombers who wreaked death and destruction upon poor working-class people. Then slowly, unconsciously, my gaze became centred upon the Girl. She too was surveying thoughtfully, unemotionally, the havoc, the pyre. Fascinated, I admired her shapely, powerful limbs, the splendour of her proud bearing, noticed how she stood out from the host of ordinary

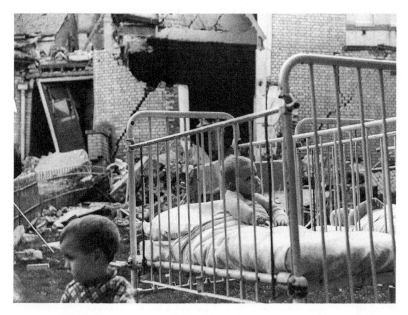

Orphans stand by the wreckage of their home after it was bombed, 27 October 1940. (*Associated Press*)

people, and commanded attention. Also I realised the full intelligence of her features, the coolness, the beauty of her. Unthinkingly I found myself regarding her as my mate, displaying her proudly, walking in high elation with her through the roads which are London, and visiting all the bombed areas. Cool and collected, abiding to the word the article by the Bishop of Norwich in today's *Sunday Times*, with which I agree, I stood there on top of the crater, looking across the abyss to the other side, and I saw the Girl…

After a few seconds, which seemed a life-time, I crossed to the other side of the crater. I looked beyond the ruins to the folly of the persons who owned the Anderson shelter on the edge of the havoc; just the bare steel shelter, uncovered, unprotected. Was that the shelter in which an eighteen-year-old boy had left this life? And just behind P.N. Motors too, which but a fortnight ago had been gutted. I crossed once again to the north side of the crater, walking up huge piles of earth to the bedroom floors, standing on the tombs of the ground floors. The wardens came and ordered the sightseers away, and I joined in the exit as the Girl went. I followed her back to the Tube; she went on towards Tooting Bec. I do not know whether I am ashamed or not when I think that on the scene of tragedy, amongst death and grief, I thought not so much of the moment, of the blasted houses and hopes, but of the Girl, just a stranger – never seen her before and probably never will again. Ships which pass in the night. But in that girl I saw everything splendid, noble, everything for which we fight and think, the hope of the new world. I forgot the past, the present, I saw only the future. I knew I was not ashamed of myself for thinking of her amongst that hell on earth, but glad. She stood so composed. I watched her out of sight; she looked back once, twice, several times. And I stood, in unconcealed admiration, on the corner by the Wheatsheaf.

As I walked home I became lost in thought. I felt happy. I had enjoyed a weekend in St Albans, I had come home inspired by the thought of all good things; I convinced myself, as I have done a million times, about Kate. Because she is the only girl I have ever known I suppose. Maybe I did so in consolation I don't know. It was after I had sat before the fire and thought of her that I went out to see the havoc, and through destiny perhaps happened upon this Girl. I think, and hope that at last the enigma of my feelings for Kate has been dispelled. She is not sinewy, wiry, strong; neither intelligent, beautiful, alluring; certainly not keen, susceptible, idealistic. Oh no, I am sure she is just an ordinary, aspiring girl, bent only upon her trail of male-baiting. I have always involuntarily thought of her, maybe because I have no one else to think of. Although I should like Kate to be as I conjure her up so splendidly, I know she can never be, will never be. She is a mere mirage.

All this talk of girls makes it appear as if I too am an admirer of the opposite sex. I have neither time, money nor patience for the average girl. I neither want nor have any desire to 'frisk around' them as Steve or Rod. I – well I just imagine the Girl. I have never kissed one, never even held hands with one

I don't think I particularly want to either. Of course they are fun – but after all what are they really? But this Girl I have written so profusely about seems different; but then isn't this journal punctuated with 'the Girls' and they have all only crashed to ridiculousness, and I have laughed at my imaginings. Steve or Rod would not have hesitated to have spoken to her but not so me. Still – if that girl had been interested, and I feel she couldn't have been, I should not have wanted her to speak for it would have dispelled my ideals. All the same, she was quite attractive.

Monday, 30 September
It was a jolly change this morning to get up to a lovely warm fire, and a breakfast steaming, waiting to be put into my mouth. Still I did enjoy the week of housework, and I think I made a very good job of it although I say it myself.

I got to London Bridge on the Tube when the alert sounded; thus I had to get out and cross over the Bridge. I did not know traffic was again running so I surrendered my ticket and had to pay 1½d extra. I boarded a No. 21 bus to the Bank; it had white boards in place of a number of windows – evidently the bus had been in a raid pretty thickly.

As the staff were late in arriving I wrote up my journal. However I am still anxiously saving up, and I trust not forgetfully, my St Albans story. I will type it probably at home tomorrow, it being my day off.

Incidentally I was struck this morning by the number of people in the Tube who were reading of God and religion. It is amazing the number of people who in these times turn to God. They do so quickly, and hope by their reading and thoughts God will help them. They try desperately, anxiously, to make up for lost time – putting it crudely. For it is now increasingly obvious that there is only one effective shelter from air-raids and all the horrors of war – that is the shelter of God – the shelter described and advocated and recommended by the Bishop of Norwich. I know it is my shelter, and I go to bed quite unconcernedly, confident in the belief that nothing will harm me. If it should – then that is God's wish. I do not by this infer I am any religious crank – heavens no. I have, ever since I can remember, said my prayers at night. I have always had, although not a church-goer, explicit faith in God, and during times of stress have asked help – and I have always, by confidence, faith and patience, received, however indirectly, that aid. But now during this time of national, rational fear, though there is to me no fear, I have not asked any additional 'favour' of God; I have just continued in my ordinary way of life and prayed regularly of a day as has always been my custom.

A New York report, and New York reports often prove correct, says that the Nazis intend to 'drench London with Gas!'

I have perceived another 'Girl in the ABC' which is awful, considering – but why? I have, it is true, just rambled incoherently about females and the one by the bomb crater however this girl is very pleasant, reserved, jolly; her eyes light with interest which display a keen, shrewd mind. She radiates kindness. She is not impassive as the other, but alive and enjoyable. Not, of course, in the sensuous way which I never infer.

Strange I should write all these strange things about strange girls. Anyone would think, reading these jumbled writings, that my orbit revolves around girls, instead of which perhaps 90–95 per cent is entirely untarnished by them: the other 5 per cent I would not be responsible for.

I feel today very much like a walk over Surrey, in the crisp, invigorating south wind of September. I see the autumn leaves, brown and withered, all the tints of Surrey in the fall. I step out briskly, crossing grassland, moor and hill. The clouds sweep by so clearly – Surrey, you're very dear.

30 September (later)

I left the office tonight just as an alert sounded. I boarded a 133 bus, and sunk my head into a very interesting issue of the *Standard* until Kennington, and I regret to state I avoided paying my fare. From Kennington I boarded a van with the words National Teapot on its sides and after being diverted round the Brixton road, past many scenes of devastation, across, rather than around Clapham Common, as all the South Side is roped off due to bombs, through a Balham smashed about like hell (the Hippodrome, Holdrons, etc. smashed up), I alighted at Trinity Road. It was good to go home to a hot dinner and lovely fire. The 'All Clear' sounded afterwards.

My people at home had seen a terrific air battle in the afternoon and the air had been filled with the staccato of machine-guns; Alan had seen one crash and vowed there were over 200 machines engaged in combat. The *Standard* tonight says that after the war when people are asked what they were in, they will say they were airmen, soldiers, sailors or, with pride, will boast they were a citizen of London. So, without effort, I am bang in the middle of war.

The *Evening News* carried a picture of a child evacuee from Carshalton in New York World's Fair, showing Lord Lothian (our Ambassador) how she took cover at home during a raid. It was Jean Doville. I was naturally most interested, and suddenly took it into my head to write to her which I did, sending the letter first to her mother. Jean and her sisters are evacuated to Canada, presumably.

I am glad that tomorrow I will have the pleasure of tearing the month of September, 1940, off the calendar. October I trust will see a new hope, of the invention and utility of secret devices for the night raiders, for they have found an antidote to every poison so far, and I see no reason why they shouldn't succeed again in a very short while.

Tomorrow I really will write my St Albans entry. I have not yet had time. At the present the guns roar again, and the bombs fall.

Stevenson Cooke broadcast and appealed to all motorists to give people lifts these days and he urged the travellers not to hesitate to ask for a lift.

Two elders of the parish Survey the destruction of the Blitz. (*Jonathan Reeve*)

London Passenger Transport Board have put up posters asking able-bodied men to refrain from using Tube stations as shelters and to give way to the aged and infirm.

Colin in November 1940, just after he had signed up to join the Merchant Navy – note his MN badge on his lapel. (*Author*)

Looking to the Future

A very ill day for me. Perfectly all right of course physically, but not in the weather or mood. So I'm short-tempered and heavy.

A lone raider bombed certain parts of London this morning, and machine-gunned the streets. We had a lot of gunfire but I saw no 'plane. No sirens were sounded in the morning.

Last night a shell exploded in the next road, and a time bomb fell not 25 yards away. Alan has had to be temporarily moved from his school. The school carries on in another road. Anyhow I'm glad Berlin was raided for five hours.

Balham was also bombed again last night.

I think as science cures disease in laboratories, fights epidemics and plagues, so too should we fight ignorance, hate and greed. We should inoculate the masses with intelligence, stimulate their curiosity. War may then be no more.

Last night I read Priestley's *Midnight on the Desert* whilst the bombers whined outside, and the guns sang their nightly serenade. I found Priestley clever; egoistic; but then it was a chapter of autobiography. His impressions of America were very true, very clearly composed. Yet it is distinctly a moody book, and I wasn't so extraordinarily keen on it.

Dad has a 'tin' (fibre) hat.

28-29 September (Written 1 October)
For a whole week I had eagerly looked forward to this weekend. I had planned, anticipated, expected a weekend of right royal fun. I had recalled all the splendid times of years ago when, twelve years of age, Steve, Rod Wilton and I had enjoyed Batchwood, roamed the fields with our airguns, dodged the cusses and threats of the game-keepers who unwittingly went to make our life worth living. Yes, after years of exile, including three years of London, I jumped with boyish enthusiasm at this golden opportunity afforded me by a chance re-union last Sunday week.

I had arranged to meet Steve on the Saturday afternoon, but the Milnes told me he was out. I had a cup of tea with them and then knocked at Mrs Wilton's: 'Rod and Steve have gone to the library,' she said. I came across them eventually. I had all week mapped out what we would do, but I had forgotten that my friends may have changed in the passing of the years. My dream of a slap-up tea, pictures, or preferably a long, strenuous walk over the fields, was doomed to disappointment. I did not have the chance to 'stand the racket.' To my utter disgust, Steve announced he had an appointment with a girl, but he would see me at 8 o'clock, when perhaps we could play pontoon. I expressed in no gentle tones that such was not my idea of entertaining a friend. Surely he could give the girl a go-by if only for that one night? But no, he couldn't. Well, I said, at least Susan wouldn't object; but it was not Susan, but some other girl. Disillusioned with Steve, I was only too glad to accept Rod's suggestion he and I should meet about 6 o'clock. Rod at least was decent.

Rod and I talked a lot. We swopped yarns, and adventures. He is still the confident Don Juan; his life revolves around cowboys, gangsters, guns, and crooks. He has always been like that. Now he is a Home Guard, the proud possessor of an old rifle and revolver lent him from the museum for training purposes. He too keeps a diary, but to my way of thinking it is hardly adolescent, merely boyish. Proudly he boasted of his ideals, his idolising of great six-foot he-men; that he longed to kill a a man, smash up white slave-traffic. Loftily he showed me his library, so full of Captain Hornblowers, Blackshirts, Raffles, Max Brands – his selection of gramophone records, in which repose many of my favourite classics, and his film-star album. To give Rod credit he is certainly an authority on music; he also would like to become a great singer. A very noble ambition. I explained many of my perplexities to him upon learning that he wanted to leave this mire and find his own life. He said, 'You know, Col, I must look up the shape of your head. Gee you are very intelligent. I think we ought to get away together someday and hitch-hike round the world. I'd do the tough work and you'd be the organiser. I really like great big fellows, but you've got something I like.' I smiled, but did not reply.

I met his grandmother who to my profound astonishment recognised me immediately. I didn't her. She is a dear old soul of seventy; we discussed her early life in India, the portrait of her when she was twenty-five, and I asked her what the world was like to her in those days. 'Oh, it was so homely, religious, contented and plentiful,' she said. We discussed, too, the war, and she is most supremely confident of our ultimate victory as we fight the right cause; and although admittedly she thought we have plundered in the past we now realise our wrongs. But Hitler – the evil cannot prevail, she emphasised. I should have enjoyed to debate all evening with her, but unfortunately that was impossible. Rod told me afterwards she liked speaking to me. I am glad.

Steve came back to Rod's at 8.20 and within five minutes I had learnt my really first card-game, pontoon. In ten minutes I was quite a veteran. As I looked around the table I saw us four boys, for Bob Crighton had joined the group; four friends of old. Steve opposite, Rod to my left and Bob to my right. I tried to picture Kate, Binnie, any girl for that matter, looking on. She looked at us four young men who were as yet mere pawns in the game of life. She liked all of us; one she would marry. Which? Each was hers for the asking, each would lead a different life. Whoever she had would lead her to an adventure, her destiny. She summed each up. Steve, with his broad tough face, square-jawed, stocky, but tall; sitting there with his piercing eyes under which appeared a sinewy, almost sadistic line. His hair, ruffled and unkempt, brown and ungreased. His sleeves rolled, disclosing smooth lean arms. She thought of his ideals; he frisked with girls, lived for girls. Nightly he kissed them and held them in his arms. 19 years old next month, he had attended the grammar school, joined the O.T.C. He worked in an aircraft research establishment. Apparently he had no ideals, was dilatory, but she thought, loyal. He would make her quite a good husband, though already he was hard, not given to sentiment, and a gambler.

She turned whilst the money changed hands over the table. Bob Crighton, whom she remembered last as a small schoolboy. He had grown to tremendous proportions, tall and willowy. His hair was black as night; his face gaunt, and his brown eyes gave the impression of temper, anger. She saw no contentment. His nose was long, almost hideous. His appearance generally was dogged, portraying the man who would never seek to further his position in life, never raise a hand to lift himself. He would chug daily the same old routine, turn the same wheel until age claimed him. He would always be surly, dissatisfied, grumbling. She softly shook her head, gave almost a little shudder. Bob did not possess many qualities, and a life with him – even now at sixteen she foresaw the awful catastrophe, dullness, marriage to him would mean.

Rod was different. He was sparkling with the happiness of life, with confidence. Full of the gay cavalier, certain of his own strength and potentialities. He had ideas, courage, ideals. He wanted to see the world, have adventure in the true screen sense. He was romantic, determined to get out of 'this life.' Music, singing, gay Span*iardo*, to him was the breath of existence. And he was good looking too; in fact handsome. His plump red face, gingery hair and blue eyes; he looked fresh, alive, almost vital. Rod had changed since she had last seen him; he had developed, gained character, exploited ideals. Girls? yes lots, but nothing serious, and he only did it for the fun; unlike Steve, who seemed drugged with sex. And even if Rod didn't have all that adventure – but she felt sure he would – his job was interesting. Already at seventeen a potential newspaper reporter, a real live-wire journalist. Yes she liked him, life would be one continual game, jolly, changing. But Rodney[23] would always be the same, ever confident, vain; the thief in the night. She smiled at him.

And there, returned to the fold, was Colin. Yes, Rod's Grandma had certainly been right when she said he had lost his boyish plumpness. His face, she noted, was thinner, paler, more matured than any of the others. He had not grown much, in fact hardly at all. He sat there losing money on this new, to him, game of pontoon quite cheerfully as if he had all the money in the world. There in his dead white shirt, his so-called old school tie, his creased grey flannels and belt, with his fair hair all tousled. His eyes too she saw were more piercing, sunk beneath their bushy brows. There was a new scar over his left eye. A marked line appeared in his forehead, one straight line; present even when he smiled. He seemed rather forlorn, content. He was four months junior to Steve. He had, too, inherited quite a new outlook, he had ideals, character. He rambled something about a new world order, whatever that may be. Yet he, too, was a lover of the world, an adventurer, traveller, writer. Totally in contrast from the others, Col had no apparent love for girls, they seemed inferior to him. They were a mystery. Rod said he was too scrupulous, but she doubted that. He seemed lean, sinewy, gay, yet calm. He was hardly a tough, yet he had that courage, that willpower which she liked. He had an unending imagination, yet he was practical, constructive. Colin believed in words and action. Nobody in the female world had ever seemed to display any design upon him, and she wondered why. True he was shy, almost reserved, yet she had known him speak to anyone from a Lord to a tinker as if he had known them all his life. Somehow, perhaps it was London, but the world appeared to have washed him more widely than any of the others; he was a man of the world, experienced. You could see the mark of the world upon him. Perhaps that was bad for an eighteen-year-old boy. Colin was an enigma. Life with him would be varied, uncertain; he had such strange ideas. He might be famous tomorrow, or an unemployed gutter-sweeper. There was no telling. He would either make headlines, or be a poor man; but, whatever, he would never lead an ordinary life. He may be exacting. He would worship his children. She mused slightly, she enjoyed her wanderings.

The boys played on. They stopped at 10 with Colin two shillings out, but he didn't mind.

But I'll leave the girl to her thoughts there.

I was sorry Steve was not able to accompany me part of the way to Dorie's. He was no longer my best friend. As I walked through a starlit St Albans, with the ever-bursting shells and the criss-cross of a hundred searchlights in the distance towards London, I thought of one of my earliest recollections – of a story Mother used to tell me, and how I would love to hear of the night in 1918 when she ran along almost these same streets from a dance at the Culver Hall to her home in Warwick Road during an air-raid, with the shrapnel bursting overhead. It had never occurred to me that one day I should do the same kind of thing.

We went up the line again at about 3 on the Sunday afternoon. But I have written about that. But I want to say how much Uncle Ted and Auntie Dorie have done for us – I love John and Jennifer. She is a sweet little girl. I took her for a walk on Sunday moming, and we collected acorns. Yes, I love Jennifer very much indeed.

This writing on St Albans was to have been quite a piece of literature, but the day, the mood, the time has not been kind to me. I have run it off in a state of depression, and cannot think coherently. But if I hadn't done it the chance may have been denied me for a long time ahead. So I seized the opportunity.

2 October

Last night the ignorance, the squabbling of some people in the shelter resulted in Mother and Alan coming indoors. They vow never to go there again. I am glad. Yes, glad. I have never felt any real trust in the shelter, and think one day it will prove a second Maginot Line. The trouble started with that damned, whipper-snapper of a bastard, Walters. I could cheerfully strangle the breath from him. Mother was in tears, and I nearly went down and smashed him; but then I stopped. I had an unexplainable feeling that fate was at work. There was that double-faced, bull-necked Connors, loud-mouthed Lines, and with Walters they were down there together. I can see no loss to the world if one night they ceased to exist. Nightly they come home, scamper furtively to the shelter, squabble and row, gossip and make unrest. Their whole minds are infused with rot; instead of trying to tum something out for their own benefit they have to devote their warped little brains to stirring up trouble. As if this war is not exacting enough to others, yet they have to wage their own private, crawling war in the shelter. Such people do not deserve to exist. I would that I could be present at their Day of Judgement.

I was not in the shelter when the trouble started. If I had been I should have stood up and pointed to Walters and said, 'Are you prepared to listen to the contortions of a person who said the finest thing which could happen in this war would be for a bomb to fall on Churchill? If you are, we are not.' For that Churchill business has rankled in my brain for a very long time, and I shall not forget it, ever. One day I will expose it.

Last night, therefore, we all went to bed in the normal, peacetime manner, which from now on will be the practice of Mother and Alan, thus following the example of Dad and myself. Mother trusts in God, and is not in the least perturbed. Mother only went down the shelter in the first place for Alan's sake, but he doesn't care a jot. It's ironical to think we really came to H.C. primarily due to Dad's looking into the future, for he had faith in the air-raid shelter. Now, however, we haven't any. I have always felt supremely confident of our safety; I never liked the idea of Mother and Alan being in the shelter. I am therefore glad fate has decided they shall not be down there. Let Walters and his Nazi ideals, his Communistic views, his deceitfulness, his lack of principle, his scared, mouse-like manner, stick in his hole along with his other fellow mice, and may they perish in hell, the blasted, conceited lot of ignorant, bloody fools.

Colin and Binnie in 1942. (*Author*)

A number of bombs whistled down as I lay in bed just after midnight. I felt very indifferent, immune, so to speak. I knew they would not fall upon us.

This morning I arrived at the office by way of a car driven by two R.A.F. Officers. I got the lift from Trinity Road to Whitehall. I saw much damage on the way, including the revengeful sight of the blasted walls of the Houses of Parliament. But Whitehall looked splendiferous, invincible, British. The crisp fresh air of this delightful October morn, shining upon the green foliage and stately buildings of Whitehall was too beautiful for words. High above in the haze three white smoke trails marked the path of enemy bombers. So near, yet so utterly remote.

I caught a No. 11 Bus to the Bank. Passing St Paul's I breathed a soft prayer of thankfulness to Lieut Davies – incidentally now awarded the George Cross – and his boys.

This lunch-hour I had my hair cut; my barber has had his house blown up by the Nazis, and lost nearly everything. He served in the Palestine campaign in 1917.

Also saw walking along the street 'the Girl in the ABC' of old. Good lord. She was awful, stodgy, simply rolling along. Phew, what a miss!

We have had a number of warnings this morning.

2 October 7.35 p.m.

Arrived home tonight by a roundabout route. The sirens sounded as I left the office at 4.30 p.m. and walked to the Monument. Providentially I happened upon the National Teapot van again: as it moved off I jumped into the back, hauled aboard by a crowd of workers. Jolly good fun. This time I could only progress through Brixton (past Arlington Lodge where we used to live – little damage in comparison) to Streatham Hill station. I walked to St Leonards and obtained a lift to Trinity Road in a super American Nash. Oh, boy, it was good. I sat behind the glittering silver gadgets, the red and white dials – I was driving along an Australian highway, under a heavenly moon: Binnie snuggled. closer to me – and, oh, boy, I arrived home to a delightfully vivacious, pleasing, intelligent letter from Binnie. She seems so fine, so true; I think I will probably marry her. It's good to know she is safe away from this aerial bombardment; keeping fit and well in a grand country.

It's right the man should have the bombardment of experience, of life. Incidentally, if I am to meet a girl I would rather I did before I go into the R.A.F., as a uniform does things; and if I found my girl after enlistment I should never know if she loved me truly or merely out of glamour, the passion of the moment.

Tonight we all drove out to Mitcham. We had heard so many tales about land-mines that we determined to see for ourselves. My God, it was no exaggeration. The Church just behind the Clock Tower was completely removed; behind, a street had literally been destroyed. House after house lay in piles of dust. It was utter, complete annihilation. The famous Cricketers also lay crumpled, razed to the ground. In fact Mitcham had more than caught a packet. On the green, crowds of small boys romped gleefully over a light, or medium Heinkel 111. I surveyed this smashed, dark green vulture. Outwardly a beauty of a machine, just like a Comet. (7.50 p.m. There go the nightly sirens: we stay put by a cheerful fire.) Pitcairn Road, Tooting, also all round the Junction Station, H.E.'s have wreaked their trail of death and destruction. They are closing in. Each side of us there are time bombs. However, there is now cheering news of a new weapon; a sort of rainbow, apparently – seen over France and here – A ray? Trust the British to invent something. But I do not intend putting any more news of bombed areas in this journal unless I or my people have actually seen the areas.

I thought this evening how really savage this war is. If we move today it is not just from a dugout in a No-man's-land, but from one's own home and all one's worldly treasures. The sentiment can never be redeemed. I cannot think as clearly as I wish to this evening.

The war is here now. The doors and windows shake, the guns boom. I have just been outside wearing Dad's fibre hat – shells right overhead and the German bombers.

But I want to talk to Binnie.

Ave Maria Lane, 1940. The air raids of 1940 left
Ave Maria Lane a fire-blackened ruin.
(*Brian Girling*)

9 p.m.
Jerry still around, of course, but during his lull buses and trams, cars and
lorries have started running again. It is as if someone has given a dying
London a tot of brandy.

3 October
Hooray! Churchilll is to reshuffle the Cabinet and Chamberlain may
relinquish his office on the ground of ill-health (oh, yeah). At least that solves
many little feelings of doubt amongst many people. We want none of this old
Pétain sort of thing. Fine, Winston, keep it up.

Last night was not so rowdy until the early hours of this morning, when
bombs dropped around us, and the guns kicked up the very devil of a stink.

Today is very wet and miserable. The clouds are exceptionally low. Some
say it's due to the colossal amount of gun-fire. However, it is another typical
day for the swines who bomb on the Buckingham Palace scale. Guns have
been gruffing all afternoon, and I have heard Jerry slowly cross over the City
several times. It is now 4.15 p.m. and I hope to be getting along home from the
office on my 'National Teapot' omnibus soon; of course I cannot expect the 'All
Clear' will go – and anyhow I find it rather exciting going home under fire.

Last night we had an 'All Clear' between 9.20 and 10.20, and people said
'if only we could really go to bed and get a night's sleep how sweet it· would
be' – yet I looked back and saw it all as a very tiny phase. Given a week of
peacetime and we should soon forget all about the blitz.

I arrived at the office this morning by car, an Austin 10. I obtained the lift
from Trinity Road and got as far as Ludgate Circus. I bussed from there to
Bank on a No. 11.

Deposited 15/- in my Savings Account.

I ache to settle down undisturbed and write to Binnie; a terrifically long letter is in my head – but it'll keep. This has been entirely written to the tune of gunfire.

(*Later*): Chamberlain has gone! A reshuffle of the Cabinet has taken place. Good. I did get the 'National Teapot' omnibus – going over London Bridge.

The journey was quite extraordinary. Passing through the Elephant and Castle, gunfire rumbled and clattered all around. On Brixton Hill a crowd of gay Pitman's girls got in. A jolly, Vera Brittainy, interlude.

4 October

I stood last night on the hall landing, holding under my arm the book of T.E.'s *Letters* which I had been reading once more; the guns pounded out, left, right, until they were like a boxer coming out for the kill. The flashes were blinding. As I looked upon this blacked-out Tooting, the solitary tram standing in the middle of the road., the glistening roofs under the flash, I thought how like Ypres it must be. Yet I could with little effort see the buses and trams running once again on their peaceful occupation, all streaming with light; I could see, too, in my mind's eye, the shoppers and other pedestrians. This was only a most fantastic phase. Yet the blast from the pounding guns blowing my shirt sleeves into little puffs assured me that it wasn't.

But I had an excellent night. Once more Musso and Adolf meet in the Brenner Pass. So now we can expect something.

Air Marshal Sir Philip Joubert was most excellent speaking on the radio last night. At least we can be assured of an antidote for these raids before a year is out. He was neither optimistic nor pessimistic. Just marvellously enlightening.

Effra Road, Brixton had a land-mine the previous night. This morning is another sunny autumn day in which London excels. I came to Whitehall in an Army Officer's car, and my passenger was a charming, versatile girl of about 18 or 19. We spoke like old friends the whole way up, and shared the love of London together. We had a lot in common. Perhaps I shall get in the same car another day. I do hope so. I am astounded to think that anyone so intelligent can reside in Tooting. She spoke very pleasantly, firmly. Not pretty by any means, but not, shall I say, homely. A girl I should like to know more about.

I intend very soon to join the R.A.F., although this grand morning makes the sea appear most palatable.

5 October

I wrote last night to Binnie in my bedroom, sitting on the edge of my bed. I had arrived home from the office under gunfire by car which I picked up at London Bridge. As I wrote, with my heart full of love, to Binnie, the rain slashed against my window, the wind whipped itself into furies, and all the while the guns dismally, disconsolately barked, and bombs shook my room. But I was not in this London at bay, I was walking in Kincumber on a hot Summer's day such as only the Pacific can provide, with Binnie by my side, and hand in hand we made our way joyfully down through the path of the waving palms to the golden, secluded beach. We were both in heaven, heart and soul in love with each other. On the beach, behind the rocks, we undressed, and ran naked into the deep blue lagoon. We were at peace, and the world outside could go on its murky way. But I dream, and the clattering of a hundred guns, almost on my doorstep, brings me back into the horrible, filthy, temporary life of rain-swept London. Yet as my mind wanders I am glad that I am now amongst this rain of death, for then in the years of opportunity; of unrevealed ambitions which lie ahead I shall be able to pick and cherish the fruit of the tree of life which offers itself to me.

To keep to the purpose at hand. I wrote Binnie a long letter of the Epic of London, the filth of the Tubes. I really wanted to write of politics, hopes, and love.

This afternoon four German 'planes approached Tooting, but were turned back by anti-aircraft fire. I cycled to Carshalton. Several poor cottages by the *Skinner's Arms* were demolished. One house near the Wallington crossroads also was down. Carshalton, this sunny, bustling, autumn day, was very delightful. I spent perhaps an hour on the green by the bridge and looked at my initials carved upon the tree in the days of infant love; but they were past. I watched the Wandle dismally churn its dirty bed. I thought the summer was prolonged this year. And as little snatches from my past flashed across my mind, as I beheld the same, yet different houses, tangible symbols that life was not all dreams, I vaguely wondered that it only needed the sirens to prove to me how everything changed, was changed. I could not console myself, or make myself, a Londoner, believe we were the front line of civilisation. Then, as if by decree, the roar of Hurricanes passed above, the sirens wailed, the hooters of the factory booted. A low-flying monoplane zoomed and dived at the earth. Squadrons of our fighters were in the air. And as I stood upon the Wandle Bridge, listening to the zooms, watching the maze of white trails like marks upon an ice-rink formed by the 'planes, I realised it was to Carshalton, the place of my youth and Kate's that war had come.

I cycled back from Carshalton to Mitcham where I paid 6d to the Spitfire Fund in order to look over the Heinkel 111 shot down in Kent, and placed on show to swell the Fund. The aircraft was of special interest to me. I scrounged two souvenirs – a piece of dialing with the number 15 upon it, and a piece of mica from the nose of the machine in which the forward-gunner is positioned. This aircraft had carried a crew of four – two baled out and two came down safely with the machine. As Alan said, it is remarkable to think that the 'plane was manufactured in Nazi Germany, a short while ago was taking off to bomb London, and we are now able to view it on Mitcham Green. It's almost as if a Martian had stepped from the pages of a Wells novel. But there, I would write more of it; how I poked amongst the controls, engines, wings. But I want to read a murder novel, *The Death Coins* – and I have been writing all day it seems to Binnie. For today I received another two long letters from her. And I am fed up with constantly writing for myself now. So I'll stop until the mood moves me.

Monday, 7 October

I have rather a lot of odds and ends to pen down, so I'll try to do so systematically.

On Saturday morning I watched a party of the Bomb Disposal Squad on Tooting Bec Common wash out the charges from Nazi time-bombs. The detonators had previously been removed. The bombs were massive projectiles, weighing I guessed several hundreds of pounds. Without the explosive with which they were packed they were an ugly enough thing to have drop on one's house. I said to one of the party 'You're busy these days' to which he replied 'Just a wee bit' with a broad grin and twinkling eyes.

Yesterday it was pouring with rain all day. The clouds were low and grey. I cycled over to Clapham, and it seemed I was 'going along the line' so to speak, for the guns had been growling off and on all morning. I stood by the four huge naval guns on the Common as the sirens shrieked. They swung round, elevated, but did not fire. It was rather absurd for by the side of these monster guns, on a common riddled with shrapnel and bomb craters, with a Jerry groaning about somewhere in the grey bank of clouds, walked mothers with babies in prams, men and boys on bikes. It says much for the British.

In the afternoon during a raid alert I cycled over to Croydon Airport, with a head wind; blustering and whistling, and the rain swept on my face in torrents. It was simply grand. I watched the Hurricanes at Croydon for a long while, enviously, until I could stand the sight no longer. Gosh, these Spitfires and Hurricanes do something to me. However coming back past the Heinkel at Mitcham in the fresh wind I felt grand, glowing with health, and, boy, I feel fine this morning.

Last night was incredulous. We had the sirens about 8.30 (incidentally I had not expected the 'All Clear' from the noonday raid until this morning) and the 'All Clear' sounded within an hour. Of course we expected the sirens to go again, but, lo and behold, we got into bed and dropped off to sleep without the guns, and 'planes, and bombs. It was weird. I would have given a lot to have heard just one good blast from our guns. Just to make me feel homely. I believe the sirens went for a short time just before dawn but I only heard the dying notes of the 'raiders past' signal. I still can't comprehend that London has had its first quiet night for two solid months of bloody hell. But how those two months have educated me… wow. I used to long and think wistfully of the time when we could again go home and read a book by the fire, drink cocoa and then go to bed in peace. But after the first week or so I did so, unperturbed, and I enjoyed all my peacetime delights as usual except that as I read and went to sleep the guns poured forth their death and the bombs smashed down outside.

This morning is invigorating. I arrived at the Bank by the good fortune of a lucky lift in an extremely battered old Ford car. I picked it up at Trinity Road. I sat next to a fellow as far as Clapham South who had run away from his people in the Isle of Wight and slept last night in the Tube; he was going to Manchester. He said his people were 'narrow-minded.' Ah well, we do see life. I sat in solitary state, amongst old iron and sacks, from Clapham North, and everyone seemed to be looking at me. It was rather a delightful sensation, sitting there in that old car which looked as if it had come from Arizona or out of one of those Middle West ancient cowboy films. And as I perched high up on the back seat, enjoying the full glory of the early morning sunshine I sighed as I rode through this new London, this invincible 'Front Line' citadel of freedom; the wind whipped my face as it came through the windowless sides. But it was good, and how much better than those stinking Tubes. I alighted from that ridiculous old iron in the middle of the pompous dignity of Princes Street, to the stares of all and sundry. But I did not care a damn, I felt splendid, young and full of the Joys of Spring... tral lah, and what's more I had again saved a sevenpenny fare. 'Will this do you, Sir?' the man asked as I alighted. 'Fine, thank you,' I said. 'Yes, James, grand,' I wanted to say.

On the wireless this morning I heard something about a 'New World Order' – I must find out more about it.

I have sent a pile of newspapers to Binnie and written one short letter. I love Binnie as I visualise her, strong and vital, fine and intelligent – oh God is good. I hope.

I do not think the Nazis came last night as the weather was so terrible. Electric storms, ice, wind, gales, and drenching rain. Better than all anti-aircraft guns. In August I prayed for such a gale.

8.20 p.m.

During the afternoon I stood on the arched roof of Brown, Shipley & Co. and watched a lone Jerry cross over the City flying at a great height. He left a short trail of white exhaust behind. A mass of anti-aircraft shells surrounded him, showing white against the blue sky. However he had the usual luck. I tried again this evening to get a lift home, but I walked over London Bridge without success. I had just got to the Borough, the sirens had just sounded, when looking up I beheld an intense barrier of anti-aircraft shells, and saw four Jerries, somehow sticking together in a widely separated formation, zoom low, bank and swoop round in a huge S.W. semi-circle; the barrier of gunfire was too much for them. I walked on and soon afterwards I got my lift

– on top of a huge lorry conveying cylindrical objects – upon which I made comfortable. The lift took me as far as Balham – I thoroughly enjoyed the ride, London is so beautiful in autumn sunshine.

As I write this the nightly Blitz is on in full swing. In all its old intensity. As Alan has just remarked, 'it is just like old times'; but then it's a fine night; bright stars in the heavens and perfectly damnable moon. The. shells, though, look very pretty.

I had two mags from Binnie tonight. All about Australia. I shall go there – but will bring my Binnie back to London.

We shall win this war.

THE FUTURE

9 October

'...do not let us dull for a moment the sense of awful hazard in which we stand. Do not let us lose the conviction that it is only by supreme and superb exertion – unwearying, indomitable – that we shall save our souls alive.

'No one can predict, no one can even imagine, how this terrible war against German and Nazi aggression will run its course, or how far it will spread, or how long it will last.

'Long dark months of trial and tribulation lie before us. Not only great dangers, but many more misfortunes, many shortcomings, many mistakes, many disappointments will surely be our lot. Death and sorrow will be the companions of our journey; hardship our garment; constancy and valour our only shield.

'We must be united; we must be undaunted; we must be inflexible. Our qualities and our needs must burn and glow through the gloom of Europe till they become the veritable beacon of its salvation.' So spoke Winston Churchill to the House of Commons yesterday.

His speech will cause the world to wonder and speculate; how can the British people in the midst of the greatest affliction in their stormy and glorious history withstand such a gloomy prospect, so truthful, so barren? And the world will respect Britain the more because of that fortitude.

What is the prospect of Youth today? Upon the distant horizon there is no break in the war clouds, no dawn of respite from death. Youth can only see wars and sorrow, destruction and annihilation. Their ideals they see already cast down, trampled upon. There is no incentive to urge them to study for the higher extremes. Guns, bombs, 'planes are imprinted in our minds.

My brother: 13 years of age. The war came – his promising school career upon which he had just set step in a London Secondary School was severed. Evacuation, jumble. And now, as he attends a private day school locally, he cannot see a resumption of his pre-war aims; when he leaves school, probably

Winston Churchill surveys the Blitz-damaged House of Commons.

at 18, he can visualise no secured position. He can see only a mad and half-starved world, bewildered, endeavouring to recover from the financial and human stress of total warfare.

Myself, 18: I am able to see all the tangles and perplexities. I know that my whole life will be altered utterly, that my dreams of youth will not materialise as I had planned. I no longer see my path with my company, progressive, ambitious, but I see a void to which I drift the nearer. I know that soon I shall be in the fighting services, and am glad. But my worry is that perhaps my people will have to remain in the battle of London, and I feel confused, and cannot concentrate. It is one thing to go to war, and another to have the war come to you and yours.

9 October (later)

The night of the seventh was as per usual. Yesterday morning I watched a host of German bombers whip overhead, like five invisible paint brushes trailing a white line across the blue sky. Hot upon their tails were our fighters, and the 'planes were so high that only the white trails could be seen. The Germans power-dived, twisted, banked. Our fighters tore across, twisted and looped as the Nazi fighters made to intercept, and the Nazi bombers twice pursued their course, like horse racing at Epsom. On the second lap they twisted and loped off into a huge, squat figure of eight, and the brushes of the invisible painter continued madly erratic. Forty minutes the fight lasted, and all through the morning many more were the alarms and excursions of the Luftwaffe.

Chancery Lane was bombed in the morning rush hour. Charing Cross station was hit, 8 killed and 27 injured. Another bomb fell near Odhams reducing a building already scheduled for demolition, knocking in several shops and killing a number of people. Victoria too – the Queen's and the Palace theatres are no more. Buses in Chancery Lane were also hit, and the passengers killed, or seriously injured. Such is the battle of London, and as I write this by the Bank of England at any moment the Dorniers and Junkers may whip from the clouds and blast us all to smithereens.

Last night was exceptionally brutal. Symphonies of guns, bombs and fires. I watched a fire blossoming south of Battersea. Miss Mann, who lives in Gunnersbury, has had a bomb 80 yards from her house, losing all her tiles and windows. I fear London is slowly getting worse. The *Daily Express* says that all our citizens should wear a badge which says: 'A Citizen of London – 1940.' How proud I am to be one. I can see now that Destiny has trimmed my wings, shot us out of St Albans and Southampton so that I may be present in my City's most noble hour. Thank God.

Flares were dropped over the Clapham gun positions, and I know sooner or later a concerted attack will follow on their positions. It is usually the practice after a flare survey by lone aircraft.

Mother and Alan slept in the hall last night. I went into my room to bed. De Havillands was also bombed early last Thursday morning. I have written to Rod as to the safety of Steve and Bob.

Also wrote to Pewsham yesterday after a period of six weeks or so.

I managed to get a lift in a Home Guard van to the City this morning. I sat next to a cheerful young fellow in the Merchant Navy. He has been everywhere, but said most of his journeys since the war have been to America and Canada. I also learned that I could quite easily get in the M.N. – I may try my hand. At least it would offer me my travel ambitions. It is also a very important and patriotic job. And I may see Binnie and Australia. If I apply it should be to the Shipping Federation, Leadenhall Street. This young fellow was in mid-Atlantic when the blitzkrieg upon London commenced and he said how horrible it was to feel that hundreds of 'planes had raided one's home town. But as he truly said the world would be amazed if they really saw our City, instead of just conjuring up pictures of a London just a huge smoking shell.

Perhaps the peoples of Berlin and London will soon have something in common and a common feeling of sympathy.

10 October

I was employed yesterday in the refreshing, enjoyable task of churning out 'one of my letters' to Binnie; the opportunity was afforded me by the gruesome fact that Miss Mann was away due to a bomb falling 80 yards from her house, taking with it her roof and windows.

Yesterday afternoon I sneaked to the third floor when the whistles shrilled and beheld scattered formations of Nazi bombers twisting and turning across the City. Right overhead they were like so many pieces of paper being blown by the wind. Of course they may have dropped death – but they were immediately up above, there was a strong wind, and I wasn't worried. Another squadron appeared from the west but apparently our fighters were on their tails for they swooped in a prodigious bank and fled like bloody hell for the coast.

Roehampton Hospital was bombed – very many casualties among the aged and infirm. Bombs on City Road – and many other places. I wonder if Tower Bridge has been damaged? The roads were raised[24] when I came over yesterday morning – there was no alert in progress. Whatever the rumoured damage it is but superficial I feel sure.

Last night the blitz was awesome. At 11 p.m. a red parachute flare, approaching from the east, sailed serenely over the flats. I thought at first it was a red glow caused by a fire. After this two bombs whined down with great gusto, and Mother and Alan just stood in the hall for a few moments, but no one was worried. The clamour of the guns was devilish; searchlights too played quite a part in the proceedings.

Blitz damage at The Nag's Head, Whitechapel Road, Whitechapel. The landlord was a Mr Joseph Perkoff. The pub was rebuilt after the war. (*Brian Girling*)

A bomb has fallen slap bang in the middle of Cornhill opposite Birchin Lane. Despite the mass of twisted pipes and the huge size of the crater the damage was negligible, for providentially it chanced to fall in the one part of Cornhill where blast could be absorbed – i.e. by the Royal Exchange – Peabody Memorial. I suppose one day concerted attacks will be made on the Clapham guns and the Bank of England. Bully for No. 6 Lothbury!

Places hit which I have not seen – Lep Works, Cherry Blossom Polish factory, Chiswick, Victoria once more, Edgware Road and again the West End.

I had a fairly good night's sleep until a nightmare woke me at 6 a.m.; the guns were still banging away and the Jerries still overhead. But I got in another hour's sleep before 8.

Again had a lift from Trinity Road, this time in an Austin 12 and to Wood Street. Jolly convenient and expedient.

The *Express* says all citizens of London should be issued with badges.

I am still lining up this Merchant Navy affair. Naturally like everything else of my crazes it is probably only built upon air, but meeting that chap as I did reminded me of Fate. Dad I don't think would object to my going in the M.N. but I loathe to leave my family in this London, and moreover I don't think I want to leave London anyhow.

Our tracer guns shot out the parachute flares. What marvellous shooting!

11 October

I got home last night with my usual good luck. I managed to pick up the 'National Teapot' van once again. The evening was drizzly, and as we went through Kennington there was a double rainbow almost like an arch enveloping the whole of the City.

Come the nightly blitz – it was exceedingly hot. Jerry came over just like old times every few seconds, and rarely was the air free from his angry growl. It was a perfect moonlit night. One could see the exhaust left by Jerry as he fled across the night sky, great long puffy white trails upon a sea of black studded with sparkling lights. As for the guns – the flats groaned from under their pulse. But it was magnificent. One bomb fell some little way off, and by God it was a big one, the flats literally creaked under its impact.

Dad called me to G.65 about 10 p.m. The wardens had just salvaged a Nazi parachute, which had come down attached to a flare. I had seen the flare a little earlier. As I felt the hot canisters which had contained the magnesium, felt the flowing pure white rayon silk, I thought how but a few minutes before it had been installed in a Nazi bomber. It seemed positively ridiculous. The 'chute bore the marking of the Nazi eagle and swastika, also the date of manufacture – 30 August, 1940, and the number 1065, which I concluded was the parachute's number that day. So on August 30 1065 parachutes at least had been made by the Jerries. Also it is heateningly significant that the Nazis are using such recent materials – 1940 'planes, bombs, 'chutes, etc. There will be the time when supplies will be used up as

The dome of St Pauls Cathedral stands resolute amidst the devastated buildings in London, 1940. (*Associated Press*)

fast as the Nazis can turn them out. It also shows the blockade is taking effect and their present stocks will soon be used. The wardens exhibited it immediately and collected £1.12.7 for the Spitfire fund. This morning the Air Ministry have sent down for it; they will doubtless be pleased with this intact, perfectly made, flare parachute. Had a good night's sleep none the less. Mum and Al slept in the hall.

Got a lift to work by private car. Foggy morning and a girl in the car said just the weather for them to use gas – sticky. Huh – well I've never yet carried my mask. Past Buckingham Palace and the Mall at the Admiralty end was roped off, due to time-bomb presumably. Walked down to Trafalgar Square, the sun came through, and a bomb had fallen slap bang in the middle of the road at the back of Canada House. Thos Cook, Pall Mall and Hamptons, etc., had no windows.

Passing St Paul's I breathed a sigh of thankfulness. Still I suppose I should say a bomb on an empty cathedral is better than on a house with people inside. A notice informed all traffic to drive not faster than 6 m.p.h., to ensure vibration will not upset the foundations or structure. Oh, St Paul's, Mother of London, what would we do without you?

Had letter from J. P. McCulloch. Posted from Manila on July 29. He was en route to the U.S.A.

Deposit 17/6 in P.O. Savings A/c.

Posted long informative letter to Binnie, along with cuttings and photos.

I 'phoned the M.N. lunchtime. I learned some details but am dubious about the 'contract' which I have heard is for 12 years – if it is I shan't join. I should hate to be organised and floating for the best 12 years of my life, especially when Binnie is so much in my mind. I wrote fully to Pewsham about the M.N. hoping we may get together on some ship to foreign ports and climes. But come 19 I shall be too old for a deck hand: but I hate the thought of training at Gravesend.

The authorities did not send for the Nazi parachute after all. The wardens of G.65 kept it on show and Mother says streams of people came along to see it all day. I am sure all Tooting must have turned out. At any rate the Spitfire fund is many, many pounds in pocket – so Tooting thanks the Nazi airmen. As the flare came down last night, I am wondering if it is tonight they intend bombing their 'target': if so – wow!

Came home after a deal of waiting in a beaut. car – Borough to Balham.

Sunday, 13 October

Yesterday we had a number of daylight raids, and during lunchtime nine German bombers passed directly overhead.

Last night, a clear, moonlit night, the sirens sounded as soon as dusk fell. Stan Reuben, a new-found friend recently moved into the flats, and I sat on the steps of No. 1 block watching the shells burst and the guns flash. It was quite momentous, and I am glad Stan has come to live here. Like me he too scorns the shelter and its host of crawling, narrow-minded, piggish persons. We came up to the flat and digested all the evening papers. During the nine o'clock news we heard three bombs whistle through the air, to be followed by the terrific retort of our guns, with their customary hollow whirling sound as their shells sped up into the night sky. Come midnight and we heard another bomb scream earthwards on its deadly mission; it echoed through the air like an express train. I went to bed at one this morning, having stayed up late listening to idle jabber. I did not wake until 9, so got in my eight hours. Apparently the surprising happened – Jerry only came over very, very spasmodically, and the 'All Clear', so I've been told, sounded about 2.45 a.m. I can understand their new tactics, especially considering the exceptionally fine night for bombing. I will be glad when this moon goes down.

This morning we went to see the damage done last night. We knew it not to be far away, and it wasn't – just in Garrett Lane. It was swarming

St James's Garlickhythe from Upper Thames Street, The debris of the bomb damage litters Garlick Hill. (*Brian Girling*)

with humanity laden with cardboard marching along smashed streets. Pubs everywhere were down. A huge pile of wreckage marked the spot where a heavy explosive bomb, probably a land-mine, had come down. Wardens were still digging for bodies as I passed by. I heard over 26 people had been found by then. Literally the whole area was blasted, and I marched along 'that City in civilian clothes amongst the smashed, dead and homeless'.[25] But on this devastation, which but 15 hours ago was a suburb, I could write for hours, penning the cheerfulness of people, the calm, resolute, unshaken morale; how in the sight of this ruin and death little children laughed and played on swings and see-saws. But to do it justice I would have to be in the mood and I am not. Tooting Broadway also had a light bomb near the traffic lights and outside of Burtons the Tailors. So – the bombs come ever nearer and perhaps, who knows? Tomorrow this block of flats could be but a small pile of rubble, and its occupants being extricated from the debris.

Yesterday afternoon Stan and I cycled to Tooting Bec, where the previous night we had heard the bombs come down. Tooting Bec Common was roped entirely off, a land-mine had fallen and was ticking away outside the mental home. Every road in the vicinity had been evacuated. Church Lane, near the church we see from our window, had been riddled with bombs, but fortunately they nearly all fell in the middle of the road. We continued by diversions to the road near the running-track; several houses were blasted clean away, and there was not a window in the remainder. Just on our left was another roped off area and we saw the hole and posts marking the exact locations of a time-bomb. Pretty awful. Evidently Jerry was trying for the railway line, which today is one of the worst places to live near. Continuing on my route to Boots in Streatham I saw more dreadful damage.

Ah well, I am in the middle of war. I looked in the looking glass; I thought how at this precise moment Binnie is safely tucked up in bed, for in Sydney it is nigh midnight. Yes I looked not too bad, and I endeavoured to remember that any moment the bombers may strike, that we live a life of insecurity, that – well, I feel fine, normal, ambitious.

Roosevelt has made a fine speech. He speaks highly of the tenacity with which democracy can fight, does fight, and how he praised up us British. He must retain his presidency.

Monday, 14 October
Stan Reuben and myself were playing draughts at 9 last night; suddenly, as the Nazi bombers went over, we heard a woosh, a scream, the draughtboard jumped inches into the air, our contesting strategy of draughts was no more. Together Stan and I sprang into the hall, to the front door. We expected to see the Holmbury Court shelter no more, expected to see destruction. But no damage was visible. We waited expectantly, and we prepared ourselves for the rest of the salvo – but they did not come. I felt remarkably cool, and did not feel one bit of fear. We returned to the game; but Dad called and what a spectacle. Over Clapham three bright yellow parachute flares were

Bus in bomb
crater. Balham
underground,
14 October 1940 .

descending, and cascades of red rockets soared high into the air, anti-aircraft pom-poms spattered away, all in an endeavour to extinguish them. The moonlight was intense. More flares, more rockets, but we returned to our game after going to the top floor to get a better view. Then the news came through – that bomb had fallen not 150 yards away, in Hebdon Road. Four houses were down, six killed. One woman had died with a length of drainpipe sticking through her bosom. And this is Tooting.

Stan, who lives in the top flat, did not fancy going to sleep alone there so he kipped down in Alan's room. But I do not care for him much. Another load of bombs, and our wardens dashed to Balham. They say there is a crater large enough to hold a charabanc in the middle of the road, between what was once Woolworths and once the Times Furnishing Co. I also hear something went down the Balham Underground ventilating shaft. Good heavens, only a few hours before I had passed over that spot on my way home.

I look around me as I write: at the beer bottles, the match boxes, the newspapers and pictures, the radio, goldfish and canary – they are all symbols so secure which make bombing seem so utterly fantastic. Yet a German bomber roared overhead and I knew at any instant death and rubble may mark this spot. I hate to see canaries and goldfish; it brings home to me the futility of their lives, so completely devoid of anything but isolation. They cannot attain any end. It would drive me mad.

Near midnight there was an enormous red glow; it lit the whole of London. It was ten times brighter than the brightest summer's day. Then a series of explosions, more and still more, and the redness made us wonder. It was the new bomb I spoke of yesterday. A basket full of splitting death. Very near too. London is grotesque, insane. I cannot describe it – it's all too enveloping. Yet I live here in this city of death, of shocking reality and see my people's homes and persons killed and razed to the ground. I know any moment my turn may come. Yet, paradoxically, I know it won't. I know that despite the blood, the death, the absurdity of this life I shall survive. And I feel not one atom of fear or perturbance as I contemplate my future. Last night I slept as usual.

Hell & God

HELL

Sunday night, the 13th, saw one of the heaviest raids of the war upon South London. Balham, the suburb of ordinary people, was again bombed. One bomb has fallen in the centre of the High Road (obviously aimed for the railway close by) and I do not know whether the bus which I saw sunk in the crater this morning drove into it or whether it was blown there. Whatever, only a few inches of the double-decker is peeping above the roadway.

This bomb I think penetrated to the steel-encased Tube below the ground, and I hear too that something, by a million to one chance, went down the ventilator shaft of the underground station. The water main was burst and the flood rolled down the tunnels, right up and down the line, and the thousands of refugees were plunged into darkness, water. They stood, trapped, struggling, panicking in the rising black invisible waters. They had gone to the Tubes for safety, instead they found worse than bombs, they found the unknown, terror. Women and children, small babes in arms, locked beneath the ground. I can only visualize their feelings, I can only write how it has been told to me, but it must have been Hell. On top of this there came a cloud of gas. People not killed outright were suffocated, the rest drowned, drowned like rats in a cage.

GOD

I have only heard this from a friend, and I can therefore only say that I believe it to be true.

A boy went to bed during the nightly raid. He awoke suddenly in the middle of the night to find no walls surrounded him, no staircase by which he could walk downstairs. Instead his bed was open to the four winds, resting on a floor held together only by girders. A bomb had struck his home and opened it completely, yet he lay in his bed, unharmed.

14 October (later)

Pewsham has written to say he is really keen on joining the Merchant Navy. Excellent.

A new type of 'Molotov' bomb was dropped over London last night. A canister sort of affair, it comes down and then splits and spills some 16–20 high explosive bombs over a large area. For all that, and the anouncement that the raid was much more fierce than for a week, I slept fine, as did Mother, Dad and Alan. Yesterday afternoon, on the roof of Holmbury Court, Stan Reuben and I watched two formations of Huns vainly attempt to penetrate the City. It was quite intriguing, but I imagine bad luck on the Jerries for all the 'planes left a trail of white smoke behind them – condensation, making them easy to observe.

This week I am once more sole cashier at the office. I find I can get much more done, and enjoy myself much better.

I came up again in a car this morning and a house in Stockwell was hit last night, and several pubs. Pubs seem to catch it pretty hot. Trafalgar Square was hit, and I think, judging by the position of the huge crater that here was the underground station given out to have been hit. The Paymaster's Office in Whitehall also bombed.

This lunch hour I wanted to attend the service in St Paul's, and had just left the office to go along when the sirens sounded (this is the 215th alarm of the war, I think – the 200th was Saturday). I knew St Paul's would be closed upon receipt of the alarm but anyhow I walked in that direction. Going along King Street I heard the guns. The day is too grey and overcast to see anything. I was amazed at Cheapside – again hit, this time on the buiding next to 'my' ABC. The ABC of memories old, and the ground (nearly) for friendship new, is now finished off completely. The whole roof has caved in, and outside is debris of every description. I do not think this ABC will be able to tempt me until after the war. Hope Bros, the men's outfitters opposite, which optimistically put in new windows only last week, is finally in ruins. And the *British General* public house is pretty badly shaken. Bow Church, however, stands out amongst the shambles, ever defiant. The whole of Cheapside, from King St to St Paul's is in shambles, every building is either absolutely reduced to rubble or damaged almost beyond recovery.

This street is how I guess the world thinks London is entirely. I suppose that the Nazis hope to bomb Guildhall, Bow Church and St Paul's when they drop their loads here, in order to damage public morale – which in any case they wouldn't.

Only hosiery and milliners are really in this quarter. I walked along Watling Street and took in the row after row of gutted buildings, Friday Street, Bread

Opposite: A typical example of a bombed-out London home, 14 October 1940. (*Associated Press*)

Above: The banqueting hall of the Guildhall was destroyed by the Luftwaffe in the Blitz. (*Associated Press*)

Street – all no more, but neat tidy piles of charred ruins, razed to the ground. Twisted girders, etc. Rather ironically all over this quarter of the City are plaques saying 'so and so – destroyed in the Great Fire of 1666' and I suppose soon, which my son will think about, will be another: 'Bombed by the Nazis 1940.' Anyhow it's razed to the ground once again. The smell of camphor and paper still fills the streets, and I am in a way glad this Cheapside will in the glorious future of London proudly show itself to the world with fine new buildings. Yet I shall be sorry to see the tiny, typically ancient London streets of Watling and Milk, etc., disappear. *Northwest Passage* will not be so interesting from the reader's viewpoint. Langdon Towne will not have his art shops.

Read Lawrence last night as the bombers came over. On sex.

I just missed getting my photo published throughout U.S.A. *Time* took the other side of the crowd with Winston; I think because a couple of girls were giggling – I looked too formal!

Friday Street, City, 14 October 1940.

15 October

My line was out of commission this morning so I came up to Lothbury in a car. The fellow wanted to get to Lambeth Bridge but I directed him wrongly, for my convenience, to Westminster. Passing along Kennington Road during an alarm we passed a house just that second bombed. The dust was rising and bricks and timber lay scattered over the road. But that is all in our life these days and we think of the danger from bombs as we do when we cross the road. The 'All Clear' sounded whilst I was in Whitehall. Fleet Street was roped off, the part where I had been stuck in a traffic jam for twenty minutes the previous morning. My No. 11 bus made a diversion right round Holborn, but again the jam was so great that I walked from Farringdon Road.

St Paul's struck 10 as I came by, and as she struck so the sirens sounded. I passed the Mansion House and two bombs crashed near Cannon Street. Mother and Alan, either today or tomorrow, are going to St Albans again. I don't mind the prospect of another indefinite period of housework or the like but I do hate the snag of going home to no meal. But I soon hope to be in one of the armed services.

Pewsham wrote and he seems pretty keen on the Merchant Navy idea, but I am wondering if he has the guts to stick it through.

Rod also dropped a line. Crighton was near the bombs which fell on de Havillands, but was unharmed. Apparently only one 'plane carried out this raid – it was shot down.

I wanted to call my entry of yesterday 'Dante's Inferno' and make it one of my rather special descriptive pieces, but lack of time and urgency of work (I am cashier for the week) force me hastily to tap out a lot of incoherent ramblings. I have not done justice to the raid last night which was pure bloody hell, nor made clear my feelings of remoteness from the whole affair. How easily I can imagine the return of peace to London. And how reassuring it all seemed as I sat there at home in the dining room, thinking and reading, as the bombs dropped outside, and the 'fourth catastrophe' was being played out around me. But work calls – pity I have had to overrun this momentous twenty-four hours so quickly – but perhaps I will soon have something far better to vent my literary mind upon.

Stan Reuben remarked how unusual a chap I was. So has Rod, so has Pewsham, so have lots of people. I am almost beginning to think I must be. Why? What then must an 'ordinary' fellow of my age feel like? Do? But I must confess I believe if more people thought as I do and seethed with the spirit I have the world would at least get somewhere. I can feel, especially when I walk in the crowd over London Bridge, that I shall rise above them all, and can see the great men of the day as acquaintances of mine. I can literally feel myself speaking to the world, ruling, and commanding. It seems natural to me that some day I shall rise and lead a people. How gloriously egoistical – perfectly neurotic I suppose, but insane or no it's me, I guess. I wish I had the time to write down all I feel. One day I will read this journal and see what I used to write at eighteen, in winter and contending the Nazi air force. It'll be interesting or else I shall feel so mad at this piffle that the whole bally lot'll go into the fire.[26]

Perhaps though one day I may be glad of this mass of hastily compiled notes, impressions and thoughts.

15 October (later)

Mother has just told me over the 'phone that she and Alan are going to St Albans today. Another bomb dropped near home this morning. I can look forward, therefore, to an indefinite period of housework, and to crown it all we have to get to the office at 9 a.m. commencing Monday. Hell's bells. We are to finish at 4.30.

I caught a glimpse of a letter from Mr Hamilton in San Francisco to Graham Spry, and he remarked how entertaining my version of the Croydon raid had been. Roy Lebkicher is going out to Arabia for a while. Garry Bower arrived early in September in S.F. from India, travelling via Cairo and South Africa. Mr McCulloch took a Dutch boat from Calcutta across the Pacific.

I wrote an eight page long hand essay in the early hours. I want to write an article entitled 'ME' also another long foolscap one on my journey to the office this morning. These are intended primarily for my interest in later years, and I hope I will have a son by Binnie who will also read them in, say,

1967. I know I wish Dad had kept a record of his life at 18. Whatever, I try to capture my thoughts and life today comprehensively, if not hastily, and store them all away in my battered old case. I want to pen down how I feel today. Consequently my ramblings in literature. I do not mean to be egoistical, for anyhow nobody but myself is supposed to read this litter of papers. But I am so varied that it is indeed a job, but once done, I know, will be worthwhile. I mean to lock this part of my life away as soon as I enter the Services, for there I do not believe in keeping records. Before I enlist, therefore, I must make haste to complete all the articles I wish to. I am thankful this office provides me with golden opportunities for writing. But I think of so many efforts and titles that forsooth I could easily keep a staff of typists busy. It may yet pay me – or someone – for if Adolf had kept a diary at 18 what wouldn't it be worth today!

I trust age will preserve these pages; and that I shall live to re-read them. I will.

16 October

The B.B.C. says last night was one of the heaviest of the raids on London. I am sceptical and think the previous night, as the Press states, was heavier. However, I managed to get home last night in a tiny Ford driven by a woman. Mother, of course, had left with Alan for St Albans, so I hotted up my dinner. Another letter from Pewsham was awaiting me and joy oh joy we may join the M.N. together. He mentioned joining as a ship's writer, but I think I should prefer something involving more physical exertion. We shall see.

Jerry came over exceptionally early, and after I had washed up and tidied the rooms I lit a roaring fire and settled down to write an epistle the proportions of which I did not conceive. But I was so absorbed that I branched off here, ran off there, and the excursion the epistle took me on is long and varied, hilly and bubbling, but it isn't finished for I got not to my intentions – but perhaps tonight. But whilst I wrote my building shook and went in and out with the crump of bombs. It was like an earthquake. Over the sky, I saw the trails the Hun left behind. A fire glowed red over the City, and I knew it was a dreadful night. Come 11.30 I went to bed, but near midnight there was a terrific din, of pom-poms and the Jerry's hum, and all our guns, it seemed to me, went clatter crash bang and bang boung bang. A shower of shrapnel flew around, clattering like hell on the rubbish heap. A shell slid through the air with a scream. Suddenly a crash, a tinkle of glass, I looked all round but saw no sign. This morning, though, I found in the front bedroom the bottom of a shell which had smashed clean through the front bedroom window, and but for the loosely hanging blackout curtains would have hit Dad in bed:

The B.B.C. announcer as he announced the 9 o'clock news was interrupted by a crunch, the shout 'Carry on' and the world heard the bomb on the B.B.C. London.

I journeyed up to Lothbury again by car and lorry. Kennington was havoc, water and glass. The Borough lay smoking and all on fire. It was a sick London I beheld today.

The City has again been bombarded, from Broad Street to Throgmonon Cafe. Our windows are out in the office again.

I am annoyed that the Police have fined the men of Lieut Davies' suicide squad for pinching, just as anyone might, a stick of shaving cream and hair oil. Hell, and the work they do – thank God Davies stood by them. If I had been one of those men I'd have yelled at the Judge, 'You bloody old bastard.' And not risked my neck for such ruddy men.

The office is talking of moving to Oxford or Cirencester. I hope I go, for I should save much money and be well-fed and kept. But not really. I should hate to leave my City in this her hour; and the Services' call I cannot allow either to go unheard.

Coming home tonight, I got a car from London Bridge to Streatham. Oh the gruesome sight of Kennington Park! A bomb fell clean on the underground shelters there last night and screens were erected around the park. A.R.P. rescue squads still toil there, along with soldiers – but it is a tomb. If only the dead and maimed had stayed in their tenements opposite and trusted in God they would have been unharmed.

I had to walk across Tooting Bec in the pouring rain, and evaded the authorities who guarded the Common. I saved myself a long walk but risked death as I passed just near the 1,800 lb time-bomb, upon which experts were working in an attempt to render it harmless. Apparently it is a new kind of bomb.

16 October (later)

Today I stand on the crossroads of my life. I can remain as I am, secure as these days will allow, or go forth into the unknown, ahead into the course of my life.

Amidst this City, wrecked by air raids, I have to choose my destiny. My roads are varied, wide and narrow; one is bumpy, stoney, the other broad and smooth. At the end of one of them lies peace and happiness, supreme content, the other leads to an awful abyss; I cannot see whether it be life or death. But I am done with the smooth. I want the uncertain, because without struggle I shall never be content. But here I will summarise the choice of my roads.

I can stay at this desk, with my firm when they move. Can enjoy luxury, change and new faces. I can walk in the Oxfordshire countryside for the office is moving away from this City. I can leave all the bombs and the guns, the 'planes and all this death and destruction. My bank book, too, can swell with ease and my aim of wealth be achieved. And after a while I can see my way to money, security and a foreign land. But I hate the thought of leaving my City in her hour of peril and need. ... ave lived in her so long, been bored with her ways, that if I should go when ...t last she has changed I feel that I should be running away. And, therefore, I shall not quit.

Yet I cannot stay so very long for despite it all I've had my fill, and conquered all and every fear, and I have once more become impatient with all this routine. The Merchant Navy is a very tough job, but one I cannot hope to see as much different from home; for these nightly bombs offer nothing worse than a torpedo out in the middle of sea. By doing so I can fulfil my ambition, of travelling around this world, in insecurity, by dint of slogging, roughing it, that is the trail I cleave.

But I do want to feel the speed of an aeroplane. I want to fly, and shoot the Nazi eagles. I want to be a pilot in the RA.F.

Yet I must make a name for myself if I do want to write a book and write of all my childhood, of high ambitions, frustrated hopes, and all my enigma of thought. I want to lead this very world unto a better way of life, and point out all our futile ways and make a name for the very brave.

Above it all, this puzzle of roads, I see my aim at every end, it is a girl, Binnie's her name, and she I vow, just come what may, to marry someday.

Thursday, 17 October
I visited this morning the once famous Dutch Church in Austin Friars. I have made countless journeys past this church, and as I used to walk under the shadow of its greying stone, buy a bar of chocolate from the peculiar little stall inside its railings, and get headaches from the dirt and grime of the tiny twisting streets, I always promised myself I would one day take a look inside. The church was the only Dutch one in the City and dated back hundreds of years. It looked so strong and fine, massive in fact. I used to wonder at the men who had built it. And now – on Monday night the German bombers flew over, and dropped a land mine right on top of the church. I have just been walking over the complete ruin. I have at last been inside the church, but inside of nothing. The Dutch Church is as if a giant hand has reached forth and picked it all up and let the bricks and timber fall wide. There is nothing left, nothing. The only intact article I saw was a chest, padlocked, for the Poor.

The surrounding offices will all have to come down; they are cracked and smashed. Everywhere within half-a-mile has been divested of windows. As I stood on the litter of debris I looked into the future, and as an old man, with my son and my wife, we walked along Austin Friars. I pointed to the green, and said this was a comparatively new London square. For fine new blocks of offices stood in place of those dirty, mingy ones, and in the centre of this City square I showed them a memorial 'Here stood the Dutch Church – destroyed by Nazi bombs in the Battle of London, 14 October 1940.' 'I knew that church,' I said, and I could see my son was impressed. Yes, one will grow

Wreckage of the
Dutch Church,
City, 17 October
1940.

acclimatised with all these new 'Here stoods' which will be erected on all the new buildings in the new London which is to be.

Last night being so stormy I did not hear Jerry quite so incessantly. I was glad of the rain and the low clouds for the moon was blotted out. One bomb screamed down, however, with an awful din; and the wardens say it landed along the Mitcham Road.

I came up to Blackfriars by car; along the Embankment next to the Oxo building smoke was still rising thickly from a bombed factory, the firemen still played their hoses upon the ruins. As I looked at that sight, from under the trees of the Embankment, I again saw how true the prophets of war had been when they saw in their mind's eye the bombing of London. I thought that I must wake up from this nightmare at any moment, and in that perspective I thought how after all our lives are but nightmares. Just a body which runs like a clockwork toy, indefinitely.

In the early days Britain was fighting for Poland, freedom, prestige, and other academic matters. Last week Britons were fighting for hedgerows, chimney pots, foggy fens, swift foxes and horses with heart, the Derby, cabbage and boiled potatoes, squabbles in the House of Commons and in every man's kitchen – things that grow and flourish and are loved in Britain. They were fighting for His Majesty George VI, King and Emperor by the Grace of God. They were fighting for their past, and for the right to make a new Britain. Upon that there was national resolve... They were glad to be fighting alone at last; no one could now say "Britain fights to the last Frenchman" or "What can Britain do for Poland, Finland, Norway, Belgium?" Their feeling was not bravado. Nor was it always realistic – but great courage is seldom born of the practice of meticulously weighing facts. The things they feared worse than bloodshed boredom – were no longer fearful. British reserve had melted... Britain's determination – which even the German press noted last week with "the admiration that the strong may grant his foe" – was not necessarily an accurate reflection of the military situation... In France, only a week before Paris fell, a wave of desperate optimism swept the country, electrifying even the indifferent French workers. But Britain is not France. The rest of the world might wonder whether Adolf Hitler would parade one day soon from Trafalgar Square to Piccadilly, up Regent Street and across to Hyde Park – and down to the gates of Buckingham Palace. But there was no question in the minds of British men and women. They boast the world's greatest poet and the world's greatest confidence. With both they said last week.

"This England never did, nor never shall,
Lie at the proud foot of a conqueror!" '

The above quoted from the American magazine *Time* of 9 September, 1940.

The war. We British have no doubt whatsoever but that we shall win this war. The worry is after. We should certainly never allow Germany to rise again, we should occupy Berlin. But besides the problem of feeding all these peoples, one has to consider the attitude of other countries. Russia? If they do not enter into this war, will they allow us to dictate Germany's policy or when they see us winning will they march into Berlin and hope to snatch the spoils from under our feet? If they did should we be glad they have taken over part of the enemy's country and thus relieved us of the burden, or would we risk yet a further war with the Soviet? And in any case would not Poland make herself heard and clamour for Soviet liberation? There is the problem – after. I do not think, though, Russia or Japan will enter into the war for, basing my facts on the Bible, it would seem that this is not to be the last war in the world. There is to be another. And I foresee with certainty that fact if Russia and Japan do remain neutral. So I think during the intervening period I will make haste to Binnie and enjoy what I can of life whilst I can. But for my son and the next generation I can see nothing the world can offer. All the world I have known will be no more, I shall never know the things of my young days again. Never know the meaning of real peace. Education, convention, society – gone. Squalor will infest the slums. Oh God is this all this Life can see? If Hitler won – he could control the world, he would be able to make a new form of money. Gold would be valueless. America, one of the richest countries in gold in the world, would be bankrupt. America must realise this factor of gold, and how Hitler would be able to render her useless at his will. Will she act? – she must!

I wonder sometimes what we are, where we're bound and why and how. Oh, to hell with war.

I Swear

18 October

Churchill promised us 'blood, sweat and toil' – how true he was. I have already sampled sweat and toil. Last night I sampled blood.

Just gone 8 last evening, Dad, Miller, Todd and myself were sitting in the dining room, comfortable in front of a roaring fire. I had just finished sweeping out the rooms and washing up my dinner things, and was just about to settle myself in *The Distant Drum*, a novel. Dad and the others were debating a Holmbury Court register, to be filled in nightly showing which tenants were down in the shelter and who remained in their flats. This was to be handed to G.65 at midnight, thus in event of a bomb the rescue parties would know where to commence digging. As this procedure was going on a German bomber growled overhead. Off-handishly I listened, subconsciously, as one always does. I started to read my novel. He, that Jerry, had gone, I thought. Suddenly there was a roar like an express train, a hurtling, a tearing, all-powerful, overwhelming rush. Together we sprang to our feet. We got no further. The earth seemed to split into a thousand fragments. A wrenching jar I thought signified the splitting of our outside wall. The subsiding rush of materials took, it seemed, all off the back. We reached the hall. We all thought the bomb had fallen just a few yards outside the back, in Scotia's scrap yard. I quickly but calmly donned my suit-coat, put my keys in my pocket and my wallet in my inside pocket. I did this groping in the dark for I saw at a glance our blackout was no more. Strangely I found myself contemplating all this with a very aloof mind, almost of indifference, and I quietly smiled to myself; I was very unimpressed and for all the world it appeared to me as though this bomb was a normal occurrence. 99 people out of 100 would, and did, complain of a turning of the stomach; not so me. Yet I knew then that death had nearly come to us. Outside there was a stifling, forbidding atmosphere. I stumbled over two masses of debris, clattered over piles of glass. The moon shone wanly upon this uncanny nightmare. Women in the hall were dizzy.

I rushed outside in the front. I saw at once all the windows of the flats had been blasted open or out. This I pointed out to Dad and Miller who together went down to the shelter, which since the explosion had rapidly filled, and told all the tenants to be extremely careful when they went into their flats in view of the torn down blackout. I meanwhile pelted headlong under a barrage of bursting shells along the Upper Tooting Road, past shopkeepers resignedly clearing up their smashed shop fronts, up Beechcroft and so into Fishponds Road, which as the crow flies lies not fifty yards at the back of us. It was a turmoil of rushing, calm, tin-hatted wardens. Two demolition squads and rescue parties roared up. I counted ten ambulances. I quickly entered into the centre of the crowd, a crowd only of nurses, wardens, firemen. And there, amidst the dark suburban street, standing on charred debris of every description, I found a new Perry. I confronted war in its most brutal savagery, I beheld blood, wounded, dying. I stood transfixed. My stomach did not turn, but from afar, yet so intimately, I found my brain dully registering sights of gore; I found I stood by the side of a little boy, his head a cake of blood, his arms – I knew not where they were. A small, plump, efficient voluntary nurse put her arms round him. He cried, every so often, very sobbingly for his Mummy. His Mummy was not to be seen. Quietly the nurse fingered his wounds – in a concise, firm, business-like voice, as if she was talking to a Mothers' meeting, 'Take him away immediately. Hospital case' and turned her attention to the next. That nurse was in complete charge, she swayed her audience. The little boy, head wrapped in towels, was gently laid upon a stretcher, passed softly along inside the waiting ambulance, still sobbing, though fainter, for his dear Mummy. I turned from that pathetic, heart-rending scene. I was oblivious of the falling shrapnel, of the clamouring guns, of the German bombers still roaring overhead. I heard from afar the wardens tell me to get under cover, for I was the only one without a steel helmet. Yet somehow that seemed very silly and petty to me then. I moved under the shielded light of a warden's torch; so shielded for we knew instinctively that the bombers might at any moment rain fresh death upon us. I saw through the waning moon the wrecked dwelling-houses, saw a warden rush headlong up the stairs of one of the doomed houses. I moved nearer to death – sitting on a chair, sobbing, convulsing, making distant moans, was a stout old lady; I judged that by her red and yellow spotted dress. By her side stood a quiet and silent girl, holding her arm, as if the contact would assure this wounded, bloody carcase that she was in the hands of God. Her face I could not see. It was covered with a huge piece of cloth, slitted for the nose to breath. Underneath seeped streams of blood, and as I watched the blood clotted itself into little mounds. I shut my eyes tight for one instant. I wanted to shriek defiance at those bombers prowling even now above our heads. Then, as suddenly, this passion left me. I felt weak, impotent at the sight. My mind flashed back – if only – but I knew no first-aid, and I had never before so much wanted to be a doctor. The wardens formed a protective barrier around this slowly heaving woman, and under the light of a torch I saw her legs, cut and bleeding. A two-inch-long red mark signified where a piece of metal had embedded itself into her leg. They lifted her skirts – I did not look. I walked across to a young, it seemed, and slim woman. She was sitting so patiently on a chair, drinking water. I saw only the back of her head – it was enough. Blood, blood, blood, it oozed from her scalp, formed cakes on her skin. Oh God ... I breathed a soft prayer. All this while I had bit hard upon my pen which I had been holding in my hand, and after I had put it into my pocket I could not find it, and next to those wounded, smashed bodies I felt in all my pockets and in my wallet. I found my pen ... I wondered how I could trouble about such a trifle when around me lives were being fought for. I turned, I spoke to Mr Humphreys the post warden of G.65, now in supreme command. He asked me to stand by ready to take a message after I had voluntered my service. I was amazed at his efficiency: I admire the man. Some minutes later I ran back along the soft moonlit road, soft due to the mist which hung on the evening, as if a cloak to hide this wounded City. I went up to the flat, and surveyed the damage. But firstly I stood and said a prayer, to ask God to relieve their suffering and to give us strength to fight this war. I then looked at the photograph of Binnie, then at my own – it dawned upon me that death had struck just fifty yards away, in a straight line with our flat, the other side of Scotia's – that's how near. War had come to Tooting, to Holmbury Court, to me. War? nay murder, worse. Just a second later or a second earlier and that bomb would have struck at me, and I saw those blood-caked people ... I thanked God, and wondered if I had deserved to have been spared. After all, was I so good and righteous as those people across the way? They were an ordinary family, probably never been out of London in their lives; they had been no doubt just happily, as present conditions would allow, eating their supper, thinking the war very remote from them – and then, their lives were cut, they were victims of Hitler's massacre. I SWEAR that I'll revenge them, I swear I will! I will not be a member of a bomber crew – never! If I thought for one moment I was a cog in bringing about such terrible tragedy I would rather be shot. My job is clear. I will be a fighter pilot, and I will shoot mercilessly the bloody Hun from out of the skies. I will fire callously at their bombers' crews, I will know no pity. I will blast these murderers, assassins, devils of all that is evil from out of the skies. May God grant me strength. For I have experienced the horror of war, the blood which has to be paid. If they had been soldiers – different. But women, children, my breed – I will not rest until I have fulfilled my vow.

More bombs screamed down. We were in Miller's groundfloor flat and again the express roar, but wide of us. Strange, Mrs Miller had had a premonition of this bomb which nearly pinned us into our graves. Later Dad and I went up to bed; Dad slept in the hall, and I in my bed – after shutting all the windows,

Not all children were evacuated during the Blitz.

and aiding Mr Miller temporarily to replace the locks on the flat doors, for a large number had been blown clean off. But I could not sleep in bed. More bombers went over, the shrill scream of their missions of death filled the air. Dad and I stood on the landing, watched the ghost of a moon, heard one, two, three, four, five, six, seven, eight bombs hurl down upon shadowy Streatham, saw the crimson flashes, the smoke rise from those tombs of living death. Again at 2 this morning fresh cascades of death descended upon our neighbourhood, and I, sleeping in the hall, knew that I slept in the midst of death.

After a very restless night, due not to nerves for I know them not (touch wood), but to the painful realisation that the scene of which I had been a removed witness was being played around me in greater torment and anguish of mind: and, the more real, to the noise of guns and bombs and the ever droning 'planes. I woke refreshed and quickly put the flat in order. I found the windows all intact, except for one small pane in the kitchen which had previously been cracked – that was out. The fastener of the bathroom window was ripped away from the frame. Outside I could not see far as a mist prevented vision, but there appears to have been destruction opposite our back windows for I can see no houses this morning. The strongly-built fence is down, and many, many windows broken in the flats. I walked to Trinity Road, and it is obvious that we were so near to the bomb (which for all I know may have been aimed for some reason at our flats in mistake for a military objective) that the blast appeared to have missed us a little. All the Tooting shopkeepers are sweeping up their glass, and indeed everyone seems to be this morning – like sweeping the snow away at Christmas. It is confirmed that it was a land-mine, and accompanied by two heavy explosives, followed by a rain of incendiaries.

Many were the diversions encountered as I travelled to Whitehall in an Officer's car this morning. St James's discovered a time bomb just as we approached, and a swarm of police descended and turned off all the traffic. Whitehall and the vicinity of Dartmouth Street was a nasty pickle of smashed windows and piles of masonry. I could not however pin the exact location of the bombs. One more had fallen in Trafalgar Square.

I should like to comment upon the remarkable efficiency of the Civil Defence services. No sooner had the bomb cannoned into Fishponds Road than a host of breakdown lorries, ambulances, and rescue parties were fighting for life. It was amazing the will with which they worked, and I felt terrible to think how in recent months I had condemned the A.R.P.

Mother telephoned from St Albans this morning to me in the office. Everything fine. Pewsham 'phoned too, and we meet under the Tivoli Arch of the Bank at 1 p.m. on Tuesday to pursue our desires in the Merchant Navy. Though I believe I shall not join, for I swear revenge, and I think to do that justifiably I must be a Spitfire pilot.

Monday, 21 October

Dad and I motored back from St Albans in the early hours of this morning. We left St Albans at 5 a.m. having risen at 4. It was a perfect drive, the moon, drifting on high, shone brilliantly through a very slight haze. We needed only the shaded side lamps on the whole way. There was something compelling about the drive, it was literally a drive to the Front Line in the heat of battle. At the end of our route lay not home but war in all its grim savagery. On the road to Barnet, on the threshold of the 'doomed City' we passed lines of dark silhouettes – lorries – waiting for daybreak before venturing into the gates of hell. We continued, alone. I snuggled deeper into my old sports outfit, but it was not cold. Binnie, I thought, would be just having her office tea in a wonderfully carefree and sunny Sydney – did she think of me? Yes it was an adventure, an experience, this journey. We entered London at its extreme north about 5.30 in the morning, a time when the German bombers are unusually active, and continued at twenty m.p.h. to the Central Area. We learned, however, from three policemen guarding a time-bomb area near Camden Town that the 'All Clear' had been sounded at 3.30 a.m. and I believe I was secretly disappointed. We went along Southampton Row, past

Colin's parents escape the devastation for a few hours on a jaunt to the country during 1940. (*Author*)

the Holborn Tube, and finally arrived at the *Herald* office. For Dad had to do his work before he could take me home so that I might go to mine. We had just got out of the car at the *Herald* office when we heard gunfire and our old friend Jerry. However the warning was not given, and in any case we paid no attention to him. We heard Hammersmith had had a bashing. At 6 a.m. the moon had gone in and it was nearly pitch black. I read a copy of the *Herald* and was startled to read that Mecca and Bahrein had been bombed by Italian aircraft. Well we went through the pitch black London all round the West, and finally arrived back home. Holmbury Court still stood and Dad and I went indoors and I changed my sports togs for my office suit and then we dashed back to Town, and I was in the office by 9 a.m. which is our new time – I was of course the very first. I sympathised with the charlady who has been bombed out of her home. Dawn broke, incidentally, at about 7 a.m. Thus I end an experience which I wouldn't have missed for worlds. Entering London at night – in the 1940 blitz.

I will merely add that my week-end, of perfect weather, was delightful. The peace of St Albans seemed almost impossible, yet it was true. Dad, whose nerves are a little strung, benefited a power. The country was made the lovelier by the warm sun, by which I could set light to paper with the aid of a magnifying glass. October too… Mother was very well, but Alan is not so good and I suspect measles – at Dorie's too.

Saturday afternoon I walked right across the rather harsh, to me unfamiliar, clime of the Hertfordshire fields, and I once again sat and watched the Abbey sink into night. Over all stole a mist, and over me a dream… a rumble of distant heavy guns, the sharp staccato of machine-guns accompanied me on my walk. And I knew the battle for Britain was in progress…Yes, I am at the turning-point in my life – 'He who puts his trust in God shall go forth into the darkness.' I purposely avoided any chance of seeing Steve, or Rod or any friend. I wanted to walk alone, my own pace, my own trail, which lay across forbidden fields (as if I could not even get a kick out of that even in wartime) and moreover I have changed my opinion of Steve – he is too effeminate, sunk in girls, unmindful of the more worthy of life's problems. Is it the M.N. or R.A.F.? I cannot make up my mind. The M.N., Ted considers, is the most dangerous job of all, always on duty when at sea – not in the air then down for a while like the R.A.F. – will that decide me?

22 *October*

Perhaps the events of today will direct my future. Indeed until yesterday I was enwrapped in an awful complex muddle. Today I feel very much more settled. I have partially allayed my dilemma. I will record this, to me, and, no doubt, to Pewsham also, heartening, stimulating, wholly significant day.

Pewsham and I had agreed to meet and pursue our ambitions, or at any rate enquiries, as to the possibility of joining the Merchant Navy, with which Service I am deeply intrigued as a result of a chance meeting with a member of the M.N. as already explained.

Pewsham cycled from Dagenham over to my place, reaching here at 11.40 this morning. It was foggy, though the sun was making every effort to penetrate this typical London cover. Temporarily it succeeded. So in weather, to me so strangely elating, I dragged forth my old iron and together we wended our way past bomb-battered buildings into the City. We cycled via Holborn. The fog came down upon us from Clapham, and our eyes smarted and trickled. Down Whitehall, up Shaftesbury Avenue and along New Oxford Street. Certainly the damage was complete and widespread. Holborn was by far the worst. And as I cycled across Southampton Row and by the Holbom Tube my mind flashed back to my momentous seventeenth birthday. I recalled longingly, comfortingly, even with unrestrained admiration and love my Lise: yet that day, as only yesterday, seemed sunk and trampled beneath the hoofs of time, under the indelible mark of the Nazis, and I knew she too was a Nazi, probably even as I thought so of her as I went amid the destruction of my City, Lise was in Germany, thinking 'Gott strafe England.' But I felt no hatred, no sympathy – she was a memory, but an experience. She was a nurse, tending and healing the wounded Nazis that they may recuperate and live again as fodder for the German war machine. She did her duty to her country. She did what was right in her eyes. I respected her, and would have it of her. But this time I was not to meet her in the Tube – Pioneer Corps soldiers commanded my attention, slaving with pickaxe and spade, crane and drills to clear up this High Holborn of gutted buildings. Yet I thought more of the brief, spontaneous action of two crossing-sweepers who upon the passing of a hearse raised as one their sweeper's hats until the coffin had passed. The dignity and bearing, the amount of feeling they displayed, unconsciously impressed itself deep into my mind. The Ypres effect of Holborn was drowned in their noble, generous act.

Pewsham and I lunched in our Lyons of date-pudding days, now ringed with bomb-strewn debris. I paid after tossing. Then we set course for our objective, the Offices of the Shipping Federation in Dock Street, E.1. Negotiating the glass of Aldgate we went along Commercial Road to be re-directed back to Leman Street. The utter destruction of this gateway to the East End appalled me, in a superficial, sub-conscious, indifferent way. Dock Street proved to be typically East End, dingy, smelling; a mass of unshapely dark, forbidding buildings. Men lounged on the steps of the Red Ensign Club, men sallow, dago, bronzed, M.N. men, perhaps companions of our destiny. A door, looking more like a churchdoorway of ages past, neglected, locked, unused, splashed with notices to men of the Merchant Navy, attracted our attention. We were astonished to witness a continual influx of tough, slouching, almost fugitive men enter and disappear inside this seemingly unused, disreputable-looking entrance. We debated, was this the door of adventure? Was this the threshold of our future? I said the words of the Bible, 'We put our trust into the hands of God and entered forth into the darkness.' Nothing ventured, nothing gained. Inside, after heaving open the sighing door, proved to be a small, even more grim and furtive, but this time open doorway. We saw a greasy, dim, green hallway. Upon further investigation a surprisingly smart and educated clerk rebuffed our prying eyes and instructed us to proceed to the building opposite for Mercantile Marine enlistment. Rather relieved, certainly extremely amused, we retraced our steps, and found the Shipping Federation proper, marked and proclaimed to all and sundry upon a fair-sized, well worn gold plate, reposing upon a much battered and begrimed light-green swing door. We could feel the eyes of a sinister-looking Chinaman peering at us, felt the almost repulsive atmosphere envelop us. We knew we were greenhorns. I pushed the filthy door open with a grimace and one finger. Pewsham, frowning, to me almost stupid-looking, followed in my wake. A large, spacious room of green, furnished, as a quick survey showed, with tarnished desks, littered tables, and a grease-worn counter. A flight of dark, creaky stairs vanished into unknown heights. A group of five men, smoking and talking over a copy of the *Star*, looked uninvitingly at us two young innocents. I stated our desire, to be greeted simultaneously by a deep, barking, concise voice which forbade further enquiry. The man who had spoken appealed to my sense of romance. He was thin, almost gaunt, displaying a mass of furry, pointed beard, which enveloped his whole features. He wore a creased and ancient-looking sea jacket, offset by a ring of dirty gold braid, which sufficed the more to intrigue me. His long, tapering fingers turned vexedly, nervously the pages of the *Star* and he puffed hurriedly at a cigarette. It was he who had defied query, he who had flung the door in my face. I was quick to retort. A pinkfaced, blubbery man spoke up, 'Beginners, eh. Maybe but we do need 'em.' Again the gaunt, bearded seaman with ne'er a glance in our direction silenced the gathering. The moment held suspense, to me frustration, amusement, gladness. 'If this falls through I'm meant to be a pilot,' I conjectured. I poked the fire. 'If we do get to sea we needn't train first need we? I mean if we do start as Deck Boys I suppose we can work our way up?' Evidently this exasperated the monosyllabic seaman. He sarcastically spat out, 'Oh, no, you'll start as Captain right away.' I responded laughingly, 'That's fine.' Once more the blubbery man came to our aid. 'Come along Thursday morning. We'll need two galley boys then.' This we learned incredulously, for after the supercilious seaman it was difficult to comprehend the rough and ready ways of the M.N. required no training. This apparently gave Pewsham encouragement for he timidly asked the rate of pay. Upon which we were told to apply at the next door, which we did, very perplexed at this Shipping Federation of five unapproachable men.

The next entrance appeared from without as unthinkable we should enter. We dimly perceived in the dark interior sprawling, sleeping, lounging figures which we swiftly calculated were human. We went through. It was just a room, furnished with but one long, greasy seat. Conversation was easy. I engaged the confidences of two other aspiring seamen, one a tall, drawlingly pleasant Irishman. His manner was condescending, yet most agreeable. Despite his potential past I would there and then have attached my trust in him, a good, loyal friend for someone. His over-riding passion was to get to sea. His person radiated mystery, almost crime. His companion was a Scotsman, smiling and patronising. Persistently, he fingered caressingly an ivory-handled knife. Undoubtedly he was infused with twopenny bloods. A wizened Maltese attached himself benevolently to us. I soon obtained his knowledge after telling him I knew something about Misida. According to him 'Frisco was the finest, most utopian city in the world. Brazil though was heaven as it was without police and the host of regulations. 'London' the Maltese exclaimed, pointing at Pewsham and me. 'Ireland, Scotland,' he said, gesticulating at our two friends, and contentedly, contemplatively walked away.

A tall, powerful man, more commanding than the rest affixed himself to us. From him we learned all the ins 'and outs of the Service, all the wangles, heartbreaks and joys. As a lad of eighteen he had gone on a voyage – then intended to quit. He was still on the voyage. He was evidently a superior man

– he told us we were freshmen and admired our spirit. He gave us tips on how to get aboard ship. His seaman's book and ticket were intriguing. After a chat of an hour we parted. The 'All Clear' sounded and we were quite surprised, having no intimation a warning had been in force. Pewsham and I are fired with ambition, of foreign lands and climes.

So now we intend to try the New Zealand line or Cunard, and heigho for the high seas. We are in a fever pitch of excitement, impatient to be away. Oh Sydney, Binnie Patterson, this time in a year. In the dingy precincts of the M.N. offices we had felt the camaraderie of the sea; it was grand; it was exhilarating.

Hallo, the globe!

Whoever but Fate would have thought my ambition to see the world would have seen fulfilment in this war!

23 October

I survived a crisis today. It had been pending for several days, and to me was of the utmost importance. The paramount issue at stake, held before the eyes of Fate and destiny, was nothing less than my life.

I have served the California Standard Oil Company Limited since the seventh of July, 1937. I obtained the post of office boy there through the City of London Labour Exchange. When on that day I first entered its office I was awed, spellbound by the majestic beauty of the place. I trod silently, almost reverently on the fine, luxurious expanse of grey carpet, I admired from the depths of a comfortable leather chair the finely grained walnut doors, the superb finish of this most rich office. Surely I never could tread those carpets, walk boldly into the rooms within those splendorous doors. Yet it came to be; I became the lowest member of that extravagant richness. At first I worked, revelled in the exquisite deliciousness of red plush and grey and walnut furnishings. I met Mr Roy Lebkicher, to whom, timidly, I was introduced. His manner and bearing completely over-awed me, then almost fresh from school and fifteen years of age. His eyes seemed to pierce my very soul. I looked up to him in something approaching reverence; would that ice being, that man of iron control ever speak to me, a mere office boy? But work became long hours, nine until anything up to eight at night. I lived amid a hive of industry, clattering machines, laughing, superior, society-like girls. I made tea, oh how many pots a day. Strawberry tarts, chocolate biscuits, ginger snaps, black tea with lemon. Then a flood of mail, piles of letters whose very addresses left me in wonder and bewilderment. Gradually I got on top, gradually my fifteen shillings per week suffered acutely in buying new well-tailored suits, stiff collars, ties of variety and cheeriness, shirts of every texture. My salary was spent on travel alone. Yes I was content to work amid the overpowering atmosphere of the City, in that office of well-being, for – so to say – nothing. My education gained, my speech became more cultured. I became aware of politics, the world, countries became so familiar that I thought of them as mere towns. I found authors, and read literature considered at school as 'dry', with zest and zeal. I discovered and cultivated, not a passion, but a love for Arabia, Ibn Saud, and, in particular, T. E. Lawrence. I made a study of him, read his *Seven Pillars*, and in his thoughts found mutual understanding, sentiment, the mind of a scholar. His feats of physical prowess I endeavoured, and not unsuccessfully, to emulate. From T. E. I turned to Wells and a New World Order. From these studies, I met characters, men of every walk of life. The presidents and vice-presidents of the Standard Oil group, the Texas Company, the Bahrein Petroleum Co. – I made contact with the directors of Indian Oil Concessions Limited, South Mediterranean Oilfields, and a host of others. I marvelled at the way in which they had only to lift a finger and they visited any country, in the most expensive manner. They spoke to me, wrote to me, sent me stamps. I became firmly established.

And so time went on. Until early this year and my interview with Mr Lebkicher. How I admire and respect this man. He told me of the world and her ways. I knew from him my future was in faithful hands. His last words to me before he finally left for San Francisco were, 'Don't do anything silly until I come back' – almost paternal, certainly benevolent, and not in the least intimate.

So as I look back upon my years I have no regrets. I recall St Albans, the simply superb, daring days of adventure in Highfield, Southampton.

Kate over the garden wall seems a dream, but a precious, treasured, jealously guarded dream. The West Central, the masters 'Podsy', 'Jenks', 'Froggie' and the host of pranks – the inevitable daily caning, leaving school at fourteen and my first days of work in Sier's, the paper merchants in Blackfriars; the mystery of London. The Dovilles, Mrs Howarth. I found Binnie and foreign correspondents. Cycling – Southampton, Llangollen – fractured collar bones. Love, lust, filth, beauty. I became a generator of intelligence, I probed into myself, I discovered the higher fundamentals of our existence, of our progress. I became Empire, England, World-conscious. And I attribute the foundation of all my past three years – the years which either make or mar a man – to the California Standard Oil Company, and to Mr Lebkicher and the many other Americans who made me aware: and to Mr Graham Spry, from Canada. And not least to London, the City of my birth and dreams and ambitions, and to the green of the Surrey Hills, the breath of her air, the change of her face, in whose sublime beauty I thanked God for the wonderment of the miracle of life and the globe, and where I realised the greatest adventure of all is to live Life.

And so I come back today. I have summarised my training ground and illustrated how destiny has been kind for me. I knew my future was reasonably well-assured with my company, but at that I grew restless. Twenty-one and Bahrein, fifty pounds a month and all found, perhaps. Too secure. My youth

Extensive bomb damage in Southampton *c.* 1941. (*Jeffery Pain*)

bellowed for the sea, wanderlust, insecurity – came the war. My Navy, R.A.F. and Army attempts to enlist frustrated. The Battle of London, even now in progress, proves fascinating, incredible, magnificent. A new outlet which suffices to prove all my theories of God, and in Him there is Love and Judgement and Righteousness. But the Blitz is now taken for granted – I yearn for destiny, which today I feel has kindly brushed me by the hand.

Reg Naylor this morning informed me that the Purchasing Department is liable to fold up, as indeed, the whole office may after April next. He therefore intends to join the Army or Navy this week in order that his salary may be made up. He advised me to pursue my R.A.F. endeavours; however, I pointed out my M.N. ambitions, and have succeeded in obtaining his aid and influence – I now await his friend's comments. This friend, Mr Gray, who works in Escombe, McGrath & Co. Ltd., is in constant contact with all the big shipping companies and may possibly be able to secure me a berth as a purser's clerk or in the wireless room. The wireless room I would prefer, but I know nothing whatever of radio. I now await the outcome from this line.

In the afternoon Graham Spry interviewed the whole staff. Miss Parkin has two months' notice and Braithwaite one. Everyone else, with the exception of Miss Green and myself, were notified that they would be evacuated to Wyck Rissington, near Kingham in Oxfordshire. Miss Green is to remain in London. I went in like a prisoner to the judge at 4.30. Straightway Mr Spry told me I need have no anxiety whatsoever for my job. That or some other position would always be open for me any time in Casocol. He said he and Mr Lebkicher in San Francisco would look after and assure me of my interests. Well, I am to remain in London. I am glad, for I have vowed to join the Merchant Navy. Anyhow I didn't want to leave the war for safety. Being in London enables me to keep in constant contact with shipping companies, etc. I am of course deeply gratified to think all my years, precious, irretrievable years, of work for Casocol have not been in vain. I am convinced my life is entangled in the cogs of the Standard Oil machine, and am delighted to feel I have established myself, for if they wished to sack me the opportunity was warranted. I am told that I am to be cashier in the Lothbury office, and that there may or may not be a great deal of work. But they can afford to keep me on for I am only paid 30/- per week, and everyone agrees I should get £3. So I wait, and dream, and hope.

Tuesday, 5 November

Today I left home early, and obtained a lift in a private car as far as Trafalgar Square. It was a perfect morning – an orangy sun, a slight, pervading mist. London looked her most splendid self. As the hour was but ten I lingered before catching a No. 8 bus to the Bank. It seemed impossible to realise the German blitzkrieg was directed against this City, and I laughed. London could absorb everything the German Moloch could deliver. But I was not in a mood to meditate – I was urgent, breathless, expectant, yet mindful. As I strolled along Cornhill, paused to survey the progress the workmen were making in the huge bomb crater opposite Birchin Lane, the sirens screamed. I cursed, for I wanted no untoward events this morning, so I went impatiently on. I found Fenchurch Avenue with ease, and discovered after all a tiny tremor, probably originating out of premeditated homesickness running through me. It disappeared almost as instantly, and I once again was calm, collected, supremely confident.

I entered No. 13, Escombe McGrath's offices at 10.35, and gave my name. Mr Gray was expecting me. He seemed different, somehow, than other people: he was far more friendly, almost paternal towards me. We shook hands. Then to the accompaniment of patter and bomb remarks we set out, along the narrow, homely dormitories of Fenchurch Avenue, until my whole being leapt as he took me through the entrance to the P. & O. in Leadenhall Street. Australia? Oh joy unprecedented. Mr Gray disappeared for a moment, and reappeared with a gentleman he called 'Eric', to whom I was introduced. As the alert was still in progress this gentleman had to take leave, for the 'real shot' I was to see was installed in the shelter, where his department carried on during raids. However, a very dignified, slight, imposing man came along, and introductions were exchanged. He regretted Mr Austin, whom I was to have met, was 'down at Croxley' but possibly I could call back the next day. I readily agreed, but all the time feeling a quiver of disappointment, postponement, vexation. Then, seemingly as an afterthought, he said he would take my particulars and so we went along to his office. I concluded he was the 'real minor shot'. His office, adorned with a picture of The Fighting Temeraire, was to me inviting. Cooly, concisely, and with conviction I answered his questions: about school, my work, and so on. The fact I had served so long in the Standard Oil stood me in fine stead. That, and Mr Gray so kindly introducing me. He then suggested I should go to sea as a writer. I had a short typewriting test carried out amongst a lot of pompous and dignified businessmen upon a noiseless Remington: I executed this easily, without any trouble. 'That's all right, fine' was the comment. Then how glad I was I had bathed last night, for I was told to pass the doctor. But the alert sounded again and I was instructed to wait in the shelter until the 'All Clear'. I scorned such humiliation, and bided the time, which seemed endless, outside in Leadenhall Street. Here I met a boy of seventeen boasting the M.N. badge. He told me he was a bell boy, and had sailed to Sydney in July and got back last week. My envy knew no bounds. I asked him about Sydney and conditions on board ship. A fine time he had had and Sydney girls were the goods. His trip, being on a 'voyage only' basis, had ended upon making Liverpool. He hoped to sign-on another ship, and I hope he does, for he seemed very bright. I enjoyed his talk of Freetown and the Cape, of quinine tablets, and so on. He said a writer is a very fine job, holding a rank equal to a petty officer. Good pay, too. And then I saw on a notice board in the doorway in which we were standing 'Binney & Co. Ltd.' and I was assured. But as for 'Limited'... A sailor who said he had a venereal disease drifted past, shabby, down at the heels – I gave him 1/2d., the bell boy a pile of coppers – his 'God bless you, Sirs' I found encouraging. With the 'All Clear' I rushed upstairs, had my name entered, and then to the doctor, a repetition of the R.A.F. medical. The doctor said: 'When you go out East' (tough, oh boy) 'you must be vaccinated,' and I was told to let him have a certificate to the effect. Back to the office and the giving of more details. I now have to wait until a vacancy occurs, when I shall be sent for by telephone or telegram.

I waited an hour for Pewsham – but he didn't turn up and I was glad. I then tore excited as a schoolboy, to the office, caught Miss Spindler before

Alan in his MN regalia, *c.* 1944. (*Author*)

Colin in his MN regalia, 3 July 1943. (*Author*)

she went to Wyke Rissington, told one and all the news – but I cannot go on, I'm unstable, hilarious with wild expectation. I must subside. But I cannot, it's a physical impossibility. An interview with Graham Spry lasting an hour proved of paramount importance. He told me not to sever connection with the Company, how gigantic it would be in the Near East after the war. (Guns outside are going thundering hell – left, right; left, right). Oh, Spry told me a host of complimentary things, and after writing a testimonial, enquired if it was good enough – hell, I must get a copy of it. I've read it and jove it's absolutely perfect – but I am losing myself in my fever of excitement. So I'll pack.

Any time now! Hope it's not the China station, but Australia. I know it will be – and if I didn't see Binnie my whole life would feel empty. How kind God is.

Paula Starkie came up and I talked a long time with her; she, too, is charming, fresh and virtuous – naturally.

Naylor has informed me that Gray telephoned him and said the P. & O. are very pleased with me – it's a cinch. I have 'phoned my doctor and I am to be vaccinated against smallpox on Saturday morning.

Now I positively will shut up. I am all too impatient, and sceptical about the blitz, for I am now in a fever of suspense. My dream of sending the following cable to Binnie: 'Enlisted Merchant Navy Arriving Sydney Early January' looks like materialising... it will!

And three or four years ago today I was thinking of kissing Kate. Hell!

Come Australia!

Colin took this photograph of his parents and brother on 7 November 1940, the day before he went to sea. A point of interest is the blacked-out headlight, necessary during the Blitz. (*Author*)

Epilogue

Written in 1971

Within a few hours of leaving the P. & O. offices I was telephoned at my work and asked to join a vessel in Liverpool without delay. I went home as quickly as I could by the simple means of walking into the path of an oncoming car, flagging it down, and when I explained my hurry to the woman driver she very kindly insisted on taking me all the way to Tooting. I recall telephoning my mother who, with my brother, was staying in St Albans. I took my farewell of the California Standard Oil Company the following morning: the office made a quick collection and by mid-day I had been presented with a fountain pen and propelling pencil and Graham Spry invited me to select some books – I chose two anthologies, *The Spirit of Man* and *The Testament of Man* – which he very kindly wrote in, with his good wishes for my 'Career as a Mariner'. I have them still.

My father met me in his car and we went to St Albans to collect the rest of the family, as we all wanted to be at home together on my last night. On the way back, I went into a post office and sent the cable to Binnie. On Friday, 8 November, 1940 the family came to see me off on the 10 a.m. train to Lime Street. The sun was shining and it was, I clearly remember, a beautiful morning. The air-raid sirens sounded a warning as we drove along the Strand. As the train backed into platform 13 at Euston, Father, wearing a black 'Anthony Eden' hat, opened the carriage door and rather precariously clambered on board before it had stopped moving to ensure I had a corner, window seat. I recollect I spent the first few minutes after the train had pulled out of the station standing in the corridor, with a lump in my throat.

I signed on H.M.T. *Strathallan* as ship's writer and sailed from England on 17 November, 1940. Our destination was unknown.

Colin in MN, 1941. (*Author*)

A world away from the horrors of
the Blitz, Colin poses in New York,
3 September 1942. (*Author*)

Transcription of letter from Mr Roy Lebkicher, an American director of the California Standard Oil Co Ltd

225 Bush Street
San Francisco

April 17, 1941

Mr. Colin Perry
H.M.T. STRATHALLAn
C/o General Post Office
London, England

Dear Perry:

It was a great pleasure to get the letter you wrote to me while at sea. I have no ideal where this will reach you but I hope it catches up with you before too long a time.

I rather got the impression that you like the sea. In fact I am not sure – if you had known how much you like it – that we would ever have had the pleasure of knowing you at 6 Lothbury. About the time you decided to go to work for us you would have Shipped off somewhere as a cabin boy and perhaps by now would have your certificate as a Second Officer, or something like that. From your enthusiastic account I rather gather also that you are going to find it difficult later on to confine your-self to the four walls of an office.

I always knew you had talent for a lot of things besides making good tea and doing your work well but when I knew you in London I did not suspect that you had such a flair for writing. Your account of the first air raid at Croydon, which was sent to me early last autumn, was I thought very well done and your letter to me confirms not only that you express yourself very well but that you really like to write. Just now when you have so much to write about, I have no doubt that you are at least keeping copious notes and that those who hear from you are receiving some colorful and engrossing letters.

I have been in San Francisco practically the whole time since I returned from London a year ago but just now I am getting ready to go out to Arabia for an indefinite time. Hitler has scattered a lot of us over the four corners of the earth and has certainly interfered with a good many of our plans. The way things in the Mediterranean look now he may possibly upset my present plans but I hope not, and still have the greatest confidence that the British can keep control of the situation there.

I have no idea when I may see you again but I should greatly like to keep in touch with your progress, and would appreciate hearing from you once in a while even though it may take months for a letter to reach me. If you do feel like writing again, I suggest you continue to address me at 225 Bush Street, San Francisco, as letters sent here will be forwarded to me wherever I may be.

When the office at 6 Lothbury lost a good junior clerk I am sure the Merchant Marine gained a good seaman, and I sincerely wish you every success.

Very truly yours,
Roy Lebkicher

Sinai

Barren, ragged, yet noble in mine eye,
Her mountains rise unto the sky.
Sands of deserts, piled and soft, speak
Of roughness, lost.
She sprawls, so fine, remote, reeks
Of warriors, kings, and God.
For her is not the path of time, of conquest—
Rests she proudly, content
Wrapped within her cloak of mystery
Silent, savage bewilderment.

Yet one does live, one has died
Who in her valleys, hills and soil, saw
Royalty, splendour, vast intrigue
Man's origin, and steady rise.

I see her now, so rough and fine,
Indefinably I've found my life
This new, refreshing, bracing morn.

Thank you God.
I'm now content,
If only this glimpse to me is sent.
Although I'm young,
And scarce begun,
I have pride so deep
In every sleep —
Thus so early have I achieved
My desire —

I smell the sea of Suez hue,
Feel the freshness of the morn,
See the mountains of Your hand
And the book of duty born —
Into reality.

My thoughts of the one, who died,
are right,
Of the King, His domain,
His might:
And without from all
attempted
thought and wrote,
Is proven the right, within Your sight
Therefore I do bridge my moat.

And I pray, please God to say
— grant me my pound of hay.
For I mean, some day
to write of all things, gay,
High-faluting, and what is He, Life, me.

In the achievement of desire
we know an exaltation which
is above all.

Triumphant shall he stand unto
himself, he who would act
his dream.

Colin Perry,
Gulf of Suez – Dec. 28th 1940

Endnotes

1 Mr Churchill's words were: '... while we toil through the dark valley we can see the sunlight on the uplands beyond'.

2 Mr Churchill said: 'And I proclaim my faith that some of us will live to see a fourteenth of July when a liberated France will once again rejoice in her greatness and in her glory...'

3 Mr Roy Lebkicher was an American director of the California Standard Oil Co. Ltd who, with many other Americans, returned to the United States in about April, 1940 in accordance with their embassy's advice.

4 The author destroyed the rest of this entry.

5 The names the author had determined to give his children; in the event, the author has two children – named Lawrence and Felicity.

6 T. E. Lawrence.

7 'Lord Haw-Haw' was the name given to the Englishman, William Joyce, who broadcast German propaganda to Britain. He was later executed as a traitor.

8 That was a preliminary alert. The 'yellow' was followed by a 'purple,' then by a 'red' (take immediate shelter), followed by the sirens.

9 A daily report on his work as a *Daily Herald* London circulation representative had to be made to his newspaper; he was also the 'founder' father of a union chapel (NATSOPA) of *Daily Herald* representatives.

10 Mr Graham Spry, a young Canadian who was managing director of California Standard Oil Co. Ltd. and a reporter for a Canadian newspaper; in 1942 he accompanied Sir Stafford Cripps to India as a member of the Mission.

11 Mr Lloyd N. Hamilton, a director of the Standard Oil Company of California, who in 1933 negotiated with King Ibn Saud the American oil concession in Saudi Arabia.

12 Auxiliary Fire Service.

13 Ministry of Information.

14 A part of the office of California Standard Oil Co. Ltd. was removed in the early days of the war to Coombe Cottage in Malden.

15 ARP wardens' post located in Holmbury Court about 20 yards from Upper Tooting Road.

16 Postcards of the T. E. Lawrence memorial in the crypt may be bought in St Paul's Cathedral.

17 The name of an ice cream.

18 Abbreviation for 'California Standard Oil Co. Ltd'.

19 Tom Cole was killed commanding a tank in North Africa in 1942.

20 J. B. Priestley regularly broadcast as a postcript to the news on radio.

21 Lieutenant Davies was in command of a bomb-disposal squad.

22 A new award, the George Cross, was announced by HM King George VI.

23 Rodney Wilton became a radio officer in the Merchant Navy, and after his ship was torpedoed was alone on a raft in the Atlantic for some days and posted as missing. He survived.

24 The roads of Tower Bridge were raised during air raids.

25 The epitome of a dream the author had before the war and which remained with him.

26 The author in fact destroyed a lot of this journal immediately before his marriage in 1945; this book contains most of what survives of his manuscript.